Beyond Nature

Historical Materialism Book Series

The Historical Materialism Book Series is a major publishing initiative of the radical left. The capitalist crisis of the twenty-first century has been met by a resurgence of interest in critical Marxist theory. At the same time, the publishing institutions committed to Marxism have contracted markedly since the high point of the 1970s. The Historical Materialism Book Series is dedicated to addressing this situation by making available important works of Marxist theory. The aim of the series is to publish important theoretical contributions as the basis for vigorous intellectual debate and exchange on the left.

The peer-reviewed series publishes original monographs, translated texts, and reprints of classics across the bounds of academic disciplinary agendas and across the divisions of the left. The series is particularly concerned to encourage the internationalization of Marxist debate and aims to translate significant studies from beyond the English-speaking world.

For a full list of titles in the Historical Materialism Book Series available in paperback from Haymarket Books, visit:
https://www.haymarketbooks.org/series_collections/1-historical-materialism

Beyond Nature

*Animal Liberation, Marxism,
and Critical Theory*

Marco Maurizi

Haymarket Books
Chicago, IL

First published in 2021 by Brill Academic Publishers, The Netherlands
© 2021 Koninklijke Brill NV, Leiden, The Netherlands

Published in paperback in 2022 by
Haymarket Books
P.O. Box 180165
Chicago, IL 60618
773-583-7884
www.haymarketbooks.org

ISBN: 978-1-64259-781-3

Distributed to the trade in the US through Consortium Book Sales and
Distribution (www.cbsd.com) and internationally through Ingram
Publisher Services International (www.ingramcontent.com).

This book was published with the generous support of Lannan
Foundation and Wallace Action Fund.

Special discounts are available for bulk purchases by organizations and
institutions. Please call 773-583-7884 or email info@haymarketbooks.org
for more information.

Cover art and design by David Mabb.

Printed in the United States.

10 9 8 7 6 5 4 3 2 1

Library of Congress Cataloging-in-Publication data is available.

Contents

Introduction

The way to rid ourselves of our masters is not for humankind itself to become a collective master over nature, but to recognize the imposture in the very notion of the Master.[1]

∴

1   The Soul of Animals under Socialism

I have always been a Marxist and an Animal Rights Activist, and I have always thought that it was perfectly normal to stand against human *and* animal exploitation. Over time, I have learnt that this conviction of mine was not very popular among socialists and animal liberationists: both tend to reject the other view as a 'diversion' from their main goals and both are suspicious of any attempt to find a link between human and animal oppression. I would not bother the reader with such personal remarks if I did not think that those who want us to choose between humans and animals are wrong. The more I immersed myself in the Marxist and Animal Liberation literature, in fact, the more I noticed that the arguments used in both fields to dismiss the other struggle were not convincing. This book is an attempt to show that there is no *theoretical* reason for sacrificing the human or the animal interest, no definitive argument for choosing between human and animal liberation, between anticapitalism and antispeciesism.

If this book has something to say, the reader will find it at such a theoretical level. I am obviously aware that there have always been Marxists who happened to be Animal Rights Activists and Animal Rights Activists who happened to be Marxists. The point I want to make is a different one though: my aim is to show that the two struggles can be thought of as one and the same. At the same time, I do not wish to minimise the huge *practical* problems that such a unitary vision could face. To start with, Marxism has often understood itself as a rather cold and scientific approach to reality: the confutation of 'Romantic', 'sentimental', 'Utopian' Socialism is part of its basic assumptions. The struggle for human emancipation is a hard one, the road

---

1   Žižek 2010, p. 243.

to freedom paved with violence and blood. Lenin once said that he could not listen to Beethoven because it would have softened his heart; Brecht lamented that capitalist terror made it impossible for him to write poems on the beauty of nature. Marxists who care about animal suffering have always been rather few and far between. Among them, I am proud to be in good company.

> In the yard where I walk, military wagons often arrive, packed full with sacks, or old uniforms and shirts often spotted with blood ... They are unloaded here, passed out in the cells, mended, then reloaded, and delivered to the military. The other day, such a wagon came drawn by water buffaloes rather than horses. This was the first time that I saw these animals up close. They are built sturdier and broader than our oxen, with flat heads, their horns bent flat, their skulls rather resembling the skulls of our own sheep; the buffaloes are completely black with large soft eyes. They come from Rumania, they are trophies of war ... Anyway a few days ago, a wagon loaded with sacks drove into the prison. The cargo was piled so high that the buffaloes could not make it over the threshold of the gateway. The attending soldier, a brutal character, began to beat away at the animals with the heavy end of his whip so savagely that the overseer indignantly called him to account. 'Don't you have any pity for the animals?' 'No one has any pity for us people either!' he answered with an evil laugh, and fell upon them even more forcefully ... Finally, the animals started up and got over the hump, but one of them was bleeding ... Sonitschka, buffalo hide is proverbial for its thickness and toughness, and it was lacerated. Then, during the unloading, the animals stood completely still, exhausted, and one, the one that was bleeding, all the while looked ahead with an expression on its black face and in its soft black eyes like that of a weeping child. It is exactly the expression of a child who has been severely punished and who does not know why, what for, who does not know how to escape the torment and brutality ... How far, how irretrievably lost, are the free, succulent, green pastures of Rumania! How different it was with the sun shining, the wind blowing; how different were the beautiful sounds of birds, the melodious calls of shepherds. And here: the strange weird city, the fusty stable, the nauseating mouldy hay mixed with putrid straw, the strange, horrible people – and the blows, blood running from the fresh wound ... We both stand here so powerless and spiritless and are united only in pain, in powerlessness and in longing ... Meanwhile, the prisoners bustled busily about the wagon, unloading the heavy sacks and carrying them into the building. The soldier, however, stuck

both hands into his pockets, strolled across the yard with great strides, smiled and softly whistled a popular song. And the whole glorious war passed in front of my eyes ....[2]

The above passage from a letter by Rosa Luxemburg, written while she was in prison, is proof that one can be a Marxist revolutionary and still stand against animal abuse. That you can be a Marxist and still cry for a buffalo, because sharing tears with a tortured animal means having a glimpse of the unity of oppressions ('the whole glorious war passed in front of my eyes'), something that shakes your soul *and your body*: the very place where you ultimately *feel* how unjust the world is. Caring for animals can be a point of departure for the moral revolt against a world gone wrong. Sadly, for most of the people who protest against animal abuse, everything ends there. Since they lack Luxemburg's insight in the articulated structure of human oppression, their horrified look on animal oppression eclipses everything else. The apocalypse of animals, their unimaginable suffering, torture and death, the shocking figures of this genocide, causes them to lose sight of how and why all this happens. They become blinded by the tears. By doing so, they leave behind concepts – like those elaborated by Marx – that could help them understand such horror and perhaps help to put an end to it.

Thus, as I will try to show, approaching the topic of animal suffering starting with feelings, or empathy, is not a good move. At least not in the way feelings and empathy are often evoked in mainstream Animal Rights literature. Although I heavily criticise Peter Singer in the following pages, I have always appreciated how he underlines that to fight against speciesism, one need not *love* animals.[3] What is really at stake, when we talk about the way we treat animals, is not the way we *feel* towards them: it is a problem of *justice*. The main difference between my approach to animal oppression and that of standard Animal Rightism is that justice to me is a socio-political concept. Since we are social animals, the only way for us to treat justice as an operative, materialist concept is to understand it as 'social justice'. Thus, I think it is highly problematic to talk about justice between human and non-human individuals, or between human society and non-human individuals. The question of justice arises only when we discuss the relation between human and non-human *societies*. When the question of justice is understood in terms of relationships between individuals, in fact, it becomes the object either of 'positive right', or

---

2 Luxemburg 1993.
3 Singer 2015.

of 'moral philosophy'. Both of these approaches are insufficient for a discussion of social justice: the first is too narrow and empirical; the second is too general and abstract. The question whether animals are part of human society cannot be answered in purely theoretical terms.[4] Animals express a living contradiction. Hence the endless debates between Animal Rights Theorists on how that relation is to be understood, and the infinite disputes on the legal and moral consequences of considering them as sentient beings or not. For the relation between human and non-human societies is a practical, historical one. What we 'are' and how we 'consider' and 'treat' the other animals is part of our political struggle for self-determination. What kind of 'self' is that? How should it 'determine' it-'self'? These questions fall outside the domain of positive right and moral philosophy. Animal Rightism generally considers it necessary to change the way we think, in order to change the way we act ('political subversion presupposes cognitive subversion').[5] I suggest that the opposite is true. Changing the way our society produces is the necessary step to change the way we relate to other societies and think our relation with (our own) animality.

Certainly, you cannot think of doing justice to animals if you consider them mere 'objects'. We will discuss, then, the problem of 'animal subjectivity' and, in doing so, we will re-frame the problem of 'sensibility'. Thus, in certain respects, the way we treat animals *has* to do with feelings, but only because when we put into question the human/animal divide, when we criticise the history of spiritualism and its effects on human self-representation, the entire structure of human identity changes. The rigid and dualist distinction between pure reason and irrational emotions is a consequence of a long spiritualistic tradition, but to get rid of such mystification is precisely one of the central tenets

---

4   See for instance how it troubled Weber: 'It would lead too far afield even to attempt to discuss how far the behaviour of animals is subjectively understandable to us and vice versa; in both cases the meaning of the term understanding and its extent of application would be highly problematical. But in so far as such understanding existed it would be theoretically possible to formulate a sociology of the relations of men to animals, both domestic and wild. Thus many animals "understand" commands, anger, love, hostility, and react to them in ways which are evidently often by no means purely instinctive and mechanical and in some sense both consciously meaningful and affected by experience. There is no priori reason to suppose that our ability to share the feelings of primitive men is very much greater. Unfortunately we either do not have any reliable means of determining the subjective state of mind of an animal or what we have is at best very unsatisfactory. It is well known that the problems of animal psychology, however interesting, are very thorny ones' (1947, p. 104). On the sociology of human-animal relationships, see Bujok and Mütherich 2015 and Sanders 2006.
5   Cavalieri 2016, p. 31.

of Marxism. Anthropological dualism has pathological[6] and conservative consequences. As Marcuse has made clear, to stand against a reified world, one must feel its pressure, experience it as an unbearable constriction; sensibility is not just a passive faculty: it is also an instrument of revolutionary thinking, since it fosters new ways to imagine how things should be.[7] As we will see, the problems of animality and sensibility become important for Marxism because they help us develop a consequent historical and dialectical materialism. I will try to show that Marxism is a form of 'solidaristic materialism'. Contrary to 'vulgar materialism', which understands reality as an interplay of inanimate matter and void, solidaristic materialism is a kind of 'relational ontology', in which reality is understood in a dynamic, historical way. Matter is not a static 'thing', but rather should be described in terms of reciprocal 'relations' evolving in time.

I must admit that in recent years Marxism has become more receptive to animal suffering. What was once a bizarre fixation of a few sentimental weirdos has now become a rather respectable topic even for the Left. Things have really changed since Ted Benton launched his challenge to Marxist Theory, advocating for animal justice.[8] Even those who sharply criticised him then are now trying to include the question of animal exploitation in their theories.[9] Yet, I confess that, though I welcome such developments, the overall debate has never been totally satisfactory to me. I was not happy with the way Benton introduced the problem of animal suffering in the Marxist tradition and have always felt that something in his treatment of the animal question was misleading. First, I could not find Benton's polemics against Marx either historically correct, or theoretically necessary.[10] Apart from his wrong reading of the humanism in the *Manuscripts*,[11] Benton's overall 'ecological' interpretation was distorted by his standard charges of 'Prometheanism' against Marx;[12] unfortunately, 'animal-studies scholars have broadly adopted Benton's key interpretations and results',[13] and the emerging field of antispeciesist 'critical thinking' seems to be heavily influenced by his misreading of Marx.[14] Secondly, and conversely, I found that Benton's argument *for* animal liberation was too derivative of Tom Regan and, thus, impossible to receive in a Marxist framework.

---

6   Weisberg 2011.

7   Marcuse 1998.

8   Benton 1988; 1993.

9   Foster and Burkett 2016.

10   For a philological assessment, see Burkett 1998; 1999, pp. 38–47, 105–6.

11   Stache 2018.

12   For a rebuttal of such accusations, see Foster 2000, p. 126 ff.

13   Stache 2018.

14   See, for instance, Sanbonmatsu 2011, p. 16 ff.; Boggs 2011, p. 88 ff.; Llorente 2011, pp. 125–6.

Although I appreciate his efforts and agree with much of his critical analysis of Animal Rights, our positive views of the human-animal relation go in opposite directions.

As I will explain later, my interest in fighting animal oppression came from a completely different theoretical perspective, i.e. the philosophy of Theodor W. Adorno, Max Horkheimer and Herbert Marcuse. Consequently, I think that animal suffering is not just an 'ethical' problem; it cannot be reduced to the abstract moral scheme proposed by Singer, Regan and the like. It is for this reason that I encourage Animal Studies to reconsider the importance of Marx, and realise how dangerous and equivocal Benton's allegations of speciesism were. The thesis of this book is that the Frankfurt School,[15] with its progressive critique of civilisation, has opened the possibility for a theoretical reframing of the human/animal relationship, in which both the Enlightenment and Marxism play a key role. In what follows, therefore, I will suggest that, thanks to such a strong political and ontological background, Marxism and Animal Liberation could be unified through a dialectical understanding of the human/animal opposition.

2   Did You Say 'Dialectics'?

Since this book is partially dedicated to Leftists who want to get acquainted with animal liberation theory from a Marxist point of view, I could probably spare the reader a preliminary definition of 'dialectics'. Yet, animal advocates who do not have a particular interest in Marxian thought might charge me with obscurity. Singer, who has himself studied Hegel[16] and Marx,[17] has sometimes been severe against the abuse of what he calls 'uninterpreted jargon'.[18] I fear that the present book is likely to annoy him in this regard. Singer has the old-fashioned tendency to label as 'punning' and 'play of words'[19] Hegel's attempt to use language not as a neutral method, but as a dynamic structure through

---

15   Although I do not want to diminish the importance of 'feminism, existential phenomeno-
      logy, Habermasian discourse theory, critical race theory, and queer theory' (Sanbonmatsu
      2011, p. 4), in this book the expression 'Critical Theory' is used exclusively in relation to the
      writings of Adorno, Horkheimer and Marcuse. I will discuss in Chapter 6 the reasons for
      this choice.
16   Singer 2001.
17   Singer 2000.
18   Singer 1980c; 2001, p. 100.
19   Singer 2001, pp. 73, 76.

which mind can objectify and reflect itself. In his book on Hegel, Singer manages to explain almost the entire content of the Hegelian philosophy without ever using the words 'dialectic' or 'dialectical'. Only at the very end does he mention the dialectical approach to logic and reality, but he does not criticise it.

Unfortunately, dialecticians who are asked to define dialectics find themselves in the rather difficult position of having to explain something that eludes the rules of formal definition.[20] This has nothing to do with some 'mystical' insight; it rather derives from the fact that dialectics seeks to describe reality as 'becoming'. Moreover, it attempts to describe the *movement of reality* alongside the *movement of the mind that thinks reality*, and their *mutual relation*. Dialectics has its rigour, of course: it is precisely the necessity of thinking these three different levels together. It is because formal logic does not take into account the becoming of reality in all its components that dialectics denounces its limits and abstractions. This does not mean that dialecticians always get it right, of course, but no formal, a priori objection can prevent them from trying to explain phenomena in a dialectical way. What must not be forgotten, though, is that dialectics *per se* does not imply any commitment to 'panlogism'. This means that a dialectician does not necessarily believe that dialectics is the key to understand everything. I, for example, am content to show that dialectics is the only way to make sense of at least *one* phenomenon that is central for us here: the human/animal relationship. For sure, once we understand that such relation is implied in almost every aspect of human culture, the centrality of dialectics itself and the impossibility of an a priori definition become apparent. Dialectics is a relational, oppositional structure. Thus, it is neither a method, nor the ontological structure of reality. It questions such static oppositions. At any rate, since I am myself rather sceptical towards what I call 'neither/nor' philosophy, I will spend no more time on formal and abstract remarks of this kind, hoping that the research will speak for itself.

3   Singer & Sons

I want to set out very clearly that I consider Peter Singer a serious philosopher. Maybe not a 'deep' thinker – if you love reading Heidegger or Derrida – but certainly one who is worth reading and discussing. I think he is still the best philosopher in the field of Animal Rights Activism. Much of what has been writ-

---

20   Adorno 2003; 1997d.

ten after him merely explores the theoretical landscape traced by his thought. No wonder such discussions often seem futile diatribes to those who question Singer's philosophical framework.

As is generally known, Singer grounded his positions on Bentham's utilitarianism, and such an atomistic and oversimplified conception of the human being, along with the idea that vegetarianism can be the normative conclusion of analytic moral reasoning, strongly affected the Animal Liberation Movement. But this is likely only because Singer's ideas met the latter's subterranean needs: they fitted it like an ideological glove. Thus, we probably have a reciprocal effect: while Singer became a hero of the Animal Liberation Movement, academic philosophy exerted a perverse influence on Animal activism, introducing the extensive use of formal reasoning into a field that needed a totally different approach. As I hope to show, the 'philosophisation' of traditional activism against animal cruelty has produced negative effects on both its theory and praxis. On a theoretical level, every attempt to discuss the topic of animal oppression after the success of Singer's *Animal Liberation* has been characterised by a narrow ethical outlook, the notion of speciesism reduced to abstract discussions of a moral prejudice, with endless debates on whether it is right to eat meat or 'euthanise' mentally injured people.[21] On a practical level, Singer's ground-breaking book produced (or reinforced) a fixation for personal 'lifestyle' as a means to change the world that has condemned a great part of the Animal Rights Movement to sectarianism.

The problem is that such a framework was too narrow. Thus, Singer's followers became trapped in a vicious circle, trying to make his moral arguments more coherent, rather than questioning his philosophical starting point. As we will see, the urge to 'move in the direction of a larger consistency'[22] is the central drive in what I call *Animal Liberation Ideology*. It compels activists to face the challenge posed by social and historical contradictions by assuming the task of *purifying* themselves from them: this implies either ignoring those contradictions – thus severing the animal question from other political and economic issues ('class struggle is humanistic' ...) – or pretending to solve them by reducing the complexity of the social process to the sphere of individual action ('those contradictions do not bother me as long as I do everything I can to get rid of them in my own life'). Even when they talk about 'micro level' and 'macro level',[23] Animal Rights Activists never provide a serious sociological analysis, nor a realistic description of the process that should connect individual

---

21   For a critique of this kind of rhetoric, see Scotton 2018.
22   Regan 2003, p. 5.
23   Francione 1996.

action to social change.[24] 'Social change' is always intended as a question of 'magnitude' and 'critical mass'.[25] Yet, those contradictions are *objective*: there is a *qualitative* difference between what happens on a subjective level and the *faits sociaux*. While Singer later faced such problems,[26] his philosophical heirs simply accepted the way he ignored them in 'the bible'[27] of the Animal Rights Movement. Thus, on the one hand, I agree with Sanbomatsu: 'the idealist bias in analytic philosophy is that it tends to lead either to voluntarism – for example, putting one's faith in changes in individual "lifestyle" – or to forms of analysis that seem oblivious to the many connections that link speciesism with other systems of power and dominance'.[28] On the other hand, there is plenty of research in the field of Animal Studies that does not endorse 'analytic philosophy', and whose ability to establish 'connections' with 'other systems of power and dominance' does not really change the moralistic and apolitical look on society of Animal Rights Activism.

Sure, between the emergence of Singer's utilitarianism and the recent growth in moralistic Veganism, a lot of things happened. Regan's theory of 'inherent value', Adams's vegetarian feminism, Francione's 'incremental abolitionism', the rise of the deconstructionist/postmodernist approach, etc. The problem, I argue, is that much of this theoretical debate changes nothing in the mind-set of the average Animal Liberationist, nor in his/her praxis. Set against the background I am trying to describe, they all really just look like shades of grey. With the possible exceptions of Nibert[29] and Sanbonmatsu,[30] speciesism has only been discussed as a moral prejudice, rather than as a *material social structure*. Nonetheless, even these important contributions share Benton's point of departure (i.e. his moral standpoint and his critiques of Marx) and, although asking for a political re-orientation of Animal Liberation, they fail to show how such politicisation could be possible. The reason, in my opinion, is that the basic conceptual frame is still unclear: the tension between moral assumptions and Marx's a-moral analysis of capitalism is not resolved. Under such circumstances, every attempt to formulate a synthesis is impossible.

---

24   Although I appreciate Wrenn's efforts (2015, pp. 26–7) to place 'social movement' as a necessary mediation between 'macro-structural change' and 'individual boycott', I will criticise the methodological individualism that I believe affects some of her conclusions.
25   Regan 2003, p. 118 ff.
26   Making even worse mistakes with his idea of a 'Darwinian' Left (1999), as we will see.
27   Francione 1996, p. 52.
28   Sanbomatsu 2011a, p. 29.
29   Nibert 2002; 2013.
30   Sanbonmatsu 2011; 2013.

If we look at the outcome of these nearly fifty years of history, we realise that the basic elements of this ideology were there right from the start. That is why I so often point the finger at Singer's mistakes: if he has been a sort of secret Demiurge of the entire history of Animal Liberation, it is just because the ideology of the movement is already there in his first book, in an embryonic yet powerful stage. All in all, Singer himself is probably an *effect* of the mind-set that was going to find in him such an effective spokesperson. Thus, I agree with Francione about the importance of Singer for the ideology of the Animal Rights Movement,[31] although I do not subscribe to his criticism. Francione and Singer have more in common than Francione would want to admit.

4   Against Animal Liberation Ideology

How Singer – who has worked on Hegel and Marx[32] – could find in Bentham an interesting starting point for philosophical discussion is a total mystery to me. He must have had a very quick look at the following page from Marx's *Capital*:

> Bentham is a purely English phenomenon. [...] In no time and in no country has the most homespun commonplace ever strutted about in so self-satisfied a way. The principle of utility was no discovery of Bentham. He simply reproduced in his dull way what Helvétius and other Frenchmen had said with esprit in the 18th century. To know what is useful for a dog, one must study dog-nature. This nature itself is not to be deduced from the principle of utility. Applying this to man, he that would criticise all human acts, movements, relations, etc., by the principle of utility, must first deal with human nature in general, and then with human nature as modified in each historical epoch. Bentham makes short work of it. With the driest naiveté he takes the modern shopkeeper, especially the English shopkeeper, as the normal man. Whatever is useful to this queer normal man, and to his world, is absolutely useful. This yard-measure, then, he applies to past, present, and future.[33]

I have always been puzzled by the way in which Animal Rights Activists dismiss Marx as an old-fashioned nineteenth-century thinker, while at the same time celebrating the unsurpassed 'modernity' of Bentham. As we will see, Singer's

---

31   Francione 1996, p. 47 ff.
32   Singer 1982; 1980b; 1987.
33   Marx 1962, pp. 189–90.

attempt to update Benthamism suffers from analogous problems every time human relations need to be understood in a historical and social context. Without mentioning the fact that, though regularly charged with accusations of 'totalitarianism', Marx never invented the panopticon. Singer's philosophy might advocate freedom for more individuals. The question is: what kind of liberty can we expect from a movement inspired by such a miserable concept of humanity?

Slowly but steadily, more and more Marxists have begun to seriously consider the problem of animal suffering. For its part, the international Animal Rights Movement did not show an analogous interest in Marxism or Socialism. One reason for this is evident, and we have already put our finger on it. Since the origins of Animal Rightism are to be found in philosophers who do not openly oppose capitalism ('the rights view is not antagonistic to business, free enterprise, the market mechanisms, and the like'[34]), its basic theoretical, moral and political concepts 'are tied overwhelmingly to questions of individual moral choice, a product of the liberal tradition in which motifs of social structure, institutional power, and ideology are de-emphasized'.[35] After all, the animal liberation movement developed in the late '70s, while the wave of the New Left was declining. Carol Adams links animal rights and feminist theory, two movements that emerged in those times as new forms of struggle centred on the 'personal'.[36] What is true in this insight, though, should be corrected by the observation that both theories became largely accepted in the academic discourse of the '80s, as postmodernism and neoliberalism started to celebrate the end of political illusions and the beginning of a post-utopian era.[37] But this is only half the story. Animal Liberation Ideology is a more specific form of political obfuscation.

The reason why I speak of animal liberation 'ideology' is that having been an Animal Rights Activist for several years, I have noticed the perverse effect of that ideology on myself and on the people around me. The world of Animal Rightism looks like a puzzling mixture of hyper-rationalism and utter madness. A robotic fixation on strictly rational argumentation against animal abuse sits

---

34   Regan 2004a, p. 341; see the recent hypothesis of an animal-friendly capitalism by McMullen 2016.

35   Boggs 2011, p. 87.

36   Adams 2010.

37   In the following pages I will focus on the 'classic' version of Animal Rights, from Singer to Francione. I will not discuss the recent development of post-structuralist theories on animal liberation (Calarco 2016; Acampora 2006). This would require a different discussion, centred on the works of Derrida, Agamben and Deleuze. Some useful critical remarks can be found in Bündnis Marxismus und Tierbefreiung (2018).

alongside the most extravagant beliefs about science, society, history, humans, or aliens. Sometimes all this happens *within the same person*. My personal experience as an Animal Liberationist can only confirm Regan's frank account:

> Let me be perfectly honest. My wife Nancy and I have been involved in animal advocacy for more than thirty years. During this time, we have met some people we would not want to do any baby-sitting. Misanthropic people, mean-spirited to the core. People who hate hunters, hate trappers, hate butchers, hate every living, breathing human being, even themselves. We have also met ARAs who could be described (to speak charitably) as weird, kooky, or strange, and others who have no respect for reason or science.[38]

I remember a Leftist vegan once saying that, from a moral point of view, George W. Bush and the children who were dying under US bombs were both guilty in relation to animals. She was pretty surprised that I could not follow her in making such a strict rational connection which led to absolute idiocy. Recently, another woman was so outraged by the tortures inflicted on migrants in Libya that she wished for the extermination of the human race. Asked how that statement could fit with the piety that had so passionately moved her in the first place, she answered in the same way: after all, even those abused children and women were party to the exploitation of animals. Of course, it would be unfair to generalise from this or that case. But what if this tension between abstract moral reasoning and concrete political blindness was *not* contingent? I have come to the conclusion that, in fact, it is not.

Regan, for instance, tries to correct his own description of the Animal Rights Movement, and deem it as a mere prejudice. It is too easy, he maintains, to attack an entire movement judging from the fallacies of its wackiest members. But then again, Regan himself confesses that *he* believes that using a 'fork' and bombing with 'napalm' are two forms of 'violence' that can be equated in a certain sense.[39] He even admits that while marching against the Vietnam War, i.e. against the bombing of children with napalm, he started wondering if using a fork could not be considered equally wrong from a moral point of view. Of course, I do not blame him for having thought this. I object to the *consequences* he drew from entertaining such an idea: 'I tried to avoid coming to terms with the question that was really troubling me. Instead, I threw

---

38   Regan 2003, p. 118.
39   Regan 2003, p. 3; 2004b, p. 31.

myself into asking bigger, impersonal questions – about the justice of capitalism, the future of civilisation, the threat of nuclear annihilation'.[40] Since Regan
recalls his working-class origins,[41] the fact that the 'justice of capitalism' can
be considered an 'impersonal' question denounces the alienation of both the
philosopher and the animal rights activist from *his own life*.

It is true: 'Vegans are subject to stereotyping that casts them as extremists
or even terrorists',[42] but can we really blame society for that? Is there not at
stake something more than unconscious hatred and bad faith? Carol Adams
has notoriously tried to defend the vegetarian movement from these kinds of
stereotypes:

> a history of distortion is required that would examine the problems
> embedded in how we judge social activism on behalf of animals; the
> person is viewed as dysfunctional rather than society. The explanations
> provided such as status displacement, the erosion of rural society, or a
> strong identification with pets are obvious attempts to eviscerate the cri-
> tique of the dominant culture by attributing psychological motives rather
> than political motives to those who protest the activities of the dominant
> culture.[43]

Although I appreciate Adams's work and share most of her analyses of such dis-
tortions of the meaning of vegetarianism, I must confess that I cannot totally
agree with her conclusions. Even if sometimes, or most of the time, prejudice
against vegetarianism was caused by the critical potential of vegetarianism
against the system of oppression, this would not mean that judgements on
vegetarians are *always* wrong, nor that all vegetarians are *per se* carriers of a
critical potential. Not only do I believe that 'displacement, the erosion of rural
society, or a strong identification with pets' are still relevant to understand
why some people become vegetarians in the first place,[44] but I am also convinced that their 'critique of the dominant culture' has no 'political motives'
whatsoever. At least, until it is expressed in purely moral terms, which happens continuously, even in those who are convinced that their fight for animals

---

40   Regan 2003, p. 4; 2004b, p. 31.
41   Regan 2003, p. 1.
42   Griffin 2017, p. 24.
43   Adams 2010, p. 199.
44   Anyway, these are *not* arguments against vegetarianism: 'social displacement', for instance,
      both in terms of upper-class separation from the rest of society, and underclass dissolu-
      tion of traditional communities, could explain why people develop emotional bonds with
      animals, i.e. to subjects which experience radical forms of social marginalisation.

is a 'political' one.[45] In short, from one side, critics who see vegetarianism as a form of 'individualistic and anthropocentric subjectivism'[46] have not been adequately rebutted; from the other, I am not sure that seeing animal rights as an 'assemblage of pet-extremists, eco-misanthropes, and fringe New-Agers' *only* reflects 'an intellectual myopia'.[47] By placing Animal Liberation in the context of a broader political theory, the present book traces the path to practically prove that this kind of criticism is wrong. Unfortunately, since the basic concepts of Animal Rightism have been entirely de-politicised, the path will be a long one.

Though acquainted with Adams's concept of the 'absent referent' in relation to animals, the *complete oblivion of class struggle* in the writings of Animal Liberationists is striking. While Adams made clear that the purpose of her theory was to link the experience of oppressed groups,[48] animal rightism has spent considerable effort turning class into the *real* absent referent of its discourse. This happens either by minimising human conflicts (or deeming them as 'natural', a consequence of 'violence', etc.), or by shifting attention from class oppression to some symbolic substitute, be it 'the Left'[49] or 'Marxism'. Although I am not concerned with a sociological analysis of the animal rights groups in terms of class,[50] it is interesting to note how Regan describes the world of Animal Liberation activism: either misanthropists, weirdos, mystical sectarians, *or* 'normal people', 'good Americans', Patriots and the like.[51] It is not important here to underline that sections of the working class have taken part in animal liberation activities here and there in the last two centuries. Far more

---

45   In what follows I hope to show that Veganism cannot be described as a 'symbolic threat' (Griffin 2017, p. 24) either. Antispeciesism is. But only if understood also as a 'material threat' to class relations.

46   Perullo 2018, p. 21.

47   Boggs 2011, p. 86.

48   See for instance: 'the structure of the absent referent requires assistants who achieve the elimination of the animal, a form of alienated labor' (Adams 2010, p. 70).

49   At the same time, whenever Animal Liberationists evoke the Left as a *positive* political paradigm, they make sure not to mention class struggle as a central issue: 'my focus here is not so much with the left as a politically organised force, as with the left as a broad body of thought, a spectrum of ideas about achieving a better society' (Singer 1999, p. 6). How do we define a 'better society'? What happens if we forget the *working class* and all we talk about is 'the poor'? What happens if we forget *productive* relations and to be 'on the side of the oppressed' simply means 'a more equal distribution of resources' (Singer 1999, p. 9)?

50   As I hope to show, the problem is not that 'mainstream middle-class white vegans' ignore 'the extent to which they benefit from "institutionalized whiteness"' (Griffin 2017, pp. 9–10; Adam 2018): more dangerous is that even left-wing, working-class vegans fail to understand the political nature of speciesism.

51   Regan 2004c, p. 18 ff.

relevant for us is the impolitic nature of the modern Animal Rights Movement, since it seems to imply that the working class has to put aside its struggle when it comes to defend animals from oppression: workers should march side by side with their exploiters, against speciesist workers if they want to be consistent from a moral point of view. The *de facto* conservative, unhistorical and individualistic features of Animal Liberation Ideology makes it impossible to think the animal question in its concreteness, and to assess the political nature of the struggle against speciesism. Here I try to outline the basic elements of this ideology, considering the writings of the major philosophers and the way their ideas have been received and put into action by activists.

Some will find my critique of the Animal Rights Movement too harsh. Some will surely object that I tend to generalise, and that what I describe as 'Animal Liberation Ideology' does not apply to *all* people involved in antispeciesist groups. Obviously, I am proposing a sort of Weberian *Idealtypus* of the Animal Liberation Movement, i.e. a *theoretical model* that exceeds particular thinkers and activists because it expresses the underlying structure of their conceptual and practical world. I am sure, though, that all those who have been directly or indirectly involved in the Animal Liberation Movement will easily recognise in my model some of the dynamics that are typical of these groups. My thesis is that there is a strong, uniform, unconscious *Weltanschauung* at the basis of the various strands of Animal Liberation and *this* is what I am currently trying to bring to light and attack. If I sometimes indulge in a sort of 'symptomatic reading' (*à la* Althusser) of the authors I quote, it is to show the unity and the uniformity of the Movement even where these authors seem to contradict each other. The problem, as we will see, is that the *theoretical vagueness* and the *absolute irrationality of the praxis* elaborated by the Animal Liberation Movement is one of the causes of its endless internecine wars. Even when these authors or activists underline the importance of 'politics', 'history', and 'society', for instance, these words are always intended in an abstract and undialectical way: I personally met several Animal Rights Activists who professed the political nature of antispeciesism and could not tell the difference between a revolt and a revolution, between Parties and Unions, Left and Right, a street parade and a strike. This is also the reason why I did not feel the need to distinguish between Animal Liberation, Animal Rights, Antispeciesism, Veganism, Abolitionism and Welfarism, although such distinctions are crucial for those who are involved in the struggle against animal exploitation. My direct experience as an activist, along with the time wasted trying to find in the Animal Rights Philosophy an explanation for the theoretical and practical shortcomings I was aware of, has made me confident about the explanatory potential of the model I am proposing here. It is not by chance that those who share a real political interest in social change, after years of hopeless confrontation within the world of Animal Rights Activism, have recently felt the need to go 'beyond animal liberation'.[52]

Animal Liberation Ideology is so pervasive that even attempts to denounce its limits fall victim to its illusion. Take, for instance, the assumption that capitalism and liberal democracy shape the theoretical and practical framework in which animal liberation is supposed to take place: sure, every attempt to get beyond these conceptual and political dogmas of traditional Animal Rightism is considered illegitimate and normally rebutted. Consequently, several Animal Rights Activists have now come to realise how wrong and misleading such an attitude has been in the last decades, even those who helped to spread this kind of apolitical philosophy in the Animal Liberation Movement in the first place.[53] Of course, I am happy to see that things are changing even on this side of the barricade, and that we Antispeciesist Socialists are not alone anymore in denouncing the sterility of classical Animal Rights Philosophy. Still, as I already mentioned, this is only half the truth. Liberal Ideology is not entirely to blame for the conceptual and political shortcomings of Animal Rightism. It is time we admit that there is more at stake in the inability of the Animal Rights Movement to perform a sound critique of capitalism *and* hold its moral stand against animal abuse. The reason is that what I call Animal Liberation Ideology works *deeper* than classic political ideologies. Sure, liberalism is part of the problem, its atomistic worldview blocks every attempt to think the animal question beyond the limits and possibilities of the present society. But it is sufficient to engage in some debate with Animal Liberationists coming from a different political orientation, like *anarchists*, to see that they share a very similar outlook on society. The main difference is that liberals believe that the present state of things is an acceptable compromise and that we should only work hard to extend freedom to the other animals, while anarchists believe that real freedom is to be found beyond the oppressive structure of human society. Yet, abstractions about 'individuality', 'moral choice' and 'lifestyle' work for both. The problem is that until the human/animal relation is understood in its real dialectical structure, social and historical concepts will remain obfuscated and distorted.

---

52   Assoziation Dämmerung 2013; Best 2014; Bündnis Marxismus und Tierbefreiung 2018.
53   See, for instance, Cavalieri 2016.

5   Critical Failures

It is from this point of view that it will be clear why Animal Rights Activists'
critiques against Marx are always wrong. Had they understood the basic elements of historical materialism, they would not have fallen victim to Animal
Liberation Ideology in the first place. Usually, in fact, Marx is criticised in a
rather standardised and sterile way. Some object that in the Soviet Union, animals were exploited just like (or even worse than) in capitalist society: thus, the
mode of production is considered irrelevant to the question of Animal Rights.
Any real discussion of such theses is impossible: one should start by knowing the difference between Communism and State Capitalism, or between
a theoretical analysis of capitalism (Marx) and a State Doctrine (Stalin), for
instance. In Marx, there is no hint of a sociological model with instructions as
to how society should be organised once capitalism is defeated; furthermore,
one should not ignore how problematic it was to realise such a model in isolated countries while capitalism was still the dominant mode of production in
the rest of the world, and so on.

Other authors attempt a theoretical confrontation with Marx, trying to trace
back socialist 'coldness' towards animal suffering to some original mistake in
Marx's oeuvre. We will later present a detailed discussion and rebuttal of such
accusations of 'humanism' and 'anthropocentrism'.

The problem is that, although it can be questioned whether Marx and Engels
sponsored a total domination of the human being over nature, they surely
did not advocate animal liberation. Thus, Animal Rights Activists can keep
on ignoring Marxism. From all that has been said, though, there is more than
one reason to believe that such reciprocal indifference must change. This book
hopes to show how much Marxism and Antispeciesism could gain from enga-
ging in a serious dialogue on the real origin and structure of 'dominion relationships'.

In any case, one point should be clear. While I believe that Marxism has
much to learn from the critique of speciesism, I think that such acquaintance
with animal suffering would only complete its already deep understanding of
history and of capitalism, making its politics more coherent and unambigu-
ous. On the other hand, the Animal Rights Movement has hitherto shown a
very weak understanding of human society and its basic political tenets are,
at best, naïve. This is the main reason why the present book seems to attack
Animal Rights: while Marxism can easily criticise Animal Liberation, in fact,
exposing its theoretical and practical weakness, the opposite, unfortunately, is
not true. And this is a pity because there *is* a certain ambiguity in the way Marx
and Engels treat the problem of nature and human liberation. When I defend

Marx and Engels from criticism, quoting and interpreting their works word by word, I am *not* assuming a dogmatic position: I am simply trying to show how weak such criticism is, how it misinterprets their texts and intentions. But I do think that their theories need to be reworked in order to make room for animal liberation. In this respect, there is a lot of work to do if we want to articulate the role of animals in capitalism and in the history of civilisation. At any rate, we do not have to start from scratch. I believe that a 'Marxist' critique of Marxist anthropocentrism has already been elaborated by the Frankfurt School in the 1940s.

6   Hegelian Animal Spirits

So, what is new about that? Do not many Animal Rights Activists today quote Adorno's motto: 'Auschwitz begins wherever someone looks at a slaughterhouse and thinks: they are only animals'? Surely they do. Unfortunately, as Susann Witt-Stahl has shown,[54] this quote is a *fake*, even if it derives from various similar Adornian reflections on animals.[55] However, quoting Adorno is one thing; understanding him is another. It is important to underline what Adorno really means when he talks about our indifference towards animal suffering: he is not just criticising some ethical 'belief'; rather he is pointing out how human consciousness works; he is unveiling the hidden structures that *produce* such indifference. Moral indignation cannot explain why our mind sees itself as something *different* from nature; but this is precisely what we must understand, if we want to put an end to our animal alienation.

Among the most important results of Adorno and Horkheimer's *Dialectic of Enlightenment*, in fact, is their progressive interpretation and critique of *Naturbeherrschung* ['domination of nature']. According to Adorno and Horkheimer, humans had to take control of nature to defeat their own *fear*; such domination implies what Marx called the 'appropriation' [*Aneignung*] of outer and inner Nature, i.e. the repression of animality which traces an important break in the process of estrangement of consciousness from the material world. This is the fundamental structure of civilisation – i.e. the history of hierarchical societies – the hidden core of both material and cultural progress. Such structure cannot be overcome unless its basis – the domination of nature – is also transformed. As Adorno, Horkheimer and Marcuse made clear, a free,

54   Witt-Stahl 2003.
55   Mendieta 2011.

classless society cannot be imagined without the liberation of nature.[56] If we want to find an organic link between Socialist struggle and animal liberation, then, it is necessary to demonstrate that violence against animals and violence against humans share a *common root*. According to Frankfurt Critical Theory, this root is our animal self-hatred, i.e. the fact that *we despise our animal-being*.[57]

I believe that the chief theoretical contribution of the Frankfurt School to both Marxism and Animal Liberation is this stress on the centrality of the historical *Übergang* from animality to humanity. The persistence of our prejudice against animals and animality, its continuity through the ages, is not in itself an explanation; rather it is what needs to be explained. In *Dialectic of Enightenment*, Adorno and Horkheimer make clear that we need to investigate our detachment from our original animal consciousness, i.e. how the human consciousness *as something 'other' than animality* came into being. Human consciousness is not something that has always been there, since the beginning of time. It rather derives from a process that makes 'obvious' and 'natural' a divide we later discover in ourselves.

Sure, we are unable to investigate analytically the origin of such a process, and not only because it begins in the darkest prehistory. Our *a posteriori* look reveals that the domination of nature has always produced and widened the splitting between human and non-human beings. Humans' dominion over nature, thus, is both cause and effect of our alienation from nature. Hence, the complexity of such research.

At any rate, the origin of human consciousness cannot be formulated in anthropological or biological terms – i.e. as something that belongs to humans as 'natural' beings. It is rather to be explained in socio-economic terms. The very language which insists on terms like 'nature', 'natural' or 'biology' is trapped in this process and is unable to describe it.[58] There is no way in which the escalating control that humanity exerts over outer and inner nature could be 'deduced' from our physical constitution. As we will see, even if violence and aggres-

---

56   The concept of 'nature' is multidimensional and stratified, thus any immediate use of it could be misleading. However, I do not believe that univocal definitions offer a real solution to such ambiguity: no differently from the case of the concept of 'dialectic', the concept of 'nature' will be clarified in its crucial aspects through the argument itself. The two questions are linked, since, in the end, I intend to support an open, relational, 'dialectical' notion of nature. The issue will be addressed in Chapter 6.

57   Maurizi 2005a; Bell 2011; Mendieta 2011.

58   *Contra* Singer 1999. The idea that nature is a *relational* and *practical* concept, rather than a substance, makes the opposition between subjective constructivism and objective biologism inadequate.

sion could be reduced to biological mechanisms, they would still not be able to describe the complex structure of *institutionalised oppression*.

> Man's avidity to extend his power in two infinities, the microcosm and the universe, does not arise directly from his own nature, but from the structure of society ... the totalitarian attack of the human race on anything that it excludes from itself derives from interhuman relationships rather than from innate human qualities.[59]

Two points are important here. First, human relationships are *conflictual*, and such conflicts shape not only the material production of society but also the whole development of civilisation. It is through social organisation that human consciousness becomes self-conscious, posing itself as something other than nature. The elevation and improvement of the human 'spirit' is only possible through privilege and dispensation from material labour. Secondly, the 'Self' is embedded in societies on which individuals entirely depend. Self-idealisation is mediated by material and symbolic structures. 'Domination of nature involves domination of man. Each subject not only has to take part in the subjugation of external nature, human and nonhuman, but in order to do so must subjugate nature in himself'.[60] Human beings internalise as individuals the oppressive praxis that they exert on nature as species, learning to domesticate the animals they are. Our escape from animality becomes the *conditio sine qua non* of our own social existence. Nobody can avoid such *self-domestication*. At every level of social development, animality must be extirpated from humans, as it becomes a menace to society. The self-conservation of the species through the individual becomes, through social organisation, the self-conservation of the collective, the inescapable destiny of each and everyone. Moral theories usually do not want to be reminded of the *impotence* of individuals. They usually forget that the division of labour, bureaucracy and priesthood (or 'the beginnings of state power', as Engels called them)[61] gradually transform the organisation of society into an autonomous being, something that transcends individuals and, at the same time, shapes them from the inside. Adorno and Horkheimer describe this form of universal (self-)deception as *Verblendungszusammenhang*.

Human dominion over nature is not proof of our 'unnaturalness'; the cliché of the human as a 'crazy animal' is just the counterpart of the religious belief,

---

59   Horkheimer 2013, p. 76.
60   Horkheimer 2013, p. 66.
61   Engels 1962b, p. 166.

according to which the human being is the 'King of the Earth'. Defining human beings as 'unnatural' beings would simply restore an idea of transcendence. On the contrary, we must recognise that what human society does to nature is a consequence of the *illusory* opposition between spirit and nature. This means not only that by defining nature as something 'other' than spirit we perpetuate its humiliation, but also that such otherness is the very lie that sets our unconciliated spirit ablaze: *the inner struggle of human culture is the perpetuation of a natural, internal war.* All human culture is mediated brutality. What we do as *homines sapientes* is to reproduce at a higher level the violence of nature, its relational and oppositive structures. The very concept of civilisation implies the idea of being or going *beyond nature.* It is precisely this idea that ought to be articulated in a different way. As I will try to argue, it is not by ignoring or deconstructing this contradiction, but rather by going through it that we can hope to put an end to speciesism. We need an idea of transcendence *inside* nature.

Thus, any attempt to get out of the present catastrophe must ground its efforts on a simple, materialist notion: that the human being is, after all, still an animal. At the same time, only by superseding the dialectic of civilisation does the human being become *properly human*, according to Engels's formulation: in socialism, 'for the first time, man, in a certain sense, is finally marked off from the rest of the animal kingdom, and emerges from mere animal conditions of existence into really human ones'.[62] It is only by recalling its own naturalness that the human spirit can solve its inner contradiction, its furious opposition to the rest of the natural world, its urge for power and control. Such a move discloses the historical process as a self-referential natural process: history is nature's attempt to go beyond nature. The 'dialectic of anthropocentrism'[63] is not mere ideology: it is a material, natural process.[64] Nature is intrinsically divided and seeks a way out of its own condition of general violence: it aims at a state of universal reconciliation that only human society – violent as it may be – could guarantee. In its inner drive towards universality, in its attempt to recompose the pain of a fragmented nature, human reason proves to be something more than just the logic of cold extermination. As a socially liberated force, reason is an instrument of universal justice, solidarity and peace. The hope of the oppressed. Even those who are oppressed by nature.

We will discuss the *dialectical theory of animality* that derives from this. Its decisive, paradoxical thesis can be defined as follows: until we consider ourselves different, we are nothing but animals; yet it is only by considering

---

62   Engels 1973, p. 226.
63   Bell 2011.
64   I suppose this is where my version of the human/animal contradiction departs from Bell's.

ourselves as nothing but animals that we can make the difference in nature. This means that our alienation from nature will torment us, until we theoretically accept our own animality; at the same time, by practically putting an end to animal exploitation, humanity could really emerge from nature as a different kind of animal. What could be called, in Hegelian terms, a 'universal animal'.[65]

7   The Structure of the Book

The book is divided into two parts. The first, entitled 'Critique of Animal Liberation Ideology', is an attempt to define the concept of 'speciesism' in a historical and social context. It presents a critique of the common notions of 'speciesism' and 'violence' which can be found in mainstream Animal Liberation discourse. At the same time, it also criticises apparently more radical brands of Animal Liberation, like those oriented towards anarchism and primitivism. I hope to make clear that Animal Liberationists generally ignore how society actually works, and therefore never understand speciesism as a political problem. I outline a critique of current Animal Rights Activism in the last chapter entitled 'Animal Rights Activism and its Discontents'.

The second part, entitled 'Marxism and Animal Liberation', tries to articulate the relation between animal exploitation and capitalism in the context of Marx's critique of political economy. The first chapter – 'Marxism and Animal Rights' – is a defence of Marx against the classic accusations of 'speciesism' by Animal Rightism. Here I show how little Animals Rights theorists really understand Marx and try to explain why they fail. The second chapter – 'Marxism and the Repression of Nature' – denounces the theoretical limits of orthodox Marxism in understanding the role of animals in human society. Here I use *Marxist* arguments to show the limits of Marxism. The first and the second sections, thus, mirror each other: I use Marxism to define speciesism as a socio-historical phenomenon and I use antispeciesism to put capitalism in the wider context of the domination of nature. The last chapter – entitled 'The Dialectical Animal' – presents a sort of synthesis of these two perspectives from the point of view of the Frankfurt School.

In the 'Conclusion', I try to outline a concept of social progress which *includes* Animal Liberation among its goals, as well as a theoretical perspective where Antispeciesism and Anticapitalism become two sides of the same struggle.

---

65   I find myself here very close to Timofeeva's treatment of the constellation Kojève/Bataille/
       Agamben (Timofeeva 2018).

Since the book is organised in such a way that the first section is an inversion of the second and vice versa, I cannot avoid some overlapping of arguments here and there. I hope this will help the reader to bear in mind the crucial task of the whole research, rather than being a cause of confusion. The core idea of the book is that human-animal relationships are not only related to historical and social structures: they are a fundamental, dynamic element of *history and society as such*. This means that animal exploitation is not eternal: it changed, and it will keep on changing, hopefully with the final abolition of animal slavery. For the same reason, it implies that those who are interested in such change will never succeed, unless they take the socio-economic structure of capitalism into account. The consequence is clear: *without the abolition of class relations, no animal liberation is possible*.

In a way, the book presents the *same history*, i.e. the history of domination, from two different points of view (Animal Liberation and Marxism). It is not a detailed history of human-animal relations, though. This is *not* a history book. What interests me is rather the *phenomenological* description of domination as an intersubjective, economic and cultural structure. Since the conclusion of my argument is that the human-animal divide is essential to the understanding of history itself, it would be proper to describe the perspective and methodology of this book as a *Philosophy of History*. At any rate, such expression usually implies a positive, quasi-teleological meaning, while my approach is negative and critical.[66] In the end, history has *no* meaning and *no* direction: yet this does not mean that it is 'nothing but a meaningless jumble of events'.[67] History is something *we make*, by progressively dominating the material conditions of our existence. At the same time, though, the making of history is the making of *ourselves*, and in this 'self' the entire question of human/animal dialectics is enclosed.

Most of the following chapters were written separately as talks held, or articles published, in Italy, Germany, Austria, Switzerland and the USA between 2004 and 2012. A slightly different version of this book was published in Italian and German, respectively, in 2011 and 2016. I present here these materials in a somewhat chronological order: the structure of the book is thus similar, but not identical to the Italian and German versions. Though I have kept an eye on the most relevant literature published since writing these essays, and have reformulated some of my original arguments when I felt it was necessary, I have not tried to completely update them. There are two reasons for this.

---

66   Adorno 1997b.
67   Singer 2001, p. 15.

The first is that it is essential to the aim of this book that my critique of Animal Rightism stands on its own ground. Though similar to that of authors whose works were published later (or of which I was not aware), the theses presented herein are not only independent, but distinct in their premises and scope: rewriting my essays would have blurred this distinction. To avoid any misunderstanding: the point is not to defend some original and independent 'discovery' of mine. Quite the contrary. I want to show that there is nothing new and original in my work: everything I wrote against Animal Rights Theories and in favour of Animal Liberation is to me plain, good old, even orthodox, *Marxism*. The point here, then, is not to defend the originality of *my* ideas, because I hold my essays to be banal applications of *Marx's* discoveries.

This crucial fact changes both the starting point and the consequences of my theses. Marx does not need any update to disclose the shortcomings of the Animal Rights debate, surely not those currently circulating in that debate. It also offers a consistent and powerful framework for a critical Animal Liberation Theory. At least, this is how the Animal Liberation Theory here presented was originally constructed. To give a few examples: I read of Nibert's distinction between oppression and ideological justification *after* I wrote about the double nature of speciesism; similarly, my denunciation of abstract individualism and of vegan moralism had nothing to do with the diffusion of Francione's sect and its critique by Best (although it is important to underline how it was propelled by an analogous experience with several vegan Gurus in Italy and Germany); again, I started using Adorno's theory of the domination of nature when the Frankfurt School was largely ignored in the Animal Rights debate. Now it is very common among Animal Liberationists to quote Adorno *against* Marx, and this leads us to the scope of my book, which is altogether different if not opposed to that of authors who might use similar arguments. I do not want to deny that their contributions changed the Animal Rights debate in the last years, and for the better. Yet, they also cemented, rather than shook, the opinion that Marx is obsolete or useless for the cause of Animal Liberation. While I was updating the literature quoted in the book, I was faced with the necessity to stand against such belief. Thus, I have obviously connected my theses with those of sympathetic authors in the Animal Rights debate; yet I think it is important to underline that they are parallel, not derivative, and certainly not totally overlapping. I hope the book itself will make clear where the similarity ends and the conflict begins.

The second reason is strictly connected to the first. Though the debate has changed both in Marxism and Animal Rightsism, I believe that the basic theoretical and practical problems I was discussing in 2005 are sadly still with us. I think this proves that the two main theses here presented were correct:

those who reject Marx using the standard allegations of 'anthropocentrism' did not understand the essence of his anticapitalist critique; without a dialectical theory of animality, it is impossible to articulate the critique of speciesism in political terms. Though today I would probably write this book in a different way, I would not change such theoretical outcomes.

PART 1

Critique of Animal Liberation Ideology

∵

CHAPTER 1

What Is Antispeciesism?

1   Three Different Definitions

Antispeciesism is the theory and praxis of those who fight against *speciesism*. Then, in order to understand what *anti*speciesism is, we should first have a notion of the latter. Unfortunately, the animal liberation movement does not offer a clear insight into the essence of speciesism. As a matter of fact, speciesism is rarely ever defined, and when it *is* defined, the result is something different from what the average Animal Rights Activists believes it to be. I will now try to show that one can give a 'restricted' and an 'extended' definition of speciesism. I will then discuss a third definition, which, although rather absurd, is also important. My thesis is that these three versions of the concept of speciesism are more or less all present in Animal Rightism. Consequently, the object of its critique is never totally clear.

The first definition derives directly from the work of Peter Singer and can be summed up in the expression: 'moral bias based on species-membership'. 'Speciesism' in this first sense is a fallacy of *moral propositions*. Simply put, Singer shows that all moral arguments proposed to justify our treatment of non-humans can be reduced to the fact that they belong to a different species: it is therefore a fallacy analogous to racism.[1] Although today it is rather common among activists to speak of 'speciesist society', 'speciesist violence' or 'speciesist humans' as entities characterised by a distinctive quality called 'speciesism', there is no trace of such use of these expressions in Singer's and Regan's original works. They very rarely talk of 'speciesism' and, whenever they use the adjective 'speciesist', they use it to describe a moral bias, i.e. something that technically does not work in ethical reasoning. It is only as a consequence of such philosophical bias that we could talk of 'speciesist' *actions* inspired or justified by that prejudice.

The 'restricted' theory of antispeciesism, thus, clearly shows that speciesist moral arguments actually exist. But it does not at all show that there is an *entity* we can call 'speciesism'. This is what the 'enlarged' theory of antispecisesism is all about: starting from the speciesist nature of certain moral arguments, such theory supports the existence of a *mental attitude* or *habitus* called 'speciesism'.

---

1   Singer 2015, pp. 18–23.

This is an already problematic *essentialisation* which can be hardly justified on a logical level, since we derive the existence of *speciesism* from speciesist arguments. Speciesist arguments do exists in the empirical world as forms of real or hypothetical utterances, but what about speciesism? How do we infer the existence of a unitary essence behind and beyond the propositions that *we* defined as 'speciesist'? Is not 'speciesism' what philosophical nominalism would call *flatus vocis*? Is it not just a subjective construction? Of course, according to the 'enlarged' theory of antispecisesism, we might try to work out another hypothesis, and start to consider speciesism, i.e. the result of a process of abstraction from singular biased propositions, the *mental cause* of these very propositions. As if to say: speciesist arguments are caused by speciesist thinking. Speciesism, in this sense, can be defined in various ways: animal hatred, human selfishness, 'human chauvinism',[2] the assumption that humans are the centre of the universe, that we have primacy over any other living being, etc. Usually, speciesism in this sense becomes a synonym of 'anthropocentrism'.

Unfortunately, there is another version of antispeciesism, which I consider to be the worst. I call it 'metaphysical antispeciesism'. Metaphysical antispeciesism considers speciesism as a moral *habitus* and the *real* cause of exploitation of and violence toward animals. Thus, in this version, we take a step further in the wrong direction: not only do we essentialise an abstract and autonomous mental entity from speciesist moral arguments, but we also consider this entity the real, historical cause of animal exploitation. With the result that the entire history of civilisation becomes a manifestation of speciesism. This is not only absurd. It also prevents us from explaining the complexity of real history.

2   A Sociological Fallacy

Now, there is no doubt that something like a mental attitude or a moral *habitus* that emphasises the human interest above that of any other living thing exists. But it exists *socially*, not individually. It is the product of the interaction between people, the effect of a specific organisation of society. Furthermore, it is not an interest shared by all humanity: our societies are usually organised in *classes*, since humans have conflicting interests and needs. These cannot be explained in biological or psychological terms (such as a natural 'desire to abuse', the expression of some 'innate violence' and so on). Francione, for instance, writes: 'we do not find carriers of interests in the natural world; rather,

---

2 Cavalieri 2001, p. 70.

that an entity is or is not a carrier of interests is a conclusion we come to after we engage in moral reasoning about whether the entity may be said to have interests'.[3] Such explanation presupposes the *homogeneity* of the human interest and the fact that we impose our will on natural beings that we have already reduced to *passive* and *meaningless* things 'out there'. Both presuppositions are wrong, both diminish the importance of relations inside and outside human society: nothing like this ever happened in history. Surely, the idea that the role of animals in human society descends from 'moral reasoning' is pure fantasy. As a consequence, every discussion on the human-animal relationship that tries to distinguish what is 'necessary' or 'unnecessary' in our use of animals is meaningless.[4]

Those who denounce the speciesism of contemporary society are confusing the effect with the cause because they interpret society as an effect of individual interactions. They do not see that society is precisely what makes those interactions possible. Since animal exploitation underlies the economic structure of contemporary society, it is indeed presented and justified as 'natural' from the cradle to the grave, thus determining the cultural horizon which shapes our conscience. Consequently, one can surely argue that speciesist arguments are caused by speciesism – strictly understood as a mental habit – but only if one acknowledges, at the same time, that this habit should be explained in sociological terms. It is not the primary cause of exploitation, since exploitation, unlike 'violence', is not a psychological phenomenon, it implies the entire organisation of society.

Sure, there are Animal Rights Activists convinced that animal exploitation exists because of speciesism and that human culture itself is nothing but a creation of speciesism. Such theory is indeed consistent. Unfortunately, it ends up in an absolute *idealism*, explaining social facts through an ideology which has no explanation. Speciesism exists because human beings are speciesist, i.e. because they believe that humans are superior to animals. Yet, if speciesism is an idea *universally* shared by human beings, how could it be present in different minds at the same time? Is it a platonic idea? No wonder that many, starting with Singer himself,[5] resolve to a biological explanation. As we will see, though, speciesism is neither 'universal', nor just an 'ideology', and, more important, it is easier to explain it as a social, rather than, a natural phenomenon. It is misleading to ground animal exploitation on speciesism, because to the

---

3 Francione 1995, p. 37.
4 Francione 1995, p. 17 ff.
5 Singer 1981 and 1999.

extent that one can speak of speciesism as a (cultural, social) entity, speciesism is itself a consequence, rather than a cause of exploitation. In other words, *we do not exploit animals because we consider them inferior, rather we consider them inferior because we exploit them.*[6]

3   Metaphysical and Historical Antispeciesism

I will briefly summarise the characteristics of metaphysical antispeciesism in nine theses, marking a contrast with what would be a proper, i.e. historical, understanding of speciesism:

1.   *Average antispeciesism (metaphysical) and the antispeciesism we need (historical)*
     Metaphysical antispeciesism knows only the abstract opposition between the human being and the animal, it is unhistorical and considers the human being as an individual. Historical antispeciesism, on the contrary, has a concrete and dialectical understanding of the human-animal relation and knows that the human being is essentially a social being.

2.   *The fallacy of metaphysical antispeciesism*
     Metaphysical antispeciesism is characterised by the following way of reasoning: 1) it looks at human history from the point of view of the 'dominion' over animals; 2) it turns this concept into an objective reality and places it over history; 3) it considers this phantom ('speciesism') as the cause of all violence inflicted on animals up to the present.

3.   *How the fable of metaphysical antispeciesism was first formulated*
     We find a first example of metaphysical antispeciesism in Peter Singer's work: according to Singer, speciesism is the 'ideology of our species', the attitude that we 'dominant animals' have when we confront other

---

6   Nibert 2002, p. 243; Maurizi 2005b. In a typical move, Dunayer (2004) affirms that we do not know *how* speciesism was born and what comes *first*: the exploitation of animals or their discrimination as inferior beings. As I will later briefly try to show, such scepticism is a consequence of sociological and historical confusion. Contrary to what some Animal Rights Activists object to my thesis, I never assume we have a *detailed* knowledge of what happened in prehistory. Such precise knowledge, although precious from an historical point of view, would be useless for my purpose. I always work on a *phenomenological* level, outlining the conditions of possibility of social stratification. So, for instance, though *empirical* research might change some details of how *this* or *that* society really evolved in the past, *which* animal or plant was domesticated, what role played religion in the construction of a *particular* elite, and so on, empirical research cannot contradict the fact that class society without exploitation of nature and surplus-product is simply impossible.

animals.[7] Yet, the human being is not at all in itself a dominant animal. His physical minority in comparison to other animals says exactly the opposite. Humans *become* dominant animals, and they become dominant animals only as *social* animals, not as a species.

4. *Why antispeciesism needs to be historical*
    The question of how speciesist conscience justifies (but does not produce) various speciesist behaviours (to raise a certain kind of animal as an alimentary resource, to use another kind for clothes, to sacrifice another one for certain rituals etc.) cannot be answered *in general*, as a real explanation can only be found in the historical relationship of the human being with its different environments. On the contrary, Singer's 'Short history of speciesism'[8] is not a real history – i.e. a history made by individuals who live in a concrete society, with determined needs etc., but a history of *ideas*. Singer quotes various thinkers who have proposed different conceptions of animals, as if real history were made by philosophers. But it is rather obvious that the theories of philosophers can only mirror their social existence (Aristotle, for instance, justified slavery because the Greek society of his times simply could not exist without slaves). It is in the way in which human society is organised that we must explain the origin of speciesism and not the other way around.

5. *Why historical antispeciesism is not relativistic*
    To understand how different societies and eras have justified the use and abuse of animals does not mean that every historical society and epoch has a 'speciesism' of its own (as if the concept of 'speciesism' was a relative one). On the contrary, historical antispeciesism seeks the *common* origin of the various speciesist habits.

6. *Metaphysical antispeciesism cannot explain racism and sexism*
    Metaphysical antispeciesism has no relation whatsoever with racism and sexism. Either it explains speciesism through an *analogy* (hence, it does not explain the relation between the three terms), or it holds speciesism for a 'more general' concept than racism and sexism (and it thus falls victim to the abstraction fallacy – see thesis 2 above – in as much as it sets a concept as cause of a real event). Finally, metaphysical antispeciesism sometimes gives a pseudo-historical explanation: speciesism is the cause of sexism and racism because humans first subdue the other animals, then the other sex, then the other races ... (or: because humans first

---

7 Singer 2015.
8 As delineated in Singer 2015, p. 186 ff.

subdue the other animals, then the other races, then the other sex ... and so on). As a matter of fact, this is another fable disguised as a historical explanation.

7.   *Historical antispeciesism can explain racism and sexism*
     The historical process that casts a light on speciesism, sexism and racism is the birth of the *Human/Nature opposition*. This splitting inside the human consciousness, i.e. the illusion of a spiritual reality superior to nature, is the precondition of speciesism, sexism and racism, as the human being considers itself as the bearer of spirit and projects on the Other the inferiority of a not-spiritual nature (animals, women, other 'races'). It goes without saying that such opposition is in itself a social process, not something that happens in our heads.

8.   *Historical antispeciesism explains the human being as a social being*
     The dominion over nature has always been justified in the name of the spirit. But it is in fact grounded on domination *inside* society, on social hierarchy (i.e. on violence perpetuated by humans upon other humans). The autonomy of the spirit and its opposition to nature is only possible when some individuals live upon the work of others and can eventually dedicate themselves to 'spiritual' activities (from theology to science). This process begins in human prehistory (when the human being – like other animals – did not need a *justification* for its own violence) but was strengthened with the first hierarchically organised human societies. The whole of human culture is built on the exploitation of both humans and animals.

9.   *Metaphysical antispeciesism severs the human being from the animal*
     Metaphysical antispeciesism believes humans should drop 'speciesism' for other species' sake, as speciesism merely means pursuing the interest of 'humans' against that of the other animals. In this way, the human being is again severed from and counterposed to the other species. On the contrary, historical antispeciesism maintains that the human animal is a victim of speciesism, too, and that we should put an end to it for our *and* other animals' sake.

As a matter of fact, speciesism – our belief that the human being is something other than and superior to every other animal – is the cause of nothing; it is rather the effect of something that metaphysical antispeciesists have not yet explained.

4   Animal Liberation and Human Liberation?

The real problem with antispeciesism is that it lacks any *historical* understanding of human society and it lacks any *social* understanding of human history. History could tell us *when* speciesism began. A critical look on society could tell us *how*. Animal Rightists have good reasons not to answer these questions: their theories only work when we forget such questions. These two mistakes can also be expressed synthetically as the lack of any *political* understanding of human history and society. It is not surprising that many animal rights activists dismiss radical politics, preaching animal liberation as a moral choice that concerns 'every man': it is not important to know who s/he is, where and when s/he lives or even if this 'every man' factually exists. According to this theory, polar hunters and New York policemen should both adopt a vegetarian diet and advocate for animal rights, even if this means that the first should try to grow plants on ice or become a New York policeman himself.[9]

It is true that many animal rights activists share the assumption that 'animal liberation is human liberation', although often for different reasons. Singer, for example, argues that the diffusion of vegetarianism and the abolition of factory farming would increase agricultural production for human needs, and therefore lead to the end of world hunger.[10] However, according to this thesis, the relationship between human and animal liberation is entirely extrinsic and contingent. First, it simply means that the consequences of animal liberation would produce benefits even for humans. Second, it forgets that world hunger is not the consequence of insufficient production: the imbalance in the use of resources is the effect of human exploitation, and, as long as the latter produces unequal distribution of power, there cannot be any equal distribution of wealth.

A second version of the motto 'animal liberation is human liberation' tries to go deeper into the connection between animal and human oppression, but it is equally incorrect. This idea is held by those who believe that speciesism is a form of discrimination which includes racism and sexism. From this point of view, it is claimed, those who fight against speciesism must necessarily fight against racism and sexism. Therefore, they must fight for a more just *society*.[11]

---

9   Noske 2004.

10 Singer 2015, p. vii.

11 It is on such a basis that many deny the possibility of extreme right-wing antispeciesism. Such a conclusion would be true only under the following conditions: 1) that racism and sexism must always be *explicitly* professed; 2) that racism and sexism must always be grounded on *biology*. It is quite clear that the first condition is false. Very few racists

Yet, all this is totally inadequate to a rigorous concept of human liberation. One can well imagine a multi-ethnic and non-sexist society in which all ethnic groups and genders are equally exploited. After all, we already live in a world which professes hostility to racism and sexism, while not an ounce of human liberation is in sight. Class inequalities are stronger than ever. The problem is that human liberation – as well as animal liberation – cannot be fought by the pure statement of 'moral principles'. It requires *the real abolition of exploitation*. Therefore, there can be no human liberation without facing the problem of class society.

It is interesting to note how Animal Rights Theorists fail to see the difference between sexism, racism and speciesism from one side, and class oppression from the other. Whenever they talk about prejudice and discrimination, the problem of class is often mentioned, although in the traditional, pre-Marxist form of opposition between the 'rich' and the 'poor': 'In the world at large, a few people are very wealthy, many more, very poor. And so it goes. Humans differ in many ways. There is no denying that. Still, no one who believes in human rights thinks these differences mark fundamental moral divisions. If we mean anything by the idea of human rights, we mean that we have them equal'.[12] Yet, the problem of class is not one of 'difference'; class does not distinguish the rich and the poor in the same way as religion distinguishes a 'Jew' from a 'Christian'. This becomes apparent when Regan expands Rawls's theory of justice to include species among the characteristic of the blind ruler: 'as would-be contractors, Rawls invites us to ignore those characteristics that make us different – such characteristics as our race and class, intelligence and skills, even our date

---

or sexists accept to be labelled *as such*. Although their deeds betray misogyny and intolerance for immigrants, the assumptions that support their actions will probably remain implicit. Thus, people who consider themselves to be strict antispeciesists (vegans, animal liberationists, etc.) can be *factually* racist and sexist without admitting it: they would be right-wing antispeciesists, no matter how they try to deny it. But even people who are explicitly right-wing, racist and sexist could profess antispeciesism without coming into conflict with current antispeciesist theories. As we have seen, traditional antispeciesist theories are grounded on the assumption of a moral bias towards animals based on *species* membership, i.e. on biological reasons. Now, even in the 1930s biological racism was just one of the forms in which racism was professed and defended. Many Fascists nowadays would probably prefer other arguments to defend their idea of a closed, ethnically homogeneous, traditional society. They might for instance believe in the need to close the borders and send home immigrants ('it is for *their own* good') or to limit freedom of choice for women ('is *their* nature'), remaining 'good' – and maybe 'radical' – antispeciesists.

12   Regan 2003, p. 27.

of birth and where we live'.[13] 'Classism' is mentioned but never really discussed as 'analogous' to racism and sexism, because the mistake would be suddenly apparent: Bill Gates does not need to despise his workers to make a profit out of them. Human exploiters can be very nice guys: generous, environmentalist, Buddhist and vegan. In the end, being a material structure of oppression, and not a prejudice, *class must be abolished, not deconstructed.*[14]

Whenever antispeciesism is understood as a way of fighting a form of 'discrimination', we imagine ourselves heroically taking away the foundations of human society: yet, as a matter of fact, we are only waging a war against an 'analogy' (speciesism = racism = sexism). The problem is not, as it is usually said,[15] that here the subject of liberation is cleaved: since animals cannot free themselves, the liberated subject does not coincide with the liberating one. This is, indeed, completely false, it is even a surreptitious form of speciesism: humans *are* animals and it is not clear why animal liberation should not concern us as subjects *to be released* from animal oppression. It is in *this* sense that animal liberation and human liberation may coincide: Humans are animals repressed and exploited by the same civilisation that has subjected non-human nature. The *circularity* of domination *must be broken*: the enslavement of nature needs the enslavement of humans, social hierarchy and the division of labour, religious alienation and anthropocentrism, so that everything tends to a more efficient control over nature and humans. Only if we take these two goals as one (free the animals, free the humans) can we avoid the viewpoint of a liberation movement that patronisingly cares about others[16] and that often, because of a lack of analysis, ends up in extinctionist nihilism ('human nature is evil', 'humans are wicked animals' etc.).[17]

The concept of animal liberation advocated here is opposed both to current vegan theories that see animal liberation articulated in two different subjects

---

13   Regan 2003, p. 43.

14   Maurizi 2018.

15   Benton 1993, p. 93; Luke 2016, p. 150.

16   Even Best accepts this conclusion: 'Animal liberation is a movement of and by human animals for nonhuman animals' (2014, p. 36).

17   Extinctionism is utter nonsense. It is absurd from a mere *logical* point of view. If humans could understand how *evil* they are, and come to the collective decision of voluntary extinction, this very act would put into question their evil nature: matter-of-factly, humans would be the most selfless animals ever seen on the face of the Earth! Therefore, we have to choose: either we think that humans can consciously accelerate their own extinction (thus proving that they are able to accomplish ethical tasks far beyond the range of extinction), or they cannot (and then the voluntary extinction movement is meaningless).

(humans free the animals), and the primitivist ideology that understands the unity between these two subjects, but proposes to return to a pre-Neolithic stage of human development.

The first assumes a *static* and *unhistorical* distinction between humans and animals and ends up with the thesis that once animal exploitation is abolished, no further *interaction* between them is possible, reciprocal *indifference* is the only way in which our society can deal with other species.

The second recognises that the opposition between humans and animals is something *historically contingent* but knows no other possible relationship between these two subjects than the simple interaction typical of hunter-gatherer society. Everything that has been produced by civilisation is alienation and failure. Primitivism, in particular, makes no criticism of *predation*, which is justified as 'natural'. Thus, as can be seen, the historicity of the human being is recognised only to be denied as degeneration and a mistake! History is possible, but it should not be. Humans can be dynamic, but they should be static. Consequently, as in the first case, the assumption of a static *human nature* is also working behind the scenes: 'culture' is just an attempt to deny an unchangeable nature.

The antispeciesist perspective here defended recognises that the relationship of alienation between humans and animals is *a product of social history*, an effect of a patriarchal, hierarchical and oppressive culture. Therefore, this perspective recognises (as primitivism does) that oppression is not an inevitable destiny of humankind, but rather something that can be fought and defeated. Unlike primitivism, however, it does not see civilisation as an aberration of nature, an unnatural mistake. Culture is rather the *continuation of nature* in a specific form: it is what Žižek calls *Unbehagen in der Natur*.[18] Civilisation allowed the development of new practical and cognitive tools, the production of new infra and interspecies relations. The antispeciesist movement was born right in the middle of Western hyper-culture, in the time of maximum alienation between humans and animals. For this very reason, it is a political project of reconciliation with the natural world that accepts principles created by humans. These principles are not taken from an 'objective', static nature; they are grounded on culture understood as interaction between human and non-human subjects. Animal liberation, in this sense, does not imply any 'return to nature', but rather a *new course of relationships between the species*. These relationships include consequences which are anything but 'natural', like a diet which is at odds with human omnivorism (veganism[19]), the idea of interspe-

---

18   Žižek 2008, p. 420 ff.
19   Yet, as we will see, veganism is just a rough *approximation* of the evolutionary potential

cific equality and universal solidarity towards non-humans (which can reach up to compassion for victims of predation). Primitivist antispeciesists might object that such a perspective is itself a product of an alienated civilisation and that its practices (veganism) and its values (animal equality) are themselves unnatural deformations. The abolition of civilisation will lead, it is said, to the disappearance of both, and their replacement with 'free' and 'natural' relationships between the species. Yet, antispeciesism can be denounced as 'unnatural' only by those who share an abstract idea of nature, as a pristine, uncontaminated state of things. Such an assumption is unproven: the concept of equality, the idea of empathy towards animal suffering, although consequences of civilisation and its 'alienation', may well represent the appearance of *new* natural relations, a possibility still waiting to be fully realised. The image of nature as a static order, forever identical to itself, is outdated and wrong. Once we accept that there is no eternal Nature, once we assume the perspective of 'natural history'[20] (i.e. of nature as incessant *becoming*), even civilisation can have its own place in this story as a moment of crisis and upheaval, a crisis that could be followed by a new world of relations between the species.

of a real liberated society. Once biotechnology has been emancipated from capitalistic control, it could easily find ways to satisfy our alimentary needs, putting an end to animal exploitation. The fixation on veganism, as a form of moral and individualistic lifestyle, is part of the theoretical and practical problems faced by current Animal Rightism.

20 'Natural history, contrary to the seeming oxymoronic ring of the expression, seeks to naturalize history and historicize nature in order to break through the reification of both: nature is not only repetition of the same, nor is history the ceaseless emergence of the new' (Mendieta 2011, p. 156). We will later discuss the concept of 'natural history' in Marx and Engels (Chapter 5) and in the Frankfurt School (Chapter 6).

CHAPTER 2

On the Genesis of Speciesism

I believe that the concept of speciesism only makes sense if seen as part of
the historical self-making of the human being. Although this may sound like a
weird usage of the term speciesism, I suggest that the human animal has been
the first historical 'victim' of speciesism. In this chapter I hope to show that this
is the only way to save this concept from the sterile abstractions of academic
philosophy and from the blind and apolitical moralism of Animal Rightists.[1]

1   The Ambiguity of Speciesism

After the appearance of *Animal Liberation*, the word 'speciesism' has become
largely acknowledged in the Animal Rights Movement. Even if many Animal
Rights Activists never read Singer's book, certain general assumptions derived
from his book have indeed become the *lingua franca* of the whole movement.
The reason why I consider Singer so important is that his success superseded
earlier attempts to define 'speciesism' in a different philosophical context. The
word itself, as commonly recognised, was invented by Ryder. Its most common
use goes beyond Singer's intention in the direction of what I have described
above as its 'extended' version: a mental habit which measures everything from
the standpoint of humanity, in which animals are always considered ontologically and morally inferior. Yet, the concept of a sort of *racism of humanity against
the other species* had already been developed by various 'continental' philosophers like Adorno, Anders or Baudrillard.[2] Indeed, the critique of anthropocentrism is an essential part of modernity itself, from Montaigne to Schopenhauer.[3]

By reducing 'speciesism' to a logical mechanism for the analysis of ethical
propositions, Singer *emptied the concept of any historical, social and political*

---

1 In the following analysis I agree in part with Calarco (2016, p. 55 ff.) who suggests we should
   drop the concept of 'speciesism' and make 'anthropocentrism' our main focus. As I mentioned
   before, though, I believe that most Animal Rights Activists *already* use the two concepts
   interchangeably. My main interest here is to show that such confusion derives from an undialectical understanding of the human-animal relationship. There is something at stake in that
   confusion. We should work on it.
2 Adorno 1993; 1996; Anders 1968; Baudrillard 2016.
3 Montaigne 1993; Schopenhauer 2010.

complexity. As a matter of fact, the great success of his book was largely the result of its shocking central thesis that *vegetarianism was a moral obligation*.[4] But while vegetarians had thus found their Bible, Singer's theses provoked a heated debate that has not ceased to split public opinion. As I will show in the next chapter, the debate rested on a faulty premise. Let us for the moment focus on the simplification that this concept of speciesism brought to the Animal Rights Movement.

Animal Liberation defines speciesism as the moral privilege accorded to one's own species, i.e. we assume the interests of human animals to be more important than those of non-human animals, just as white racists do with black people.[5] This is a strict *theoretical* definition of speciesism. But Singer himself introduces a *historical* description of the origins of speciesism in his book; his sources are indeed poor but he cunningly manages to quote Aristotle, Augustine, Thomas Aquinas, Descartes and Kant to unveil the speciesist nature of Western civilisation.[6] The problem is that speciesism is a *praxis*, not only a moral prejudice: it has a *material* and not just an ideal side. It is not clear whether Singer is here describing how speciesism as a praxis came to exist in history, or how different human societies *a posteriori* justified their attitude towards animals. The fallacy of most Animal Rightism depends on the fact that it does not make such a distinction. First of all, because it does not seem to see it. In his 'Short history of speciesism', Singer merely juxtaposes the ideas of philosophers and the material treatment reserved to animals as if the latter were produced by the former. It is interesting to note that Singer's 'historical' progression has been repeated almost identically several times, even by Singer himself,[7] without putting into question its radical bias.[8] The real reason for such confusion and inversion of the material and ideal aspects of speciesism is that Animal Rightism prefers the abstraction of ethics to the concreteness of social sciences, or revolutionary politics. Since abstract moral theory only makes sense in an abstract and static world, Animal Liberationists must sup-

---

4 This can be also proven with the success of Tom Regan among Animal Rights Activists. Contrary to Singer, as we have seen, Regan's theory of 'inherent value' offers a complete and absolute justification to vegetarianism, whereas Singer's utilitarianism admits exceptions. Also, Regan offers an 'intrinsic' argument against meat consumption, while Singer starts with the consequences of its general calculus. Most Animal Rights Activists probably defend the 'sanctity of life' that Singer criticised; anyway, very few seem to approve his most audacious arguments about the moral possibility of infanticide (1994, p. 128 ff.).

5 Singer 2015, pp. 18–23.

6 Singer 2015, p. 186 ff.

7 Singer 1985; 1994.

8 See, for instance, Sapontzis 1987; Kalechofsky 1988; Finsen 1988; Francione 1995; Ryder 1998.

press the distinction between material and ideal in order to present our modern society and its values as something given. Universal principles cannot apply to a world that is conceived in perpetual change. This is evident when we think that most Animal Rights Activists are not even preaching new moral values but simply asserting that our society contradicts itself if it does not extend its already existing values to non-human animals. For instance, Francione writes: 'the position that I am proposing in this book is radical in the sense that it would force us to stop using animals in many of the ways that we now take for granted. In another sense, however, my argument is quite conservative in that it follows from a moral principle that we already claim to accept'.[9]

Many Animal Rights Philosophers are of course aware that their own moral theories are only possible under certain obvious historical circumstances. If the category of speciesism was first elaborated in 1975 and not by Pythagoras, it is only because modern society forged the concepts of 'universal rights' and 'egalitarianism', while Pythagoras was probably more concerned about not eating the souls of his dead friends. Animal Rightists simply demonstrate how illogical it is not to extend such concepts to non-human animals once Western civilisation has imposed its values – and, indeed, its economic and political hegemony – over the whole world. They do not seem to be worried about such hegemony, and instead simply accept it as a fact; the moral values they play with are not questioned, their origins remain uninvestigated. Francione, for instance, believes that we should not treat animals as property, but does not question the institution of property itself.[10] To paraphrase his own words, such an approach really qualifies as a sort of 'political schizophrenia'.

2 The Origin of Speciesism

The question of the origin of speciesism must then be treated historically, paying attention to real relationships between humans and non-humans. It must therefore be formulated as follows: when did speciesism begin? As I have said, this is itself an ambiguous question, because it implies what we called a *material* and an *ideal* side: from the material side, speciesism is the praxis of using animals for our needs, turning them into mere 'things'. But such a process of reification implies an ideal side, i.e. the ideological justification that animals are indeed things at our disposal. So, what happens if we look at real history and

9   Francione 2000, p. xxix.
10   Francione 1995; 1996; 2000.

try to trace back the origin of speciesism both in its material and ideal side? Let us begin with the material side. Since Singer defined speciesism as the ideology of a dominant species, the first question is: when did we become a dominant species? Was it a heritage of our ancestors? Who was the first speciesist ape?

2.1 Dominion as Praxis

We can surely rule out the *Australopitecus*, as he could not even hunt and was himself most certainly *food* for other predators. We know that he could probably kill very small animals, but he was likely more a scavenger than a hunter. His behaviour towards nature was scarcely different from that of other apes, although he began the all-important practice of stone-tooling.

Other ancestors like the *Homo erectus* and the *Neanderthalensis* developed hunting skills, mainly based on their growing intelligence and cooperation.[11] Although they could themselves still be food for other animals, they were indeed dangerous predators which succeeded in overcoming their physical disadvantage. But this did not make them 'dominant animals' either. It is hard to affirm that their power and intelligence made them believe they were better, more important than, or even different from the animals they killed. On the contrary, the evidence provided by societies characterised by gathering and hunting is that the hunted is sacred and sometimes believed to be a god or to possess an immortal soul.[12] The hunt is commonly preceded by a ritual: the hunters pray to the so-called 'Lord of Animals' and ask forgiveness. They cannot just go out and shoot at everything that moves. Although magic and religious ideas slowly start to draw a line between our self-consciousness and our perception of nature, human attitude towards the victims seems to be characterised at this stage by a *mixture of compassion and guilt*. Hunters must believe that the animal they kill actually *wants* to be killed, that such murder is a gift from the

---

11 Fromm 1973.
12 Eliade 1978; Puech 1988. It is clear that 'analogies' with contemporary hunter-gatherer society cannot once and for all solve the problem of Paleolithic and Mesolithic human behaviour. The risks of such a method have been discussed several times. Yet, the alternative – ending up in absolute incertitude, arguing that we know nothing about the prehistoric mind – is no less problematic. 'The problem is not in attributing thoughts to people in the past in the effort to explain their actions. It is in attributing to them no more thought than might be attributed to any sexually reproductive organism that must derive a living from the environment and compete with others of its own kind for subsistence and reproductive opportunities, or, alternatively, in attributing to people in the past a simplified version of our own thoughts. Missing from the former perspective are any thoughts that might specifically be human, and from the latter any thoughts that might be more or less common among hunter-gatherers generally or specific only to those in particular cultural and historical contexts' (Cannon 2014).

part of the animal,[13] that it is indeed a 'sacrifice'. Hunting itself is part of a magic ritual in which the hunter and the hunted are peers; it is the phenomenon that Mercea Eliade called 'mystical solidarity'.[14] There is no use in saying that such ideas were an excuse for a speciesist praxis, because magic is not simply an ideological *Weltanschauung*. It is the first approach of the human mind to reality, the first symbolic description of it, the eruption of meaning: it is science, religion and art shaped into one. It would be pointless to argue that the prehistoric hunter is lying or pretending: he really *sees* the world as a system of visible and invisible forces and this system makes a stronger distinction than that between the human and the not-human.[15]

We must therefore deny that we became 'dominant animals' before the appearance of *Homo sapiens*. Anyway, we must also reject the idea that our dominion over nature is a 'natural' characteristic of our species. It was a later cultural development: totemic systems were still grounded on the identification with the animal.[16] That is why anarcho-primitivits like John Zerzan suggest that the dominion of the human being over nature began later on, during the

---

13   Ingold 2000, pp. 69–72.
14   Eliade 1978; Van der Leeuw 1986.
15   Lévi-Strauss 1966; Hayden 2003; Harvey 2014; Cannon 2014; Brightman, Grotti and Ulturgasgeva 2012; Willerslev 2007. To suggest, as Dunayer (2004) does, that we subjugated animals because we considered them inferior is a rather funny assumption. *How* should that have happened? Dunayer imagines that prehistoric humans somehow 'feel' superior to animals and start to kill or exploit them. She even believes that this is already a *moral decision*. As usual, it is not clear whether prehistoric humans convinced themselves individually of their superiority, or if it was a cultural phenomenon. Anyway, since prehistoric humans *already* killed animals, this can only mean that they continued to kill them while starting to consider them inferior. Thus, either they *changed* their moral decisions about killing animals, or they *started* to make moral decisions. Yet, if they had lived since without making a moral decision, it is not clear why they could not go on living in ignorance of moral belief. But let us suppose that all this make sense. We know that hunter-gatherers have a strong mystical relation with animals and nature in general, showing respect and even adoration for them. This is at odds with Dunayer's hypothesis. Let us suppose that prehistoric hunter-gatherers *do not* share the magic culture that is typical of this kind of social organisation. There are, though, hunter-gatherer societies nowadays that have lived for thousands of years according to the values of animistic culture. A simple explanation would be that their system of belief evolved from prehistoric hunter-gatherers and, though it probably changed historically, it did not make a substantial leap forward or outside the circle of simple reproduction and its animistic belief: thus, they always worshipped nature and animals. Again, though, this would contradict Dunayer's hypothesis. So we must assume that they started to feel superior to non-human animals and then, mysteriously, *forgot* it.
16   Freud 2009; Rees 2018; Marrone and Mangano 2018; Timofeeva 2018.

Neolithic age, with the 'discovery' of agriculture and domestication.[17] Although I will later criticise such view, it is important to underline why it is not totally wrong. The praxis of domesticating plants and animals is indeed the step that enables us to consciously change our environment, to make it an *extension of our own needs*, instead of simply accepting it as it is.[18] It is also true that this step was followed by an amazing acceleration in human evolution: between 8,000 and 3,000 years BC the political, economic, scientific and technological structures of human society as we know it were laid down. A male-dominated, hierarchical order, in which religion and knowledge justify man's supremacy, was born. Right from the start, history has been the history of dominion. From one perspective, it has been suggested that we still live in the social order brought forth by the Neolithic age. This does not obviously mean that its social changes and inventions happened all at once and everywhere in the same way. Childe's concept of the 'Neolithic revolution' must be tempered with recent archaeological discoveries which tend to underline the continuity between Mesolithic and Neolithic.[19]

2.2   *Dominion as Ideology*

Let us for the moment be content with this conclusion; we will return to it later. There is still something missing. If the Neolithic revolution laid down the basis of our dominion over nature, thus producing the *material possibility* of the speciesist ideology, it did not produce such ideology. The *ideal* side of speciesism appeared only later on in history. It is time we asked when that happened.

If we stand on the ground of metaphysical antispeciesism, we do not differentiate animal exploitation and speciesism. We end up in a conceptual confusion where there is no sensible answer to the question 'when does speciesism begin?' From such a confused point of view, there are only two possible answers, which arise respectively from the restricted or the extended definition of speciesism.

In the first case (speciesism as 'moral bias tied to species membership'), we will be forced to say that speciesism is born with the Enlightenment or even with the Declaration of Human Rights, since here – for the first time in history – human society recognises a universal right of protection to human beings *qua* human beings. Humans, and only humans, are characterised by an 'intrinsic value'. This means that fundamental rights are granted to members of our species and are, thereby, explicitly denied to non-humans. It could be argued that

---

17   Zerzan 1994.
18   Giannetto 2005.
19   Whittle 2003.

even in the pre-Enlightenment era (especially in Medieval Christianity) such prejudice was already there, since Christ's sacrifice had elevated humanity to an unprecedented status of dignity. Humans, regardless of their class origin, were all 'Sons of God'. However, it is a fact that in Ancient and Medieval society (and, to a great extent, even in Modernity), this did not automatically mean that humans were generally treated in accordance with their alleged moral 'dignity'. Quite the contrary. Human exploitation, indeed, was considered as natural as animal exploitation, even morally justified, regardless of the recognition of the dignity ascribed to human beings as such. In societies where it could happen that the life of a slave or a worker could count for less than that of an animal, the narrow definition of speciesism cannot be applied.

If we believe that speciesism is a moral privilege that humans share *qua* 'humans', we cannot avoid the conclusion that all societies that practised slavery or human sacrifice were *not* speciesist. For though they adored their king like a human God, the Aztecs used to slaughter and eat humans (though there is still controversy about the extent of such practice); the abstract moral criteria of Animal Rightism would have been a good argument in favour of Aztec cannibalism. Moreover, the case of Aztec society is also a good objection to Zerzan's idea that agriculture produced the 'fall from grace', since the Aztecs were sedentary but did not live on the basis of agriculture.[20]

Thus, speciesism turns out to be a rather recent phenomenon. And this is obvious. Speciesism is a 'universal' ideology: it needs a universal concept of species, so that we can gather on one side *all* men and women under the concept of 'humans' and on the other *all* other self-moving, living beings under the concept of 'animals'. Singer's reasoning only makes sense when such a distinction is historically established and has become the basic assumption of rationality itself. Both distinctions are in fact not at all evident or immediate and it took a long time for them to become widely accepted.

Biology here does not help. Symbolic systems rearrange natural distinctions according to their inner logic.[21] Erich Fromm, for instance, argued that the loss of primordial instincts (like the weakening of the sense of smell due to the upright position) makes it difficult for the *homo sapiens* to establish an immediate identity between himself and other humans; if the basic identity of a certain culture implies, for example, being part of a tribe, it is clear that a human being from another tribe can be – and actually has often been – perceived as not-human.[22] The other human becomes an element of a symbolic system where

---

20   Hultkranz 1988; Harris 1977.
21   Lévi-Strauss 1963, pp. 51, 95–6.
22   Fromm 1973.

the distinction between human and non-humans, 'us' and 'them', is fluid. Thus, human identity as species is a conceptual identity that presupposes a high degree of abstraction. And even when such a level of abstraction is reached we may still mess up things a bit: Aristotle surely had conceived the idea of the human being but made a further distinction between free men, women and slaves. It is only with Christendom that the idea that all humans are equal was forged; it was only with the Enlightenment that such an idea became political; and it was only with Socialism that it was put into action.

From the other side, that all not-human beings should fall under the concept of 'animal' is also problematic. We have an opposition here. Therefore, if the first term ('human') is not yet established – and we have seen that it takes a long time for this to happen – the second term ('animal') will also fluctuate. In Ancient Mesopotamia, for instance, 'despite the fact that there exist classifiers for birds, fishes, and a number of mammals which are traditionally termed "determinatives", specific terms for animals excluding or including humans and deities seem missing in the earlier texts'.[23] We may find that this distinction becomes clearer, the more the idea of the human being becomes universal. And this is exactly the case. For Aristotle there was continuity between the *animal rationale* and the other animals. In Christendom such continuity was weaker and ambiguous: 'On the one hand, this tradition is distressed by the sinfulness of the animal nature of man. On the other, it admires the innocence of the beast that does not know the difference between good and evil, the bestial naivety and innocence from which we have to learn'.[24] In Post-Cartesian mechanicism – with the possible exception of materialists like La Mettrie – the idea of an affinity between humans and animals was definitively *passé*.

3   How?

Here, it emerges that the concept of speciesism implies a structural contradiction: its material side – the physical exploitation – does not coincide with its ideal side – the ideological justification of oppression. They even form a *chiasmus*: the praxis of exploiting animals began when we did not think we were different from them; and we started to denounce our dominion over them now that we cannot perceive them as peers any more. Why? Because we forgot that

23   Selz 2019, p. 26.
24   Timofeeva 2018.

the human being is an animal, too. So, the first question should not be 'when did we start to oppress the other animals?' but rather 'when did we forget that we are animals too?'

More than 30,000 years ago, with the Aurignacian culture, human evolution began running wild. Human culture, i.e. the product of labour and of intelligence, started to developed at a rate unknown to the natural kingdom before the appearance of our species. This is what intrigued Marx and Engels, even before they read Darwin: 'Men can be distinguished from animals by consciousness, by religion or anything else you like. They themselves begin to distinguish themselves from animals as soon as they begin to produce their means of subsistence, a step which is conditioned by their physical organisation. By producing their means of subsistence men are indirectly producing their actual material life'.[25] The making of the human Self is therefore something that can only take place through such a process. History is the place where such self-making happens: human culture is something we actually *produce*. Please note: when Marx and Engels here say that the human being is 'different' from the animal, they are not talking about some ontological difference, some universal and static distinction; rather they are talking about an *activity*. Humans *differentiate* themselves from the other animals through history. History is the act of making ourselves different from the animals. From one side, the distinction is *real* because we permanently change ourselves and our environment through our labour. From the other side, it is an *illusion*, because we *are* animals, part of nature, material beings. The *super*natural aspects of human culture, the 'spirit' in whose honour the temples of civilisation were raised, is a lie. But this proves again the undeniable uniqueness of the human being: *an animal that forgets to be an animal*. History is a tale of forgetting.

If we ask ourselves when we started to forget, the only reasonable answer is: since the beginning. Or, at least, since our hands and our brain began to show weird reactions to the environment: for example, as we started to make tools that were not only useful but also beautiful, symmetric, harmonic. The praxis of making something that was not *in* nature brought forth the illusion of something that was *not* nature – i.e. the germs of the spiritualistic ideology. The first cultural expression of the human spirit can be traced back to magic and animism. Although magic did not create the split between our mind and the external world, it was anyway the first expression of a split that had already taken place. Magic implies the idea of an invisible force, hidden behind the nature we see: it is such force that explains natural phenomena and enables

---

25   Marx and Engels 1969, p. 21.

the magician to produce effects in the real world. It is the beginning of the spiritual illusion, but it is also the beginning of an explanation of nature. As we have said: magic was religion, art and science at the same time.

We also said that magic did not produce the split between the human and the not-human, although it was the beginning of the historical process that led to it. It did not 'alienate' us from nature because magic works through the law of *similarity*. As anthropologists Mauss and Hubert expressed it, the principle of magic is: *one is all, all is one, nature triumphs over nature*.[26] Magic expressed the beginning of forgetting but did not cause it. Such forgetting was in fact gradually imposed on the human beings through education, sexual restriction and alienated labour. The question about *when* all this happened, is therefore inseparable from the question about *how*, i.e. from the question of social organisation.

Marx's idea that humans produce the material basis of their existence only makes sense when we consider humans that live in society: i.e. real human beings, not the Cartesian 'solipsists'[27] who inhabit the world of moral philosophy. The sphere of material production has always been inseparable from constriction. Whenever society establishes rules through which it can reproduce itself, everybody must do their part. Although such a social order implies the dictatorship of the collective over the individual, 'primitive' human societies are at least characterised by egalitarianism. When those societies become 'tribes' and later 'chiefdoms', the social order becomes hierarchical and centralised: a central authority, which is religious and political at the same time, starts to organise the distribution of the economic resources.[28] Such authority, probably caused by natural differences (like physical or mental cleverness), starts to detach itself from the person who holds it and to become a privilege.[29] It

---

26   Mauss and Hubert 1972.

27   Acampora 2006, p. 4.

28   Service 1971; Guidi 2000, pp. 59–60.

29   I am describing this crucial passage using the *historic present* because I do not want to give the impression that this is a (pre)history of social hierarchy. Both social anthropology and archaeology use terms like 'tribes', 'chiefdom', 'Neolithic revolution', 'early States' etc., although in a slightly different sense. In social anthropology this terminology describes *ideal phases* of development of social stratification. In archaeology, it describes *factual phases* and, of course, their use is influenced by material differences in space and time. Institutionalisation of Power, thus, can both evolve gradually from certain given conditions *or* be the effect of a sudden revolution, the consequence of an external pressure. Some critical histories of domination, for example, underline the importance of the Kurgan invasion for the evolution of European societies (Kohl 2007). The fact that I do not mention the Kurgan Hypothesis here is due to the fact that I am more interested in a *phenomenology* of social hierarchy and its relation with the domination of nature. Differ-

is at this stage of social evolution that the *taming of the human animal* takes place, because social constraint, religion and authority all contributed to make us accept an unjust order. Social rules start to be imposed from above and introjected by the individual as 'normal'.

In the early States, the central religious and political authority becomes an institution that not only coordinates the economic efforts of society, but makes *profit* out of it.[30] Of course, 'profit' here is to be understood in terms of surplus-production.[31] While the majority materially produces all the means of subsistence, the State stores the products of agriculture and feeds those who do not work (the political and religious elite) or whose work does not produce food: like the metal workers whose manufactured goods were also dedicated to the elite and reinforced their status.[32] It is here that individuals – 'big men' – and individual groups – 'families' – turn into impersonal power structures: 'as the surplus from production continued to grow, these individuals, or their family groups, began to form a social class which controlled a part of society's wealth. Once they formed a separate class, they began to have different collective material interests from the mass of the population. This leads to a self-identification for the controlling group as a separate class from the wider population. Increasingly the new ruling class will see the interests of the whole of society as being their own'.[33]

The *temple* – where the resources are stored for redistribution – is the axial point of the whole process. The authority of the chiefdom *discorporates* and power becomes *impersonal* (this is what Maisels calls 'the movement from status to state');[34] at the same time, the State incarnates the idea of religious transcendence: the abstract product of social antagonism is imposed over society as a being-in-itself. Magic, which started as a way of comprehending the world, evolved into institutional religions and became a way to prevent criticism. Magic had a manipulative side too, and it was also an attempt to dominate the external world. But its effects were ridiculous if compared with that

---

ently from a historical account, a phenomenological description clarifies the *conditions of possibility* of social stratification, not the *series of events* that factually produced it. Domination over nature is a prerequisite of class society in Europe, Asia or America, no matter how, no matter when it happens. And *this* is the core of my argument. In this sense, though the Kurgan Hypothesis would confirm my general scheme, it is not necessary.

30 Guidi 2000, pp. 60–1; Liverani 2004, p. 28.
31 Mandel 1967.
32 Childe 1950; Guidi 2000, pp. 87, 130.
33 Empson 2014.
34 Maisels 1993, p. 211.

of later state-religions which slowly adopted the patriarchal view of a tran-scendental dominion over nature. Although religion may have offered the spir-itual weapons needed to force people to work for others, such social devel-opment surely involved a certain amount of external violence. As Mario Liv-erani writes in his wonderful book *Uruk: The First City*, the guardians were invented 'not to protect *people*, but to protect the central richness *from* the people'.[35]

It is essential to understand the difference between 'violence' and 'system-atic violence', i.e dominion, between 'conflicts' and 'exploitation', 'hierarchies' and 'class'. Violence between human groups in the palaeolithic, for instance, is not 'war'. Even if it is possible to define the clashes between groups of hunter gatherers as 'wars',[36] the difference between these clashes and neolithic war-fare cannot be denied, because it expresses a new constellation of resources, power and social stratification. It is intertwined with inner-group exploitation: 'the existence of a surplus of wealth makes war a potentially profitable exer-cise. This is not to say that pre-class societies did not engage in war or fight for resources. But with the development of classes, violence becomes inherent to society'.[37] Later, 'in the Bronze Age, for the first time, weapons were developed for the sole and specific purpose of killing humans rather than animals'.[38] The point, here, is not to resume an idyllic vision of the palaeolithic lifestyle as 'nat-ural' and 'peaceful'; the point is to avoid any interpretation of class struggle and class-derived conflicts in term of some 'natural' violence and aggressiveness, which would obliterate their socio-historical structure and trace them back to our instinctual life.

4   Speciesism and Human Liberation

What is at stake in the transition from *nomadism* (the social form that anthro-pologists call 'hunter-gatherer society') to *sedentarism* (based on agriculture and livestock)? As far as the exchange between society and nature is con-cerned, the nomadic phase is characterised by a sort of symbiosis between humans and the environment, while sedentary groups – through the process of domestication of animals and plants – start to control the environment: other species cease to be autonomous and become a 'resource' at our disposal. This

---

35   Liverani 2004, p. 24.
36   Guilaine and Zammit 2005, p. 25.
37   Empson 2014.
38   Harding 2000, p. 275.

phenomenon is accompanied by historically important changes in our social and symbolic order, which ultimately feed back on the relationship between humans and nature, by providing the ideological basis of what we call speciesism. Human groups who give up nomadism, in fact, abandon the kind of egalitarianism that characterises hunting and gathering society and give rise to forms of social hierarchy. Clearly, civilisation is not only due to the exploitation of nature: without human exploitation it would be impossible. Yet, these two forms of exploitation go together and escalate exponentially once combined. The material domination over nature has serious repercussions on the symbolic level. The magic-animist culture of nomadic societies establishes a weak opposition between the human and the nonhuman. It is only in patriarchal and hierarchical societies that the phenomenon of *deification of the human being* arises.

Our symbolic and material relationship with animals experiences a dramatic change with the birth of class society and institutionalised religions. *Totemism* expresses the ideological turning point from animism to anthropocentric religion, because 'a core aspect of *totemic* worldviews is how differences in the natural environment are used as models for human thought and as tools for "ordering" the world by categorising the elements within it. Differences between natural species serve as models for making sense of differences between social groups, or clans'.[39] Such 'animist-totemist ontologies' are 'concerned increasingly with vertical rather than horizontal social organisation'; distinctions are made 'between certain other-than-humans (specific totem animals) and the (human-descent) clans associated with them, and other other-than-human-persons (different totem animals) and the clans associated with them – involving a greater emphasis, though evidently not axiomatically, on human ancestors'.[40] No wonder that the diffusion of *anthropomorphic divinities* and the deification of the elite and its ancestors go hand in hand. With material dominance over animals, thus, identification with the animal is less real and the relationship becomes increasingly metaphorical. At the same time the ambivalence towards animals become detrimental: animals become symbols of moral degradation, lack of reason, etc. Animal imagery is frequently found in the body of religious wisdom, expressing our ambivalence toward the natural world: 'the bull was felt to be the most expressive symbol of this irrational and sometimes destructive power of wild nature, to master in order to be truly "a man"';[41] 'proverbs, hence, concentrate on the ox or bull, expressing

---

39   Fuglestvedt 2014.
40   Wallis 2014, p. 322.
41   Cauvin 2002, p. 245.

the common metaphors associated with the animal, such as its strength and vitality, but also its stubbornness or even stupidity'.[42]

The contrast between humans and animals has its origin here, yet such a divide is not propelled by 'humans' in general. It is rather those placed on top of the social pyramid that need to exert their power over all beings under their control, i.e. humans and animals; these, in turn, make the ideological power of the elite possible through their own material exploitation. Human and animal oppressions are so closely related that it is only through their interaction that the phenomenon which Singer calls 'speciesism' arises. Speciesism, as ideology, is derivative and secondary, compared to the real exploitation of both humans and animals. In other words, *without animal exploitation there is no class society, but without class society there is no speciesism.*

The ideal side of speciesism – i.e. its ideological justification – was a by-product of the institutionalisation of religion and, as such, it was a process that involved constriction and repression. But the material side of speciesism was no fun for human beings either. Surplus accumulation and the division of labour *increased the exploitation rate of both humans and animals.* It is only when someone can make profit out of them that animals become things and humans become slaves. This does not mean that Mesopotamian kings actually *saw* their oxen as mere things. Nevertheless, the yoked oxen was a precondition of the existence of the Mesopotamian State, as it made possible the necessary surplus accumulation to feed the state bureaucracy. Once animals themselves become gears in the machinery of dominion they are subjugated not to the 'human being' but to the superior necessity of the State. It is only when a hierarchy *inside* society is established that the relation between the human being and the animal becomes hierarchical: *humans control humans who control animals.* It is a dialectical process. If it is true that the enslavement of the oxen made the enslavement of the human being possible, from the other side, human enslavement reinforced the distance between the top of the social pyramid and its basis. Individual peasants may have domesticated individual animals even at the end of the Palaeolithic. But it is only with the Neolithic class struggle that animal exploitation becomes systematic and totalitarian. Although phenomena of domestication were already known to nomadic humanity (the dog, for instance), Neolithic economy establishes domination upon nature as a precondition of social rationality and of subsequent economic advances; as Childe puts it: the domestication of the ox was the first step towards the steam engine.[43]

---

42   Cohen 2013, p. 218.

43   Childe 1975.

Only if the economic necessity of exploitation is questioned, can we think of a different social order where hierarchies based on class, sex, race and species are smashed down. This can be done only if we avoid two symmetrical mistakes concerning the material and ideological side of domination.

1) Intended as material structure of power, speciesism may well be back-dated to the end of nomadism and the rise of civilisation. This thesis has found expression in the animal liberation movement, following the primitivist John Zerzan, who theorises civilisation as a mistake from which humanity must break free.[44] In addition to Zerzan's historical and theoretical simplifications, primitivist antispeciesism must reckon with the fact that even if hunting and gathering societies were not *strictu sensu* speciesist, they practised forms of animal killing that are incompatible with antispeciesism. These groups were and are completely unable to criticise *predation* (which is part of their liveli-hood) or to come up with a concept of 'universal equality' (which is impossible for them, since their symbolic systems are historically, geographically, econom-ically, and conceptually condemned to particularism). We do not find here the horrors of civilisation, nor its idea of universal justice. Obviously, primitivists believe that this idea of justice is another flaw of 'civilised thinking', and, there-fore, they will consider themselves immune to such criticism. I suggest, on the contrary, that this is another weakness of primitivist thinking. We will return on this in Chapter 7.

2) Hierarchies based on class, sex, race and species are not 'issues' we should discuss or moral advances we should demand. We must leave the heavens of moral abstraction and understand how the social machine actually works. It is a political question and since the roots of domination are so deep, a social change like the one we are working for needs a radical solution; it needs a revolutionary politics. Animal liberation and human liberation are still two kinds of separate and different oppression. Their connection is extrinsic. Their unity can only be justified by attacking a political system that Animal Rightists accept as such. For us, the statement 'Animal Liberation is Human Liberation' means something different: we see the political nature of it, we see that the core of the problem is the logic of exploitation of class society, a logic whose basis was established more than 10,000 years ago and that has since not ceased to enslave and sacrifice humans and animals on the altar of Civilisation. Con-trary to mainstream Animal Rights Activism, we believe that human liberation is part of animal liberation. The human animal is the animal that should start a revolution and smash the cage of class and species oppression.

---

44   Zerzan 1988; Zerzan 1994.

CHAPTER 3

Animal Rights Activism and Its Discontents

Animal Liberation Ideology is a closed symbolic system, an articulation of signs which regulates what is acceptable and what is not in the philosophy of animal rights. Every time one is close to unveiling the limits of the Animal Liberation Ideology and its (un)political agenda, every time the discourse begins to see through the smokescreen of moralism and abstraction, something prevents animal rights theorists from freeing themselves from the chains of bourgeois reason. The crucial information gets twisted, the unavoidable conclusion is denied, the necessity to widen the focus of the research is ignored.

Having exposed the theoretical shortcomings of mainstream antispeciesism, we shall now discuss its practical limits and contradictions. We will immediately see that they are strictly connected to the theoretical mistakes we have been analysing so far. I will not make here any distinction between the 'top-down, businesslike structure, with centralised control, that characterised the often large and always conservative animal welfare charities', and the 'radicalism' of 'grassroots activism'.[1] First, because in the meanwhile the dogmatism, lack of internal debate, and blind pragmatism denounced by Francione as typical of big organisations have become quite common in the 'radical' small groups that grew up in the 1990s. Francione's sect is a tragic example of a 'bottom-up' critical strategy gone terribly wrong. Second, because the theoretical and practical differences between big welfarist charities and grassroots activism are often irrelevant when considered from a political point of view.

1 Two Forms of Praxis: Conflict and Inclusion

Along the lines of what usually happens in the human liberation movements, the praxis of Animal Liberation essentially follows two directions. On the one hand, it is a *conflictual* movement, i.e. its protest aims at neutralising exploitation; on the other hand, it is *inclusive*, i.e. it seeks to spread its ideas and, possibly, to widen its ranks. In short, it is a matter of fighting speciesism and giving resonance and visibility to antispeciesism. No transformation of reality can do without these two aspects of praxis: if we do not fight what is unjust,

---

1 Francione 1996, p. 24.

justice will never be achieved; at the same time, if a liberation movement does not 'grow' (in a quantitative and qualitative sense), it will never have the visibility, nor the energies, nor the analysis, and the praxis that are indispensable for carrying forward its own demands.

2   Conflict

2.1   *Social Life Is Not the Reification of Individual Behaviour*
I believe that the praxis of animal rights is inadequate and should be rethought from the ground up. It seems to me that theoretical confusion is the real reason why neither the conflictual nor the inclusive strategy of Animal Rightism can be considered effective.

Let us start with the oppositional aspect. Francione writes: 'A movement is generally defined by both its ideology and its practical efforts to implement that ideology in the real world. The ideology of the animal rights movement is usually expressed in terms of the long-term liberation of nonhumans from virtually all forms of institutionalized exploitation'.[2] Francione speaks of 'ideology' in a positive, non-Marxist fashion, as a mere system of ideas. Yet, according to him, the Animal Rights Movement is condemned to never see its hopes realised unless it abandons welfarism to embrace his incremental abolitionist position. I use the term 'ideology' in a critical, Marxist sense: ideology is a mystifying conception of reality which hides the class conflicts of society. In *this* sense, Francione and the Animal Rights Movement, no matter whether welfarist or abolitionist, are all under the spell of the same ideology. Thus, not only do they mystify the reality of oppression, but they are also incapable of accomplishing their 'ideological' goals.

First of all, the Animal Liberation Movement is not yet clear against *whom* or *what* it is fighting (as noted by Cherry, contrary to traditional social movements, vegans 'do not have conventionally identified adversaries or goals'[3]). As we have seen, this uncertainty depends on the fact that there is still considerable vagueness as to the very essence of speciesism. One cannot effectively fight a phenomenon whose genesis and structure one does not understand. 'Classical' antispeciesist theories (Singer, Regan, Francione, etc.) do not help in this sense, because, as we have already seen, they consider speciesism to be nothing but a 'moral prejudice'. As a consequence, the predominant practice

---

2   Francione 1996, p. 42.
3   Cherry 2006, p. 155.

of the animal liberation movement has always consisted in fighting such prejudice by confronting individuals in a conflictual way, hoping to 'convert' them
one by one. I do not think it is necessary to show how ineffective this type of
strategy is.

From a sociological point of view, this is a form of 'methodological individualism': the theory which considers individuals to be the basic elements of
society, since only individuals 'act' according to pre-fixed goals, while States,
Classes, or Society have no 'intentions'. Revolutionary interpretations of methodological individualism often insist on the fact that institutions can also be
derived from the repetition of individual behaviour. Social structures would
be nothing but the frozen product of such iterative actions, the reified result
of continuous repetition. Even though the Marxist tradition has sometimes
worked with a similar concept of 'reification' (see the young Weberian Lukács),
the idea that social life is a 'flux' that gets ossified by institutions is a form of
late bourgeois vitalism. It parallels Simmel's and Bergson's *Lebensphilosophie*,
with its opposition between life and forms: a social ontology which has more
political resonance with anarchist immediatism. Here, mediation means losing the energetic, spontaneous urgency of life. A more nuanced sociological
approach sees in institutions forms of objectification of social life, which *can*,
though not necessarily, express reified and alienated relationships. The problem with methodological individualism is that by theorising the origin of social
structures from the repetition of individual action, it postulates that it is possible to 'deconstruct' such reified structures with a reverse operation. Yet, individual efforts could succeed in dismantling institutions only if these were mere
aggregates of discrete, atomistic elements.

As we have repeatedly shown, speciesism is not only a prejudice but also,
if not above all, a *material form of exploitation* which is justified (and certainly
reinforced) by prejudice. The current conflictual approach of the Animal Rights
Movement makes the mistake of prioritising the fight against prejudice rather
than against the exploitative material activity. In doing so, it reverses the order
of priority between (a) ideal and material, and between (b) individual and
social. The overall strategy is then fallacious in a double way: instead of fighting
the *ideas* in the heads of *individuals*, it should attack the *material* structure of
society, which is what generates those ideas in the first place.

It is true that the Animal Liberation Movement includes groups and individuals whose conflictual praxis targets material exploitation facilities – ALF,
etc. Largely inspired by anarchism, these groups open the cages, free the pris-
oners and often even destroy the private property of those who exploit and kill
animals.[4] Unfortunately, even attacking the material structure of oppression

---

4 Best and Nocella II 2004.

through direct action does not offer an effective way out of capitalism. Capital is a global, universal structure of oppression: although fighting its *local manifestations* is necessary, it does not touch its *essence*. In a nutshell: destroying a *single property* because it breeds, exploits and/or kills animals does not in any way affect the *property system* and, therefore, leaves undisturbed what makes property possible.

By opposing speciesism as moral prejudice, Animal Rights Activists believe that in order to transform society it is necessary to change the conscience of *individual citizens* and consumers. Animal Liberationists, on the contrary, think that society can only be transformed by directly attacking the exploitative activity carried out by *individual owners*. But the substance does not change: the basic social theory is inadequate. Again, it must be emphasised that the speciesist conscience of individuals, along with the various material activities of animal exploitation, are an *effect* of the symbolic, economic, political and cultural structures of society. Consequently, those who desire to fight speciesism in both its subjective (conscience) and objective (industries) side, must develop a comprehensive and large-scale transformation strategy. The limits of both these forms of conflictual praxis derive from an inexact conception of society: i.e. the idea that society is nothing but an aggregation of individuals, rather than a set of inter- and super-individual structures.

2.2   *The Juridical Illusion*

The political impotence of the Animal Rights Movement can be clarified by the very use of the word 'rights'. Tom Regan[5] is partly responsible for this shift from the animal 'liberation' to the animal 'rights' rhetoric. Singer[6] did not approve of it and only accepted using the words 'rights' in a somewhat tactical way. That is why Žižek's polemics against Singer are partially out of focus. Criticising Singer in the name of Animal Rights, Žižek affirms that in Animal Rightism humans get 'animalised'.[7] I would rather agree with Marx's objection to Bentham, and say that the problem with Singer is that animals get *bourgeoisified*. What are, according to the young Marx, human rights?

> The so-called rights of man, the *droits de l'homme* as distinct from the *droits du citoyen*, are nothing but the rights of a *member of civil society* – i.e., the rights of egoistic man, of man separated from other men and from the community. [...] Liberty, therefore, is the right to do everything that

---

5   Regan 2004a.
6   Singer 1985.
7   Žižek 2002.

harms no one else. The limits within which anyone can act *without harm-ing* someone else are defined by law, just as the boundary between two fields is determined by a boundary post. It is a question of the liberty of man as an isolated monad, withdrawn into himself. [...] But, the right of man to liberty is based not on the association of man with man, but on the separation of man from man. It is the *right* of this separation, the right of the *restricted* individual, withdrawn into himself. [...] The right of man to private property is, therefore, the right to enjoy one's property and to dispose of it at one's discretion (*à son gré*), without regard to other men, independently of society, the right of self-interest. This individual liberty and its application form the basis of civil society. It makes every man see in other men not the realisation of his own freedom, but the *bar-rier* to it. [...] There remain the other rights of man: *égalité* and *sûreté*. Equality, used here in its non-political sense, is nothing but the equality of the *liberté* described above – namely: each man is to the same extent regarded as such a self-sufficient monad. [...] And security? [...] Security is the highest social concept of civil society, the concept of *police*, expressing the fact that the whole of society exists only in order to guarantee to each of its members the preservation of his person, his rights, and his property. [...] The concept of security does not raise civil society above its egoism. On the contrary, security is the *insurance* of egoism. None of the so-called rights of man, therefore, go beyond egoistic man, beyond man as a mem-ber of civil society – that is, an individual withdrawn into himself, into the confines of his private interests and private caprice, and separated from the community. In the rights of man, he is far from being conceived as a species-being; on the contrary, species-life itself, society, appears as a framework external to the individuals, as a restriction of their original independence. The sole bond holding them together is natural necessity, need and private interest, the preservation of their property and their ego-istic selves.[8]

Such ironic definition of fundamental rights is perfectly mirrored in Fran-cione's individualistic and egoistic description of right: 'a right is a particular way of protecting interests. To say that an interest is protected by a right is to say that the interest is protected against being ignored or violated simply because this will benefit someone else. We can think of a right of any sort as a fence or a wall that surrounds an interest and upon which hangs a "no trespass" sign that

---

8   Marx 1981, pp. 364–6.

forbids entry'.[9] In a typical conservative move, right is considered important to protect individuals against the State and the majority. Such modern description, though, is at odds with Francione's universal, transhistorical conception of right: 'in *any* society, be it capitalist or communist or whatever, humans must possess a basic right not to be a resource as a minimal prerequisite to being a moral and legal person within that society'.[10] Regan, too, takes the point of view of 'libertarians', and regards rights as merely *negative*. Although justified in a pragmatic sense ('while there is disagreement over the validity of positive moral rights, there is unanimity concerning the validity of negative moral rights'[11]), such choice is problematic, since it excludes a positive point of view on social interactions. This is methodologically wrong. A proper socialist analysis, in fact, does not state that negative rights are *per se* valid and they only need to be 'completed' by the positive ones.[12] Since the distinction is false, their conjunction is spurious. Consequently, any discussion about animal-human relationship becomes grounded on a wrong premise.

Apart from being an ideological perpetuation of the capitalist *status quo*, the concept that rights are just 'neutral', practical instruments of social regulation, a 'universal', formal feature of the human world is pure idealism. Even Hegel, for whom the Law was a manifestation of the Absolute, objected to the formal-instrumental nature of rights, and recognised their universality only on the assumption that right is a historical product, the very essence of the Spirit objectified in human institutions. There is nothing like a pure essence of right: like every other social institution, the concept of right should be considered in relation to the development of human society and its inner material conflicts. Hence, it is wrong to assume that bourgeois rights have the same meaning and function as Medieval, Roman or Greek legislation. All these are not 'norms' in the same sense, they do not simply fall under the same general concept of 'norm'. The same goes *a fortiori* for rules that regulate social life in prehistoric times, before the birth of the State.

This is more than generic advice not to obliterate historical accuracy. It is a *political* problem: if the modern form of juridical protection, i.e. bourgeois rights, become nothing but the last incarnation of a universal essence, it is easy to jump to the conclusion that a critique of right as such is impossible, or 'dangerous'. Benton, for instance, attacks Marx's critique of human rights on the assumption that human nature cannot be identified with social and

---

9   Francione 2000, p. xxxvi; for the 'no trespass' analogy see also Regan 2003, p. 25.
10   Francione 2000, p. 24.
11   Regan 2003, p. 25.
12   For a critique of the liberal concept of rights see Benton 1993, pp. 99 ff.

political relations.[13] According to him, one should distinguish between a legitimate critique of 'bourgeois' rights and an illegitimate, over-politicised critique of right in itself.[14] Thus, 'the State' and 'Human Rights' become universal and de-historicised entities, something for which no genetic explanation is possible: set beyond natural history, State and Rights become ontological, anthropological structures that cannot or should not be determined by social relations. Consequently, we should not seek to put an end to the sublimation of social antagonisms in the State.[15] It is clear how Benton, in his attempt to unify Marx and Animal Rights, throws in the dustbin a basic assumption of Marxism. As I will argue in the next chapter, Benton expects simultaneously *too little* and *too much* from Marx. Too little: since he still uses in a rather generic, de-contextualised and unquestioned way concepts like 'egoism'. Too much: since he shares the traditional vision of Communism as 'a society marked by universal spontaneous benevolence, or which transcends all sources of human estrangement and suffering'.[16] The whole point of Marx's analysis is precisely that concepts like 'egoism' or 'benevolence' cannot be used to explain social relations: they should rather be explained. A Marxist critique of rights does not rely on the idea that Communism will be a Garden of Eden where people are always kind to their neighbour. Communism is the determined negation of a specific mode of production: it embodies its richness and elevates it to a superior level of organisation, where free individuality can develop *universally*, unrestrained by the *particular* interest of a self-proclaimed elite. Speculating now on what will become of 'human rights' after the abolition of class oppression is otiose: in whatever form they survive – if they will – their function will be completely different; it will be determined by the social interaction of a liberated society. To preserve the idea of State power and formal rights in such a scenario, simply means to give up the specific idea of liberation from class exploitation: as we will see, the typical move of Singer and Benton is to confuse a classless society with an idyllic age of love among humans and condemn it as Utopian and impossible. On the contrary, since the power of the State and, more recently, the concept of

---

13   Benton 1993, p. 193.
14   Benton 1993, pp. 106 ff., pp. 134–40.
15   Even those who do not believe that the State was originated by class struggle (Maisels 1993) must acknowledge that such obfuscation of class conflicts is one of its essential features in the present time. If there was a 'pure essence' of the State, a 'universal function' of the State which even a classless society could not deny, it is something that only through the end of class society could be theorised and discovered from a practical point of view. Because the particularism of class society is the practical negation of universalism.
16   Benton 1993, p. 139.

rights are part of the social mechanism which produces oppression, the theoretical and practical critique of their alleged neutrality is necessary. The political critique of capitalist economy concerns both its *material* and *formal* structures.

What a Marxist should find interesting in the concept of 'animal rights' is rather its inner *contradiction*: reactionaries who criticise the 'absurdity' of animal rights catch a glimpse of their true meaning. By radically questioning the identity of the human subject, animal rights tend to dismantle the entire system of bourgeois right. Unfortunately, with the important exceptions of feminists[17] and post-structuralists,[18] no Animal Rights Activist shares this radical view. Cavalieri, for instance, wishes to *expand* the concept of 'human rights' without dialectically abolishing it ('to undo what citizenship means'[19]). The consequence is that she welcomes the transfiguration of the underlying 'subject' of those rights into an abstract and ghostly 'agent'.[20] Yet, all the critical potential of Animal Liberation dwells in the ambiguity of its goal, which, from one side, is to *realise* Animal Rights, and, from the other, is to *dissolve* the ideological machinery of bourgeois rights. It is this dialectics that the Animal Rights Movement fails to see.[21]

In this respect, the divergence between Singer and Regan on the concept of animal rights must not be overemphasised. In a way, lacking a clear political strategy, Animal Liberation is subjected to the sort of juridical illusion denounced by the young Marx. The whole discourse about rights is nothing but an *imaginary suppression of exploitation*. When oppression is not eradicated in the world of social relations, it is perpetuated in the State where all contradictions are composed in an ideal, purely abstract, unity.

> The State abolishes, in its own way, distinctions of *birth, social rank, education, occupation*, when it declares that birth, social rank, education, occupation, are *non-political* distinctions, when it proclaims, without regard to these distinction, that every member of the nation is an *equal* participant in national sovereignty, when it treats all elements of the real life of the nation from the standpoint of the State. Nevertheless, the State allows private property, education, occupation, to *act* in *their* way – i.e., as private property, as education, as occupation, and to exert the influence of

---

17   Donovan and Adams 1996.
18   Acampora 2006; Pyke 2019.
19   Pyke 2019, p. 276.
20   Cavalieri 2001, pp. 137 ff.
21   For instance, Francione 1996, pp. 37–8.

their *special* essence. Far from abolishing these *factual* distinctions, the State only exists on the presupposition of their existence; it feels itself to be a *political State* and asserts its *universality* only in opposition to these elements of its being.[22]

Thus, impolitic indifference in the domain of economic relations makes all claims about class, sexual and racial equality look like wishful thinking. Confronted with the ruthless exploitation of the oppressed[23] the discourse on formal recognition of equality reveals its lack of socio-economic substance. But the problem is not only that juridical equality is often a mere façade which does not change the reality of social relations. This is of course also problematic and it is unbelievable how little Animal Rights Activists are concerned with the misery of the rights rhetoric. It is clear that a system of rights can only express *the composition of antagonistic forces* in a precise moment in time; that is the reason why, contrary to the widespread post-war belief that we are moving towards a time of universal rights, we are currently facing an ongoing restriction of human rights which were once considered to be definitive acquisitions of contemporary society. The juridical illusion of Animal Rightism is part and parcel of that general self-illusion of the post-war era. Singer's belief in the rise of a global ethics as a necessary corollary to a globalised world where national sovereignty and cultural particularism gradually lose their importance has not been shaken by the shocks of Brexit and the resurgence of nationalism.[24] Although Ryder appears very proud of his scepticism about religion, his old-fashioned faith in Western democracy does not seem to be troubled by the recent advance of the reactionary right: 'Socialism and Marxism were narrow-mindedly obsessed with equality and class struggle as if these were valid ends in themselves. These angry ideologies could not see that these aims were mere stepping stones to universal happiness. In America, human rights and democracy have now become the vision'.[25] Yes, he admits, 'there are still some huge problems with democracy', but we luckily got rid of that 'equality' and 'class' nonsense. One may suggest that there is a connection between the international defeat of the working class and the growth of the alt-right movement, but why spoil Ryder's quasi-religious certitude?

Animal Rights theorists who believe that animal exploitation will be defeated once a universal and well-informed 'debate' convinces the majority

22 Marx 1981, p. 354.
23 Benton 1993, p. 95.
24 Singer 2016.
25 Ryder 2017,.

of people that abusing animals is morally wrong, are wildly exaggerating the power of both moral discussion and legal protection. There is a sort of historical 'determinism, which assumes the inevitability of an ever-expanding "rights revolution"'.[26] The belief that 'moral progress' is slowly taking place in history and that we should just let it happen to see things change.[27] This point of view is so deeply rooted in the Animal Rights Movement that even revolutionary anticapitalists like Steven Best see Animal Liberation as 'the next logical development in moral evolution'.[28] There is no such thing as a moral 'evolution'.

Anyway, as we have seen, classic antispeciesism never believed that the discourse about Animal Rights should focus on 'rights' in purely juridical terms. It is not just Singer who does not accept this point of view; Regan, too, always talks about 'moral' rather than legal rights *strictu sensu*. The problem is that when such confusion between moral and legal rights ends, things get even worse. Animal Rightism gets stuck in the pseudo-concreteness of 'legalism' and the whole dialectical tension between realising and dissolving the sphere of rights is lost. The heated debate between Gary Francione and Steven Best is a good example of such simplification. Francione's approach, in fact, is centred on the idea that a progressive non-violent strategy will one day produce animal liberation through purely legal means, education and the diffusion of veganism. There is a contradiction in our laws that needs to be solved, which Francione describes as 'moral schizophrenia':[29] from one side, laws recognise animals as sentient beings (and accord them protection, under certain circumstances); from the other side, laws deny animals the status of subjects (which would make it impossible to treat them as objects, goods or properties). Best objected that this is just an illusion, that the system of oppression cannot be changed from the inside, that all legal means are, although necessary, not decisive in the last instance.

> Despite passing references to capitalism, state power, and commonalities of oppression in hierarchical societies, Francione ultimately pushes a simplistic apolitical, quiescent 'go vegan' approach pitched to a marginal white, affluent, and privileged Western audience. In their vegan outreach efforts, Francione, and the global vegan movement generally, rarely engage people of color, working-class families, the poor, or peoples in China and India – the world's most populous and rapidly modern-

---

26   Donaldson and Kymlicka 2016, p. 79.
27   Miller 1993.
28   Best 2014, p. 37.
29   Francione 2000.

izing nations whose insatiable appetites for meat pose massive problems for vegan abolitionism and, indeed, the planet. Francione thereby
reinforces the abysmal elitist, classist, and, racist stigmas attached to
animal advocacy since the early nineteenth century, and he further isolates veganism and animal rights from progressive movements and the
social mainstream. Unable to articulate a structural theory of oppression,
Francione exculpates capitalism – its destructive logic and disastrous
impact on humans, animals, and the environment – to lay the entire burden of blame and responsibility for change on individual consumers. He
identifies the problem as one of individual demand for, not institutional
supply of, animal products.[30]

Best's critique of Francione's apolitical and quietistic veganism is definitive. As
usual, though, his position here is not entirely convincing. He fails to see that
Francione's strategy is just the logical consequence of veganism as we know
it, i.e. as a moral choice (wrongly) identified with the fight against speciesism.
Considered in purely moral terms, Francione is right and Best is wrong. It is only
when antispecisism (*not* veganism) is understood as a political issue that Francione's fallacy becomes evident. Best's charges against Francione's sect could
be directed to almost *all* vegan groups: 'For them, the world is black and white,
answers are cut and dry, and complexity is reduced to the Procrustean bed of
rigid "either/or oppositions", rather than enlivened through the dialectical logic
of "both/and" possibilities'.[31] Best should ask himself why personalities like
Francione are to be found in almost all Western countries and tend to monopol-
ise the attention of Animal Rights Activists, transforming them into an army of
moralising vegans. The power of the message resides in its simplicity, which has
been part of veganism since the beginning. Francione's veganism is veganism
purified from all the distracting complications of the real world. It has nothing
to do with antispeciesism, but is a well-packaged alternative.

   As we will see, this is an inexorable consequence of the strict ethical nature
of mainstream antispeciesism: when our relationship towards animals is formulated in purely moral terms, either/or-answers are unavoidable. You cannot
at the same time include and exclude animals from moral protection; either
you kill them or not; either you consider them subjects or not, and so on.
Without an immanent (and dialectical) critique of the ethical discourse, the
struggle against animal exploitation will never be part of *revolutionary politics*.

---

30   Best 2014, p. 44.
31   Best 2014, p. 43.

The expression 'revolutionary politics' here describes a political theory in which neither the State nor social relations are considered fixed, unchanging entities. This does not mean that human nature is absolutely 'flexible' (the classic neoliberal allegation against Marx, which Benton and Singer repeat), and that everything is possible. It rather means that limits to the potential of social evolution can only be derived from our actual historical becoming. Every attempt to set these limits outside the field of historical interaction is methodologically flawed, and leads to inevitable conservative conclusions.

Although morally commendable, the 'direct actions' of the various anarchist groups are far from being a model of such politics. Best's defence of ALF's illegalism never manages to show how such a strategy should be included in an alliance of progressive social movements. Best understands the importance of mediation and does not totally side with anarchistic immediatism. No wonder he gets criticised by the same groups he would like to include in his all-ecompassing political strategy.[32] Unfortunately, Best's relation to veganism is affected by an analogous defect of immediatism.

As should be clear by now, discussing the pros and cons of illegal action never really makes room for an analysis of the possibilities of revolutionary politics. Best's intention to include veganism in a wider oppositional and anti-capitalist movement is an empty hope and is destined to fail. For their part, when Singer,[33] Regan[34] and Francione[35] face the problem of violence (and property), they, too, focus on the effects of direct action, the ALF-style operations, as well as those other groups, like Animal Militia, which resort to 'terrorist' means (like vandalism, harassment, personal threats etc.). Politics, as a long-term strategy, in which immediacy and mediation are intertwined, in which action aims at dissolving a system of bureaucratic, economic, social and cultural structures, is never mentioned. Legalism and illegalism, under this respect, are just two sides of the same coin. They both fetishise 'right' from opposite points of view.

This shows that a deeper problem needs to be discussed. It would be too simple to believe that 'rights' do not work because the State can do nothing when it comes to economic relations. That would be a rather crude argument, either a form of economism that ignores the complex relations between capital accumulation and the State, or an anarchist conclusion which believes that

32   Subservise Energy 2012.
33   Singer 1986, pp. 153–4.
34   Regan 2004b, p. 234; 2004c, p. 188.
35   Francione 2009; 2010.

the State is just an imaginary projection of the elite's will to power. The power of the State is *not* extraneous to the power of economy: the point of Marxism is precisely to understand such structural connection.

An undialectical opposition between State and Economy ends up with the false alternative between reformism and anarchism (which is mirrored in the Animal Rights Movement in the opposition between welfarism and abolitionism/liberationism). Even when the political nature of Animal Liberation is taken into account, Animal Rights Theorists oversimplify the political process. Politics here appears as a necessary evil, something we cannot do without.[36] Political parties are all considered means to an end, and they can be supported only if they promise to pass legislation improving animal moral status. Animal Rightism understands politics only in the dualistic form of an opposition between State-Power and the masses. Animal Rights Activism either tries to influence politicians or to veganise the masses: nothing can happen *between* these two poles, because society has been reduced to a *homogeneous* phenomenon. Since the only interest taken into account is the supposed interest of 'humanity' against the interest of animals, class dynamics and conflicts are ideologically hidden and mystified. Even the anarchist currents of animal liberation tend to acknowledge the abstract opposition between the State and the Masses. 'Expand the law and educate the masses' is the motto of Animal Rights Reformism. 'Break the law and educate the masses' is the motto of Animal Liberationist Anarchism.

From a Marxist point of view, a revolution is a process that, while accepting the rules of the game (in order to get a realistic picture of the wider context where action must take place), does not consider the game *unchangeable*. Quite the contrary: it constantly pushes for an active transformation of the given conditions.[37] It permanently tries to *transcend* the system, opening up

---

36   See for instance Holland 1985.

37   In *this* sense, I agree with Donaldson and Kymlicka that it is 'a mistake to focus solely on how liberal rights function once they have been legally instantiated (leading to misunderstandings of rights as largely axiomatic, hollow, or as tools of state power). To be sure, rights can become tools of governance, but they have also served as tools of resistance for the excluded to challenge existing structures of power' (2016, p. 81). At any rate, even if it is true that 'various strands of liberalism, including the left liberal strand that we endorse, have offered an extensive critique of capitalism' (p. 78), to 'criticise' capitalism does not mean to recognise and try to overturn its *class* basis. The problem with Animal Rightism is that its ideological mind-set prevents the subversion of the *productive relations*. Though such ideology does not depend *entirely* on liberalism, I see no way in which the liberal tradition defended by Donaldson and Kymlicka (with its emphasis on individual agency and subjective meaning-construction) could help Animal Liberation to overcome its moralist shortcomings.

new possibilities. The antispeciesist movement should work out a similar political strategy: this implies a theory in which antispeciesism is an attempt to
establish an *alternative social model*, rather than a new moral standard.[38]

3   Inclusion

Let us now consider the second aspect of praxis, the one aimed at convincing
as many people as possible of the necessity to put an end to anthropocentrism.
It is clear that 'persuasion', although being an erroneous way of fighting against
speciesism, could be a useful and even necessary *collateral* activity to the political fight for animal freedom. It may help spread a non-anthropocentric culture, and enlarge the ranks of the movement. At any rate, such inclusive praxis
implies two distinct goals which unfortunately often overlap in an unclear way:
a)   making people *understand* the antispeciesist message;
b)   making people *accept* the antispeciesist message.
We will now measure the effects of the current inclusive practice of the animal
liberation movement with respect to these two different phases of its communication strategy.

3.1   *Understanding the Message*
The need to make the antispeciesist message 'clearer' and more 'coherent' has
long been established in the animal liberation movement. It all began with
Singer's claim that vegetarianism was a moral obligation, and ended up with
the criticism of the so-called 'extrinsic arguments'.[39] An 'extrinsic argument' is
an attempt to convince people that they should defend animals not because it is
morally wrong to exploit and kill them, but because animal exploitation could
be *dangerous* to human beings (world hunger, deforestation, side-effects of
animal experimentation, etc.). Shortly: we should put an end to animal abuse,
not for the animals' sake, but for ours.

   It is obvious that emitting contradictory messages does not facilitate the
understanding of antispeciesism. We cannot ground our arguments both on
altruism ('x is immoral') and *selfishness* ('x is harmful'). After all, antispecies-

---

38   See Wrenn's intelligent attempt to overcome the opposition between micro-level and
       macro-level, between legal reforms and illegal protests through the concept of 'social
       movement' (2015, pp. 26–7). Such a concept is still ambiguous, its goals too vague. Animal
       Rightism, especially under the current vegan hegemony, is a rather unique social move-
       ment (Griffin 2017): we will soon see how contradictory its relation to 'society' is.
39   Perlo 2007; Stzybel 2008.

ism prompts humankind to abandon selfishness and widen the sphere of moral consideration. For this reason, the movement has increasingly focused on the so-called 'intrinsic arguments'. Although this seems a reasonable thing to do, I will argue that it is a false solution.

When Perlo, Styzbel or Francione debate whether it is more *effective* to focus on intrinsic or extrinsic arguments, their idea of 'effectiveness' is unclear. Stzybel believes that the goal of antispeciesism is to save more animal lives as possible, thus every strategy is welcome (if saying that meat causes cancer spares animal lives, why not say it?) Perlo and Francione believe that coherence is more effective because they establish a direct parallel between individual and collective behaviour: the ethical consistency of individuals and small groups will help society to change in the desired direction. *How* this should happen is never explained. Presumably, through the 'incremental' conversion of more and more people. Francione even draws parallels between speciesism and human slavery, but this can only bring us to simplify the struggles of the past: for instance, by considering the abolition of slavery a *linear* process in which the 'consistency' of the message was the leading force in the hands of the liberators.[40] The same could be said for parallels between animal oppression and class exploitation:[41] here the risk is to consider veganism a way to fight capitalism. For Perlo and Francione, action is effective whenever we convert 'one more human being' to antispeciesism. For Stzybel action is effective whenever we rescue 'one more animal being'. The underlying scheme is the same: society, as usual, is ignored, or considered just the effect of individual action.

Sure, putting extrinsic arguments aside, especially extrinsic arguments *in the form in which they have been elaborated so far*, is necessary, but this does not mean that focusing on intrinsic argumentation is the real solution to the problem. Because, again, by doing so, Animal Rights Activism gets stuck in its abstract and individualistic ethical fixation, making it impossible to decline antispeciesism in a political, collective sense. Moving from intrinsic arguments, there will never be a real, conflictual praxis aimed at transforming society. To understand why, let us analyse the logical implications of Perlo's and Francione's thesis.

The whole dispute over 'intrinsic' and 'extrinsic' arguments is based on the assumption that antispeciesism can be proposed and/or defended by reducing its content to a series of *isolated, self-referential, prescriptive propositions*. This is

---

40   See Best 2012 for a critique of this simplification.
41   Noske 1989.

what the term 'argument' means in this debate. An argument is here reduced to a proposition whose content is either the direct affirmation of moral equality among sentient beings (i.e. a *prescriptive* proposition), or is it a factual affirmation that, making its way through the selfish interest of the listener, could lead to an improvement of the condition of the animals (i.e. a *descriptive* proposition). Considered from this angle, all the so-called 'intrinsic arguments' are not 'arguments' at all, since they cannot convince anyone who *does not already share* their ethical standpoint. The *informative* value of the prescriptive propositions is zero: they describe values, not facts.

On the other hand, in the descriptive propositions, the *ethical* content is zero: they describe facts, they do not prescribe. And *this* is the real weakness of the extrinsic arguments. Since they constitute arguments in the proper sense, they can be effectively *contradicted*. Obviously, all those who make use of extrinsic arguments are entirely convinced of their truth and reliability. And this seems to me the most detrimental aspect of the antispeciesist culture: the tendency to believe in unverified 'facts' and the incapacity to ask if and to what extent they are true or even verifiable.

Now, if antispeciesism has to be something more than academic moral philosophy, if we believe that animal liberation should start a political transformation of society, such fixation with prescriptive vs. descriptive propositions becomes absurd. Political reasoning is based on a social model in which prescriptive and descriptive elements are inextricably intertwined. No political philosophy starts from purely prescriptive assumptions and deduces their practical consequences. Politics is a complex theoretical and practical process in which it is not easy to distinguish prescriptive and descriptive elements. Indeed, all political philosophies have at least a claim to be based on factual conditions and not on prescriptions. This is so true that when we criticise a political position we often unmask its 'facts' and denounce them as 'unproven assumptions' or 'surreptitious prescriptions' (i.e. we show where such reasoning falls prey to the 'naturalistic fallacy'). The interesting thing is that while nearly all political philosophies could be criticised as being based on unproven 'prescriptive' assumptions, those who profess them very rarely consider them in this way! For Marx it is a fact (not an ethical assumption[42]) that capitalism exploits the worker. For Hobbes it is a fact (not an ethical assumption) that humans are selfish by nature, and so on.

Now, we find ourselves in the uncomfortable position of having our 'normative assumptions' already prepared for us by the academic moral philosophy. As

---

42 Certainly, this means that (1) the 'fact' of exploitation emerges thanks to a theory that illuminates it, and (2) for Marx 'exploitation' as such is something unjust. But it must be

Singer puts it: 'The animal liberation movement is unique among recent political movements in the extent to which its ideas and support have come from
academic philosophers. This has meant that the case against speciesism has
been put more rigorously than might otherwise have been the case'.[43] But this
does not help us; it is rather a huge problem. Because now every attempt to discuss the animal question from a factual point of view will be easily dismissed
as extrinsic, a way to derogate from the purity of the ethical principle. From
such a premise it is virtually impossible to assume the task of dismantling the
speciesist society.

Such a political project, in fact, can only be based on the elaboration of a
coherent and articulated social model that contemplates a different conception of infra- and extra-species relations. What I have always found interesting in the use of 'extrinsic arguments' is not so much that they can persuade
people to embrace animal liberation, but the fact that they *link* human and
non-human interests (even if confusedly and erroneously). It is quite clear, in
fact, that those who use extrinsic arguments start from the direct interests of
non-humans, even if they try to connect them with those of humans. But this is
a *merit*, not a defect. The problem with extrinsic arguments is that such connection is often arbitrary or factually wrong: is a meat diet necessarily unhealthy?
No. Is veganism an effective way to put an end to world hunger? No. Are the
results of animal experiments always misleading? No, etc.

What interests me then is not so much the current shape of extrinsic arguments, but what they could mean within a social model in which there is no
opposition between human and non-human interests. The decisive question,
in fact, is that any political interpretation of animal liberation cannot ignore
the human interest: human and non-human interests should go together.

Therefore, such a political model would not focus on the current state of
society with its *contingent* conflicts between human and non-human needs.
It would seek to outline an *alternative* social model in which such conflicts
are, if not completely abolished, certainly reduced to a minimum: in a liberated society, in fact, social and scientific progress would both work out the
best way to establish an equal and just relationship between our kind and the

---

reiterated that the 'fact' of exploitation does not derive from some basic 'ethical assumption', least of all from universal and a-historical 'values'. The aversion to exploitation in
a generalised form cannot but be the product of the collective and historical action of
humanity. The ethical 'roots' of behaviour (compassion or the sense of justice) are certainly unconsciously present in every human being: the point is to understand when, how
and why they become conscious as a universal moral theory or as a situated political project.

43   Singer 1994, p. 174.

non-human world. To clarify what I mean with some examples: does it makes sense to contrast the ethical horror of the slaughterhouse to the political horror of the unequal distribution of resources if we assume the point of view of a social model in which both have disappeared? Does it make sense to contrast the disdain for vivisection with the denunciation of pharmaceutical interests if our social model makes the persistence of such phenomena impossible? Our political model will be convincing precisely because it will unify interests that present society depicts as contradictory.

Let us now analyse the immediate effects of the so-called 'intrinsic arguments' on the level of the inclusive practice we need.

Firstly, 'intrinsic arguments' state that the various cases in which animals get exploited and killed should be avoided simply because they are unjust, without adding any other consideration. As we have seen, the 'arguments' used in this circumstance are by no means arguments in the proper sense: they can all be reduced to the request to make room for non-human animals in the sphere of moral consideration. And here is the first problem: presenting themselves as 'arguments', they simplify the antispeciesist message, turning it into a *moral tautology*. We denounce *fishing* because fishing is wrong, and why is it wrong? Because animals are moral subjects. We denounce *vivisection*, because vivisection is wrong, and why is it wrong? Because animals are moral subjects, and so on. Thus, we talk of food, clothing, experimentation, circuses and fairs, but never really talk about 'food', 'clothing', 'experimentation', 'circuses' and 'fairs', i.e. we never talk about these as human activities, but only for their effects *on the animals*. Since animals are the centre of our consideration, the context of their exploitation simply vanishes. Consequently, we never talk of what could really *unify* these protests and actually give them meaning and perspective: i.e. the implicit reference to a non-violent and non-oppressive human *society*. To avoid this, it would be necessary to talk about the idea of society we have in mind; to do so we need to get out of the simple moral argument and reach the domain of political discussion; finally, any political discussion must take into account the human interests involved in these practices. All this is made impossible by the intransigent ethical and individualistic approach that underlies intrinsic argumentation. According to the theorists of intrinsic argumentation, everything that is not done *exclusively* in the name of animals is a 'diversion' and takes us away from the ethical 'purity' of the antispeciesist message.

Secondly, this kind of message confuses the practical proposals that are made to show alternatives to the current exploitation of animals with the principle that lies behind these proposals. In other words, *it confuses veganism with antispeciesism*. I know it is really difficult for Animal Rights Activists to accept

this point, and it is easy to understand why. The confusion between veganism and antispeciesism arises from two different tacit, but wrong, assumptions.

Some simply identify veganism with antispeciesism: of course, here, veganism means the 'philosophy' of veganism, thus the identification is equivocal.
The equation 'the personal is political' does not erase the distinction between
'what' one does and the reason 'why' she does it, i.e. the theory behind our
action. Antispeciesism is the theory which describes the conflictual nature of
our relations with animals; veganism is the moral choice, or lifestyle, that some
derive from that theory.

Of course, others consider veganism the *practical consequence* of antispeciesism: if one believes that antispeciesism is morally true, one is also logically compelled to become vegan. Such argument is fallacious, again, because
it understands antispeciesism in strictly moral terms. It is obvious that, if we
agree to discuss the animal question through the abstract lens of academic
moral philosophy, the ethical decision to become vegan could follow like a
logical consequence from a certain set of premises. Yet, the coherence of our
theoretical system could compel only those who already *accept* such premises.
There is no way of turning ethics into a self-evident scientific discourse. Even
if it were possible to demonstrate that a moral position is theoretically true,
this would not make that moral position mandatory in the empirical world of
individual moral assumptions, not to mention in the legal, social, or political
spheres of collective action. No moral theory can do that. Thus, if we want antispeciesism to be a *social* change, something that goes beyond individual belief
and action, we must go beyond the abstract ethical discourse. As I will explain
later, the problem is that veganism is not a 'mode of production'.

Let us go back to the negative consequences of the equation veganism = antispeciesism on a communicative level. When the message describes an alternative choice (again: food, clothing, cruelty-free products), the immediate reference seems to be individual behaviour which avoids any connection with
animal exploitation. But, as we have seen, antispeciesism cannot be reduced
to an individual lifestyle, since it implies an alternative social model, a world of
relations which should be *totally antagonistic* to the one we live in, and whose
potentialities cannot be anticipated at the present time. Any attempt to live
a non-violent life *now* cannot be but a very inaccurate parody of a liberated
world: nobody can anticipate the relationships that we may one day have with
other species, the way in which we will organise life, consumption, education,
etc. If the message focuses on the diffusion of veganism as an individual lifestyle rather than on the idea that lies at its base, it confuses the consequence
with the presupposition, the effect with the cause. On the contrary, a true anti-

speciesist message should focus on the importance of developing a sensitivity for otherness in all its forms (included human alterity); it should stimulate our imagination, propel new social, inter-subjective and ultra-subjective relationships, define humanity in terms of humility rather than arrogance, and so on. When Animal Rights Acitivists speak, their listeners should understand not *that* they do not eat meat or confine animals in cages, but *why* they do not do it. And if the reason is 'for the animals', then it has nothing to do with human society and human interests, it has no political meaning whatsoever. The reason why they do not do it (or should not do it) is that they try to foreshadow today what can only be done tomorrow by a society that has finally put an end to oppression (even among humans). The difference is substantial. And it is the difference between the always imperfect application of a principle that can be realised only *collectively* and the presumption that the principle may be realised in its *entirety*, *immediately* and *individually*.

Among other things, we are thus exposed to a series of insidious objections. First of all, the lack of coherence, since it is evident that everybody takes part to a greater or lesser extent in the violence of existing society.[44] Secondly, the fact of filling a market niche that is functional to the current system of production, which is always happy to satisfy the wishes of 'ethical' movements (from 'fair trade' to vegetarian and vegan products). Finally, the accusation of identity sectarianism, due to the fact of campaigning for a pre-packaged 'lifestyle' which cannot but be perceived as a normative intrusion into one's personal life by everybody else. Vegans are pretty familiar with this kind of criticism and, quite correctly, they often dismiss it, because of the bad faith of those who proffer it. However, they should make an effort to take such objections more seriously. It is not enough to denounce the bad faith of those who criticise us: we must refute their arguments.

---

44   Regan writes 'as long as we are alive in this world, we will be implicated in its evil, including the harmful things done to animals' (2003, p. 118) and describes how the production of 'cotton', for instance, has devastating ecological consequences. But then he wants to make clear that there is a difference between eating meat and wearing cotton clothes: 'the very lives of millions of animals is intentionally, deliberately, and systematically taken every hour of every day', while 'the harm caused to animals by the cotton industry is not intentional, not deliberate, and not systematic' (2003, p. 119). I object to the words 'systematic' and 'deliberate', since both activities are planned and both imply the killing of animals. The only difference seems to rely on the 'intentional' killing perpetrated by the meat industry (whatever 'intentional' means in sociological terms), but this does not make the slightest difference for the animals involved. Even if one admits that consumers are responsible for the killing of animals, what is the difference between consumers that kill animals but *do not want to*, and consumers that kill animals and *do not care to*? Quite aptly, here, Regan's Kantianism is indistinguishable from an ethics of intention.

It is true, veganism does not mean embracing a *life*-style, but rather giving up a *death*-style. It is not a matter of personal choice. The 'life' that we should focus on is not ours: it is the life of the animals we want to save. But first of all, the relation between our life-style and the animals that get 'saved' by it is rather vague, when not utterly mystical. For example, the idea that when vegans become a 'critical mass', a certain amount of meat factories must close[45] is a fairy-tale: the centralisation and concentration of capital makes it easy for corporations to replace smaller industries or encourage the consumption of meat within new markets. Francione's criticism of Singer, as usual, diagnoses a mistake only to propose even worse solutions: 'it is [...] difficult to understand how a boycott of factory-farmed meat will lead to anything more than a free-range meat industry'.[46] Francione's idea, which descends from Regan's theory of rights,[47] is that to eat meat is wrong in itself (i.e. it is a universal, unhistorical moral duty, justified by the principle of equal consideration of interests[48]); thus, people should become vegan as a consequence of a moral choice, regardless of its effect on the meat industry. As we have seen, Francione is also convinced that his approach will be *more effective* in putting an end to animal exploitation than that of his competitors. Why? Because more and more people will campaign for *'the incremental eradication of the property status of animals'*.[49] How will this happen? Because *education*[50] will convince more and more people to stop eating meat and 'eschew animal products'.[51] Thus, Francione's more effective method results in the fact that the world will be vegan on the day everybody will be vegan.

Secondly, let us suppose that campaigning for veganism is important. Let us ask again: what kind of 'style' are we talking about?

> Unlike other groups in society who pose a challenge through non-normative behaviour (for example, gay and lesbian people), vegans pose a threat through a failure to engage in normative behaviour, that is, theirs is a passive rejection of normalcy.[52]

But can there be a style that is defined only by *negations* (non-exploitation, non-death, etc.)? The identification of antispeciesism and veganism appears

---

45   Singer 1980a.
46   Singer 1996, p. 60.
47   Regan 2004a.
48   Francione 1995; 1996.
49   Francione 1996, p. 4.
50   Francione 1996, p. 150.
51   Francione 1996, p. 172.
52   Griffin 2017, p. 24.

particularly fallacious when we reflect on how this lifestyle changes according to times and places, how strange it is to defend a lifestyle that cannot be defined once and for all. Those who spread the vegan lifestyle thirty years ago, to give just one example, certainly could not imagine that our technical and cultural development would one day produce ecological and cruelty-free alternatives to products like leather or cheese; for Chinese culture – which did not domesticate cattle and does not normally consume milk – a vegan lifestyle will present different needs and solutions; those who live in cold climates need valid substitutes in order to give up furs, etc. Theoretically speaking, a vegan lifestyle could even include the consumption of *meat* if it were possible to produce in vitro alternatives.

This last point deserves a little reflection. Animal Rights Theory has made considerable efforts to elaborate thought experiments of every kind. It is pretty funny that very few, if any, Animal Rights Theorists have dedicated time to think about the consequences of the introduction of in vitro meat on the market. It is easy to see that in vitro meat would shake the foundations of Animal Rights Activism, since it is generally known that the most horrific figures of animal killings are caused by the meat industry. As a consequence, the commercialisation of in vitro meat would totally change the traditional perspective on animal exploitation. The main argument in favour of veganism would be *practically* rebutted, while its *theoretical* Doppelgänger – i.e. antispeciesism – would remain untouched. Thus, while the extreme right could campaign against cruelty-free meat, celebrating the virtues of traditional farming, left-wing Animal Liberationists could do nothing but help capitalist enterprises to spread this new kind of cruelty-free food. At the same time, the dramatic reduction in animal deaths would make vegans' appeal to justice look even more exaggerated to the general public than it does today. Animals would be saved, and veganism would be condemned by its own restricted and moralistic view. Yet, a world where the first cause of animal exploitation and death has been definitively banished would still be a world where anthropocentrism has not been defeated. Veganism would probably end, while antispeciesism would still have to take its first major steps. The current development of biotechnologies makes such thought experiments increasingly realistic.

Those who want to get an adequate understanding of the antispeciesist message, then, must focus on the *theoretical principles* that inspire us and not on their *individual, provisional, temporary*, and *practical implementation*. But they must also, in the first instance, understand the profound difference between these two levels of discourse.

3.2   Accepting the Message

If a message is not clear, it will not be understood. If our listeners do not under-stand it, they will not accept it. The imprecision of the message is thus the main cause of our failure to spread antispeciesism.[53] Confusion arises, as we have seen, because antispeciesism is presented as a struggle against *prejudice* (rather than exploitation), and is confused with a vegan *lifestyle* (rather than with an socio-political model) and such confusion determines the main difficulties in the reception of the message. I believe that these difficulties are of two types: (1) a difficulty in communicative style; and (2) a real theoretical difficulty.

(1) As for the communicative style, the errors we have highlighted so far lead to an inevitable stalemate in communication. We have seen how, in general, we adopt a conflictual attitude, an individualistic and non-social vision of the animal question and, thus, propose lifestyle as an alternative. This is the main reason why antispeciesist politics, so far, does not really exist. Born as a *moral* movement, Animal Liberation understands politics only in terms of *moralism*: 'be the change you want to see in the world', which, put in another way, sounds like: 'if everybody would act *like me* then the world would change ...'. Not a very reasonable, inclusive and effective form of political praxis, after all. Such a pos-ition leads us, in fact, to fight the prejudice of those who listen to us, asking them to take us as a model. As a matter of fact, what we implicitly say is: 'you are wrong and you have to become like me'. For those who have any insight into human psychology, it is evident that this kind of message will encounter many difficulties. Our 'model' should be a collective one.

(2) But this moralistic attitude is justified in part in relation to a theoret-ical difficulty that antispeciesism has not yet overcome. As I have already said, when Animal Rights Activists criticise 'theriocide',[54] i.e. the exploitation and killing of non-human animals, such practices are condemned as morally *wrong*. In this case, however, it is not a question of stating that *some acts* directed towards a subject are morally illicit (as in any normal ethical argument: is it moral to kill a human? Is it right to steal? Is it moral to lie?, etc.). Rather, it is a matter of accepting as 'subjects' those who are now treated as 'objects'. Thus,

---

53   I agree with Donaldson and Kymlicka that 'to be successful, the AR movement needs to forge alliances with other progressive causes' (2016, p. 84), but I am less confident that the problem resides in incautious communicative strategies: 'AR theorists and activists have often framed arguments and campaigns in ways that are at best strange and uncompelling, and at worst downright disturbing to progressives working on other social justice issues' (p. 85). I think the problem is *theoretical* and has to do with the very ethical premises of Animal Liberation. Donaldson and Kymlicka's inclusive 'goals' (p. 94 ff.) will never be accepted if those premises are not put into question.

54   Beirne 2018.

here the discussion falls entirely on whether or not animals are moral subjects. And, it must be admitted, both answers to this question are morally licit.[55] Because for those who kill and eat cows, these animals are clearly *not* moral subjects. From those who consider animals mere objects, no moral obligation can be expected.[56] Here we find the limit of any intrinsic argument (and of academic moral philosophy in general): it is powerless towards those who refuse to consider non-human animals ethically relevant subjects. We find ourselves in the same position as Catholics who try to convince atheists that the embryo is a moral subject. The latter can always and rightly deny that it is so, even if it is shown that the embryo is 'alive', potentially 'conscious', etc. The passage from moral ideas to action – that is, to consider the animal (or the embryo, for that matter) a moral subject – implies the necessity to *make a choice* and this choice *falls outside the domain of moral discussion*. It cannot be rationally decided. In other words, it does not undergo moral criteria, but rather *produces* them: before I consider animals as moral subjects I have no moral obligation towards them, nor am I morally obliged to consider them as morally relevant. Only my decision to consider them as moral subjects brings forth such moral obligation.

This is connected to the aforementioned problem: intrinsic arguments will never get beyond the request for an expansion of the moral circle. If speciesism is a social structure, what we need is a proper political formulation of our goals. Yet, every time we fail to demand an 'expansion of the moral circle' and we focus on the consequences of speciesism on human society, this shift is considered illicit, since it exceeds the limits of intrinsic argumentation. But a different society will be an interconnection of human and animal interests, it is not something we can describe solely from the point of view of animals. Those who attack every attempt to describe how animal oppression and human

---

55   'Who does matter? What counts as violence? How we answer these questions determines
      whether we are able to see issues regarding animals in moral terms. And, for many people,
      these answers are already given, prior to discussion and debate, operating so deeply they
      affect not just thoughts and beliefs but even perceptions themselves' (Luke 2016, p. 181).
      It is interesting that most Animal Rights Theorists make use of sociological concepts to
      understand (and often criticise) the opposite moral point of view but are rarely inter-
      ested in sociological analyses of *theirs*. See, for instance, the concept of 'carnism' (Joy 2010;
      Griffin 2017). It is as if the superior point of view of antispeciesism would severe us from
      society, as if we could contemplate the human world from above. Even Wrenn (2015), who
      has offered a sociological account of the Animal Rights Movement, mainly focuses on
      the shortcomings of big organisations, taking Francione's polemical distinction between
      grassroots abolitionism and bureaucratic welfarism for granted.
56   Benton 1993, p. 94.

oppression are connected denounce this as a shift from intrinsic arguments to extrinsic, irrelevant, selfish considerations. Yet, if antispeciesism wants to go beyond the individual and ethical dimension and elevate itself to a collective and political understanding of reality – a precondition for an actual transformation of society – this is a shift that has to be made.

4   The 'Bottom-Up' Change Is a Disguised Hierarchical Change

So far, antispeciesists have understood society as a mere 'sum of individuals' and the process of social transformation as a one-to-one process of 'persuasion' of the rest of society; moral antispeciesism, then, hopes to gradually become a social 'majority', as if social change could really happen that way. Although this perspective is totally naive and unpolitical, it is still the basic assumption of most Animal Rights Activists. Social structures, though, being *networks* of economic, political, and symbolic powers, *precede* individuals both chronologically and ontologically: they 'count' more in terms of effects. Society is an opaque and stratified structure that cannot be reduced to the will of individuals. On the contrary, these social structures predetermine the possibilities of choice of individuals – the options in their cognitive field, so to say. Therefore, it is society that makes the choice itself possible in the first place. All this has nothing to do with 'determinism'[57] (we can understand all this in mechanistic terms and say that there is no freedom or we can consider social facts as the determinant of different opposing forces, whose result can never be known in advance). Yet, if this is true, speciesism can no longer be considered the combined effect of many individual 'speciesist opinions', because the complexity of social structures that produces individual speciesist opinions has not yet been identified. 'Individual speciesist opinions' must be understood in terms of effect and not of cause.

This simple sociological evidence is anathema to mainstream Animal Liberation. Its theory and praxis were formed on texts[58] in which the social and historical element is totally absent. Here, political activism can only mean 'moral persuasion'. However, social processes do not work that way and only an idealised image of the past can suggest that women's rights and the end of slavery were achieved through moral persuasion alone. The struggle for Animal Liberation, then, appears to be something more difficult, long and complex than a

---

57   As far as I know, the only antispeciesist theorist who embraces this kind of social determinism is Martin Balluch (2008).

58   The above-mentioned 'classics' by Singer 2014 and Regan 2004a.

mere ethical protest, something that involves the elaboration of an adequate social theory and a long-term strategy, with middle-range tactical goals that do not have immediate relevance to animal suffering but which are essential prerequisites of any real struggle against oppression (for example, the fight for a free information system, for real democratic societies and for solidaristic, noncompetitive economies).

Faced with all this, many Animal Rights Activists back away in annoyance and stubbornly reiterate their point of view: the change must take place from the inside of each and every person; it must be a moral awakening ('a revolution ... of the heart'[59]); it can only be a 'bottom-up change'. Although I understand what they mean, this does not change the fact that such simplification cannot be accepted: the concepts of 'bottom' and 'up' are apparently intuitive but they are ultimately elusive and generic; they have no determined sense in sociological terms (it is about the same difference between subjectively feeling 'hot' and measuring your temperature with a thermometer). Moreover, as soon as one analyses it, one discovers that what animalists imagine when they speak of a 'bottom-up change' is nothing more than a camouflaged top-down change. Animal Rights Activists are usually convinced that they are right and they should persuade the rest of society to accept their point of view. As we have seen, animal ethics knows no compromise, no middle road: either you kill animals or you do not, either you eat meat or you do not. Thus, Animal Liberation should convince 'the masses' that the masses are wrong and animals will be free. Even if not all Animal Rights Activists would express themselves in such a contemptuous manner (using an expression like 'the mass' that clearly betrays an elitist gaze: the 'top' here is the enlightened soul of the Animal Rights Activist), they generally share the idea that others should be 'educated to change'. The 'other' is always seen as a land of conquest (we need to transform the 'other' so that he/she will resemble us); the 'other' is never seen as an *actor* in a collective process of change. Yet, a 'bottom-up change' should start from the base of society in its totality, that is, from human beings considered in their irreducible autonomy, with their thousand-faceted thinking, their needs and their expectations, even their *contradictory* desires. It should be a process that mobilises individuals and groups in a continuous dialectic of exchanges, conflicts and aggregations. But exchange, conflict and aggregation only occur in diversity, not in homogeneity. Those who think that a 'bottom-up change' means that a minority slowly conquers the majority by assimilating it simply do not know what a 'bottom-up change' actually is.

---

59   Francione 2009.

A social process is not the extension of an individual act but something of a totally different nature. Social change does not take place like individual actions do, it does not start with an 'intention' which resolves into 'action'. As a matter of fact, even individual acts cannot be described as a simple process that goes from ideas to the deeds that accomplish them: we should consider the unconscious, hidden drives and desires that play a central role in determining our actions. This is all too evident when we reflect on the composite nature of social processes. Social change is not an unilinear movement, since it is an internally articulated and even contradictory phenomenon, a *field of forces*. In the Animal Liberation Movement too many imagine social change as if there could be a centre that spreads its rays of salvation to the outside, towards an indiscriminate mass that would otherwise be 'damned'. A movement constantly seeking to avoid 'cross-contamination'.[60] Such religious heritage shows how Animal Liberation is far from the elaboration of a materialist praxis.

5   Veganism Is Not a Mode of Production

The above conclusions are strictly connected to my critique of veganism, a critique that has often been misunderstood. I have been making critical remarks on veganism as a 'lifestyle' and as a 'means of struggle' since 2005: every time, my remarks are automatically interpreted as a condemnation of veganism as such. Here again we see moralism in action. While I ask for *differentiation* and *articulation* of problems, everything is reduced to a binary code (yes/no; in/out). Either you are 'with us' or you are 'against us', either you are 'inside' or you are 'outside'; all problematic positions must be condemned because they question the underlying identity of the group. For its part, the rigidity of such identity is nothing but the consequence of the ethical dualism described above: just as morality knows no compromise, group membership is an in/out choice.

But what I say about the limits of veganism as the principle way to struggle for Animal Liberation and for the diffusion of antispeciesism is only meant to show some theoretical and practical problems. He who indicates a problem is not responsible for the problem itself. Now, the question is very simple: the fact that society is not an aggregate of individuals and that its transformation cannot be the result of the mechanical 'conversion' of individuals to veganism, does not mean that veganism is wrong or that it should be abandoned. It rather means that it is *insufficient* and that, whenever we are talking of a *social* change,

---

60   Griffin 2017, p. 26.

it is totally *irrelevant*. The aim of my criticism is to *complete* veganism (as a non-violent personal choice) with something that it lacks: i.e. social action as political struggle, something that will never be the consequence of a lifestyle. Political activism implies open and democratic confrontation, the elaboration of tactics and strategies, as well as methods to control and verify the results of such actions, and so on. The effectiveness of politics cannot be reduced to the calculation of people you have convinced to become vegan.

This point is decisive. Among the various reasons why Animal Liberation cannot consist in the mere diffusion of a lifestyle, I will here repeat the most essential one. We have already seen how weird it is that such a 'lifestyle' can only be described in *negative* terms (it means to 'abstain from' and such 'abstinence' can take a thousand different forms), and that the invention of in vitro meat could even imply the possibility of being vegan and eating meat. It is clear that, being a market choice, veganism does not say a word on how a liberated world would be *organised*, how it would *produce* its collective wealth.[61] The aim of the Animal Liberation struggle is therefore not to 'veganise' the world, but to introduce a different 'mode of production' that takes into account the needs of all human and non-human subjects involved, and that therefore will abolish animal exploitation in all its forms. Thus, no, veganism is not 'an implicit challenge to present concentration of wealth and power', as Johnson maintains, since its universal realisation would not 'require a just redistribution of global resources'.[62] Without changing *productive relations*, no just redistribution is possible. Veganism, alone, cannot defeat human inequality, because it says nothing about societal organisation.[63]

Veganism is rather an individual way of resisting integral exploitation, i.e. it is the negation of the current state of affairs, it is not a positive way of life, even less a social way of life. And it is surely *not* a mode of production: the fact that today people can live their veganism together (thus emphasising 'vegan practice as a communal activity rather than as an ascetic activity'[64]) does not transform such community into 'society'; rather it is a group within society. In the meantime, the society outside our vegan micro-world continues to be non-vegan and, among other things, makes the very existence of our vegan

---

61   When Griffin (2017, p. 11) writes that veganism 'may be understood as a form of praxis – turning abstract ideas surrounding animal exploitation and oppression into tangible actions', I reply that the 'tangibility' of such goals is disputable.

62   Johnson 2011, p. 214.

63   I think that the definition of speciesism as a 'mode of production' (Sanbonamtsu 2011b, p. 20 ff.) follows an analogous path. Yet, I would rather say that speciesism is the condition of possibility of historical modes of production.

64   Wadiwel 2016, p. 210.

community possible: through the exploitation, the killings, the wars, the blood of millions of humans and animals. Without overcoming the current mode of production, even the most extreme and strict vegan community remains part of the capitalist system and serves its reproduction.

Obfuscating the difference between veganism and antispeciesism, and forgetting the qualitative difference between social group and social totality, Animal Rights Activists fail to see another important consequence of understanding antispeciesism in political terms. It is not just that vegan individuals and communities cannot be synonyms of society: society in itself, even a non-vegan society, means much *more* in terms of global revolution than veganism. Society has *creative* and *productive* possibilities that stretch far beyond what individuals and small groups can do: it is therefore nonsensical to expect vegans (or even vegan groups) to anticipate the 'right' way of living in the present. What we can do is just to show our individual disdain for the present society, our way of interpreting non-violence as a moral, personal precept. For sure, we can bring some spark of liberation into the world in our small daily gestures, but we could never fully live the possibilities of a liberated world. 'There is no right life in the false'.[65] A free and non-violent life for all (human and non-human) will be organised freely by a society totally different from ours. All attempts to imagine the future world by composing it with the *disiecta membra* of the present one resemble a Frankenstein monster. I once read a 'vegan utopian model' that went so far as to describe the details of the private life of its lucky members that it reminded me of *1984*, rather than of a liberated society.

Just as a world without animal exploitation is not an *anti*-speciesist world, but rather a *non*-speciesist one (i.e. a world that has overcome speciesism, that no longer has to fight against speciesism), for the same reason such a world will not be a 'vegan' world but, in fact, a world that has left behind the struggle against lifestyles based on the systematic exploitation of nature.

---

65   Adorno 1997a; 2005a.

PART 2

Marxism and Animal Liberation

..

CHAPTER 4

Marxism and Animal Rights

1   One Struggle?

Let us move to the other extreme. Contrary to many Socialists, I believe that Marxism is not incompatible with Animal Liberation. As I will try to show, I even think that – by including the struggle against animal oppression in its theoretical framework – Marxism achieves a higher, more consistent materialist point of view. Sure, this presupposes a radical transformation of the Animal Liberation Ideology. In the previous chapters we have shown which direction such transformation should take. Anyway, although I believe that we face the necessity of a theoretical synthesis, I am aware that the practical convergence of Socialism and Animal Liberation is possibly even more difficult. Surely, without a clear definition of some theoretical principles, no strategic unity is possible. With the expression 'strategic unity', I want to make clear that I am not suggesting that the cause for animal rights should dissolve into Marxism; rather, I think it should embrace some basic Marxist concepts and understand that human liberation is the foreground of Animal Liberation itself.

Attempts to connect Marxism and Animal Liberation generally move in the opposite direction. The first time I started to wonder about the relation between Marxism and Animal Liberation, for example, was in 2003 when I read an article by Massimo Filippi entitled 'Can a not-vegetarian define himself a Communist?'[1] Although I later became friends with Massimo, this was a rather frustrating read. It epitomised the classic arguments used by Animal Rights Activists to convince Leftists that they contradict themselves if they do not stand against animal exploitation. Arguments that I have read and heard a thousand times since. Arguments that should, in the end, prompt Communists to become vegetarian. I immediately thought that Filippi's thesis was weak and could, at best, only lead to some 'tactical' alliance between Socialism and Animal Liberation. Anyway, if we suppose Filippi was trying to convince a Marxist – Marxism still being the most influential theoretical strand of international Socialism – it is hard to believe his arguments may have any effect at all.

---

1   Filippi 2003.

None of these arguments would ever push a Marxist to become an Animal Rights activist: not the struggle against 'world hunger', not the problem of 'water scarcity', not the 'environmental crisis', not the GMO industry. These are all problems that a Marxist would try to solve within his/her own theoretical and practical approach. There would be no reason, surely no ethical obligation, to sympathise with or embrace the Animal Rights theory, nor to become a vegetarian. Like many other Animal Rights Activists before and after him, Filippi seemed unaware that Marxism sees the solution to those problems at a political level and is not concerned by 'ethical' principles. Since Marxism is interested in solutions to social contradictions, it does not try to adequate reality to some moral ideal: it believes that the unjust distribution of resources is the necessary effect of a determined mode of production, not the consequence of an evil-oriented will. Although it is true that the meat industry steals important resources, worsening the situation of the Third World, no Marxist would accept the idea that factory farming as such is the cause of starvation. From the other side, the only Marxist (or rather Unionist) argument introduced by Filippi, i.e. the 'defence of workers' employed in the alimentary industry, is an argument that would not appeal to Animal Rights activists either (since, as we have seen, it would be considered 'extrinsic'). The result of this kind of attempt is quite depressing. Is there any hope to get Marxists and Animal Liberationists to understand each other? One thing is sure: any protest against the coldness of Marxists is pointless. We have to play them 'their own melody' – to put it with Marx.

2   Animal Rights vs. Marx

Several Animal Rights theorists have attempted to criticise Marx for his humanism and his speciesist description of animal behavior.[2] I think that these critiques totally miss the point. I will try to show why by focusing on David Sztybel, an author that best exemplifies the defects of such a (mis)reading of Marx. An orthodox Animal Rights Activist himself, Sztybel tries to show that it is contradictory for Marxism not to defend animals. Unlike Filippi, Sztybel shows no sympathy for Marx and demonstrates that he has not given *Capital* the same attention he has given *Animal Liberation*. The problem, as we will see, is that even those authors who have certainly read Marx (like Benton or Best) end up criticising Marx *exactly* like Sztybel does.

---

2   Noske 1989; Dickens 1992; Benton 1993; Charlton, Coe and Francione 1993; Midgley 1995; Sztybel 1997; Francione 2000; Perlo 2002; Garner 2005; Sanbonmatsu 2011; Boggs 2011; Best 2014.

MARXISM AND ANIMAL RIGHTS

Sztybel describes how Marx and Engels understood the Human-Animal relation in their works, pretending to find a contradiction between their stress on the 'continuity' between the species and the idea that the human being is somehow a 'unique' animal. A certain Darwinan understanding of continuity between animal and humans is typical of Marxist *materialism*, since materialism considers the human being entirely part of nature, and rejects the idea that our 'soul' or our 'reason' could make us somehow *transcend nature*. On the other hand, Marx's emphasis on the peculiarity (and 'superiority') of the human being in the animal kingdom indicates – according to Sztybel – a residue of *idealism* that Marxism has not been able to get rid of.

What Sztybel is unable to see is that such apparently opposite and contradictory tendencies in Marx's theory are in fact structurally related and delineate the core of his *dialectical* thinking. Missing the dialectical point of such inner connection, Sztybel cannot do anything but propose Animal Rights as a way of solving a contradiction he has arbitrarily projected onto Marx. That Sztybel lacks any real understanding of Marx's method is evident from the way he either unilaterally quotes the work of the *young* Marx, or badly misinterprets Marx's later writings (no word is said on the centrality of history, on ideology, on the unity of theory and praxis, etc.). Sztybel's method is, on the contrary, perfectly clear: he simply applies his all-embracing and prefab category of 'speciesism' to everything he reads. It is not difficult, then, to come up with an anthropocentric interpretation of the following passage taken from Marx's *Manuscripts*:

> Communism, as fully developed naturalism, equals humanism, and as fully developed humanism equals naturalism; it is the genuine resolution of the conflict between the human being and nature, and between the human being and man, the true resolution of the conflict between existence and being, between objectification and self-affirmation, between freedom and necessity, between individual and species. It is the solution of the riddle of history and knows itself to be the solution.[3]

Although it is true that this passage is still idealistic and obscure, Sztybel manages to take all its speculative richness away, making Marx say exactly the opposite of what he means: 'In the above, rather grandiose, passage, not only is Marxist naturalism humanistic, but claims to resolve the antagonisms between humans and nature. Given the humanistic view of Marx, it is no surprise that

---

3   Marx 1968, p. 536.

this resolution is in favor of humans at the expense of other animals'.[4] Yet, Marx is not at all resolving naturalism into humanism; he is not stating that Socialism dissolves Nature into an anthropocentric Empire, where every antagonism between the human being and nature must cease in order to grant our final victory. He is arguing, on the contrary, that Socialism can put an end to the struggle between human beings and nature and, subsequently, give birth to an epoch of conciliation in which the opposition between naturalism and humanism is definitively *aufgehoben*. No Animal Rights Theorist seems able to understand the inner dialectics of this text.[5]

Sztybel is even more idealist and Hegelian than the young Marx, as he charges him with opinions that Marx has already criticised. See, for example, the subsequent sentence which is nothing but a paraphrase of Hegel: 'nature ... taken abstractly, for itself, and fixed in its separation from man, is nothing for man'.[6] This sentence that does not at all imply – as Sztybel suggests – that for Marx 'nature has nothing of value for humanity apart from humanity itself',[7] i.e. that nature is of mere *instrumental* interest for us, a way of satisfying our needs. In the following sentences, Marx clearly explains that such separation between the human being and nature is a nonsense, an idealistic abstraction. Had Sztybel read *all* the *Manuscripts*, he would have found that: 'Nature is man's inorganic body – that is to say, nature insofar as it is not the human body. the human being lives from nature – i.e., nature is his body – and he must maintain a continuing dialogue with it if he is not to die. To say that man's physical and mental life is linked to nature simply means that nature is linked to itself, for the human being is a part of nature'.[8] Marx is here more likely to dissolve the human being in nature than the contrary. But Marx was intelligent enough to avoid such vulgar materialism; that is why he wrote that naturalism and humanism should become one. Marx underlines the necessity to see the reciprocal determination of human beings and nature, their organic, indissoluble relation. The sterile and idealistic counterposition between humans being and nature can only be solved once we look at the core of Marx's theory, something that is not fully developed in the *Manuscripts*: society, which can be understood only through the abstract laws of economy and the material process of historical becoming.

---

4   Sztybel 1997.
5   See Noske 1989, p. 73; Benton 1993, p. 35; Fracione 2000, p. 121; Garner 2005, p. 107; Best 2014, p. 93.
6   Marx 1968, p. 587.
7   Sztybel 1997.
8   Marx 1968, p. 516.

We will see what this means later. For now, let us go back for a moment to Sztybel's critique of the young Marx. Having already defined the Marxist understanding of the human-nature relation as intrinsically instrumental and anthropocentric, Sztybel can easily confute Marx, using the antispeciesist mantra every Animal Rights Activist knows so well.

> Animal rightism, of course, contests the idea that nonhuman animals should be considered to have merely instrumental value. However, Marx and Engels would have to defend the subordination of nonhuman animals like everyone else does: by pointing out morally relevant differences between human beings and nonhuman animals.[9]

Stzybel's strategy is nonsensical: not only does he mutilate Marxism (as we have seen); he also presupposes – wrongly – that Marx and Engels would use moral arguments to justify the superiority of humans over animals. Something they would never have done. One would expect Sztybel to be aware of this, as he himself quotes Engels's *Anti-Dühring*: 'We therefore reject every attempt to impose on us any moral dogma whatsoever as an eternal, ultimate and for ever immutable ethical law on the pretext that the moral world, too, has its permanent principles which stand above history and the differences between nations'.[10] This does not mean – as Sztybel believes – that the 'Marxist ethic', though preaching the superiority of the human being, is also subjected to historical change from a Marxist point of view. It implies on the contrary that Marxism – rejecting *any ethical theory* – does not at all preach that superiority; in as much as Marxism does believe that the human being is a somehow 'superior' animal, such superiority has no moral implication. Let us for the moment see why Sztybel's critiques of Marx are wrong. Then we will deal with the relation between Marxism and Ethics.

To put it simply, the problem with Sztybel's critiques of Marx is that they are pointless. Sztybel accuses Marx's definitions of human qualities of 'speciesism', on the laughable assumption that Marx is interested in founding some anthropocentric moral theory. He isolates the various 'qualities' that according to Marx and Engels define the specificity of the human being (self-consciousness, labour, historicity, etc.) and confutes them, without seeing that none of those

---

9   Sztybel 1997.
10 Engels 1962b, p. 87. The quote goes on to say: 'We maintain on the contrary that all moral theories have been hitherto the product, in the last analysis, of the economic conditions of society obtaining at the time'. This conclusion should surely appear unintelligible to Sztybel.

characteristics stands by itself. Sztybel's vivisectionist method ('another can-
didate for human uniqueness is ...') is absurd, because, according to Marx's
point of view, only the *totality* of those characteristics defines the human
condition; without seeing their mutual relation, they would not even have a
content. In the *Dialectics of Nature* Engels clearly states that all human qualities can be found in the other animals: self-consciousenss, language, intelligence, teleology, etc. As 'natural' beings humans have no *supernatural* powers
that can distinguish them from the other animals. It is only *labour* and its
ability to determine human history that shows the essential difference, the
emerging quality of humanity.[11] It is only because his self-consciousness is a
product of labour that human consciousness is different from that of every
other animal. On the other hand, it is only because his social being determines what is *productive* labour that human society and animal society diverge.
And it is only because this social labour is accumulated around and inside
the individual and determines his historical development that human history
differs from animal history, etc. Stzybel himself quotes the famous passage
from *The German Ideology* – the one we mentioned in Chapter 2 – where
Marx and Engels argue that 'by producing their means of subsistence men
are indirectly producing their actual material life'.[12] Such 'material life' grows
on itself, so to speak; it develops according to human action and, at the same
time, it is a prerequisite of it: it is both effect of our vital activity and one of
its ontological preconditions. Each generation lives on previous generations'
accumulated labour. The human being is a *zoon politikon* because its being is
intrinsically *collective* in this sense: it is historical and social; in addition to
this, as the Enlightenment has shown, it can be *rationally determined*, i.e. it
brings forth the possibility of self-determination. It is only in this context that
Marx's belief that the human being is a self-conscious animal makes sense:
self-consciousness as such is 'human', because only human self-consciousness
can be intrinsically and radically collective, rational and universal. One can
define the human being as a social animal because (1) it depends on a historical collective, (2) its history opens the possibility of self-determination,
(3) such self-determination becomes more and more global, universal, and in
this sense (4) our species imagines the rational overcoming of natural violence and contingency. Our relation to our own animality is therefore historical, not an invariant. That is why Engels writes that the human being will
only be 'human' in a communist society: 'then, for the first time, man, in

---

11   Engels 1962c.
12   Marx and Engels 1969, p. 21.

a certain sense, is finally marked off from the rest of the animal kingdom, and emerges from mere animal conditions of existence into really human ones'.[13]

Nor is Sztybel correct when he writes that since Marx defines human 'alienation' in terms of an animal condition, he must believe that animals are inferior: 'Marx always maintains there is a differential between humans and other animals; even in an alienated state, humans have potentialities that other animals do not have'.[14] As a matter of fact, in the *Manuscripts* we find a description of the workers' class condition that shows how such 'animality' is more metaphorical than real: alienation is for the human being an *unnatural* condition.[15] The cleavage between labour and capital, the division of labour and the anarchy of capitalist production define alienation as an anti-human condition. Capitalism sets the human being in contradiction with its own nature, because it negates a possibility implied in its *social being*:

> Dirt – this pollution and putrefaction of man, the sewage (this word is to be understood in its literal sense) of civilisation – becomes an element of life for him. Universal unnatural neglect, putrefied nature, becomes an element of life for him. None of this sense exist any longer, either in their human form or in their inhuman form – i.e., not even in their animal form ... It is not only human needs which the human being lacks – even his animal needs cease to exist. The Irishman has only one need left – the need to eat, to eat potatoes, and, more precisely, to eat rotten potatoes, the worst kind of potatoes.[16]

As Marx clearly states, that is not even an 'animal' condition.

Sure, Marx underlines the specificity of the human animal, but this has nothing to do with moral speciesism. Marx's description of human nature is *dynamic*: the human being is defined through history as a strange creature that 'is not an animal anymore' but 'not fully human yet'. At the same time, all human abilities and characteristics do not concern us as individuals, but as a social and collective beings; or better, as historically changing social beings. Marxism is therefore not only incomparable with current moral theories; it embodies a fundamental critique of them. Singer comes close to grasping this, but not quite:

---

13   Engels 1973, p. 226.
14   Sztybel 1997; see also Clarke and Linzey 1990, p. xv; Benton 1993, p. 23 and pp. 43–4.
15   Marx 1968.
16   Marx 1968, p. 548.

It has been claimed – by Lenin among others – that Marxism is a scientific system, free from any ethical judgements or postulates. This is obviously nonsense. It is true that for Marx morality is part of the ideological super-structure of society, is determined by the economic basis, and serves to promote the interests of the ruling class. But it does not follow from this that all morality is to be rejected. What has to be rejected is morality that serves the interests of the ruling class. This includes all dominant moral-ities up to now. Once communism has been established and classes have disappeared, however, we can pass beyond class morality, to what Engels called 'a really human morality'.[17]

Contrary to what Singer here states, and to what Benton[18] or Ryder[19] believe, Marxism does not criticise current moral theories from the point of view of another moral theory, or in the vein of Nietzschean relativism.[20] What Engels calls 'really human morality' is at the same time the *fulfilment* of traditional morality and its *overcoming*. There is no way of 'extracting' some moral prin-ciples from Marxism, if those moral principles are to be formulated in the universal, static, abstract form of current ethics.[21]

Moral theories are (1) *monadological* and (2) *unhistorical*: they concern the individual as an autonomous, separated subject, placing it in an ideal (tran-

17   Singer 2000, pp. 81–2.
18   Benton 1993, p. 99 ff.
19   Ryder 2017.
20   Those who object to this argument that fighting against human 'exploitation' implies a value judgement, in my view, confuse the ethical impulse with moral theory or, worse, with the presence of 'values'. No one denies that human beings – not being machines – react to what they feel as unjust (including Marx and Engels as individuals). And it would also be possible to admit that one 'always' acts on the basis of a 'morality' and perhaps 'implicit values'. But the point on which I would like to insist is that this presupposition fails in the face of the active deconstruction of the moral theory attempted by Marx and Engels. Because the fundamental question is whether it is permissible to 'translate' that reaction to injustice in 'universalistic' and 'individualistic' terms, or if this translation does not ideologically falsify the sense of human action instead. Human action, as Marx and Engels claim, is always social and historical, open to a becoming that 'produces' – it does simply not 'recognise' as already existent – different levels of universality.
21   After his later involvement with neo-Darwinism and sociobiology, though, Singer reframed his critique in a more traditional fashion: 'Marx wanted to bring our ethical judg-ments down to earth. They did not, he thought, come from God or from reason but from the economic basis of our society and the means we use to produce the goods we con-sume. He did not consider a different earthly possibility: that our ethical judgments have a biological basis in our origins as social mammals' (Singer 2016). The reactionary con-sequences of such biologism were already clear at the end of his book on Marx, where

scendental) world, where socio-historical actuality is suppressed. Yet, as Marx has shown, human action presupposes the existence of other beings: we have an inner, immanent connection with the other, something that essentially inheres in our being, right from the beginning, even before we start doing anything. It is striking how little Animal Rights Theorists discuss the problem of animal societies. Their main concern is how we humans as individuals treat individual animals; every time they discuss human society, they consider it an undifferentiated whole and start debating how this abstract entity treats animal individuals. If they would try and compare the way human and animal societies actually work, the question of individual agency and universalism would appear to them in a totally different light.

Secondly, every moral theory is allergic to history in as much as it pretends to have no relation with the concrete historical subject that formulated it: it springs out as a product of pure reason, not of the concrete process that brought it forth. Accordingly, the 'universalistic ethics' which could only be radically and coherently formulated in the glorious age of the European Bourgeoisie is usually considered valid for previous ages and extra-European cultures. Moral theories that do not want to know about political economy are therefore regarded by Marxists as empty abstractions.

> The idea that all men, as men, have something in common, and that to that extent they are equal, is of course primeval. But the modern demand for equality is something entirely different from that; this consists rather in deducing from that common quality of being human, from that equality of men as men, a claim to equal political resp. social status for all human beings, or at least for all citizens of a state or all members of a society. Before that original conception of relative equality could lead to the conclusion that men should have equal rights in the state and in society, before that conclusion could even appear to be something natural and self-evident, thousands of years had to pass and did pass.[22]

It is interesting how moral philosophers totally misunderstand the Hegelian notions of Reason and universality. Ethical concerns about Marxist indifference towards animals usually move from universal values which are static and

---

he explained the resurgence of inequalities in the Soviet Russia as a consequence of an innate human tendency to prevail over our peers: 'we should note that the prevalence of hierarchy is not limited to human societies. There are clear hierarchies among most social birds and mammals' (Singer 2000, p. 95).

22 Engels 1962b, pp. 96–7.

transhistorical: these seem to be true precisely because they are supposed to be eternal, valid for every human being, no matter where or when she lives. Moral philosophy, though, is blind to the idea that universals *become*, that history itself is the locus of such becoming-true of universals. Isolated from its dynamic and social nature, human universalism becomes the easy target of allegations of speciesism. Benton, for instance, accuses Marx of ignoring the phenomenon of animal 'culture',[23] as if animals could raise their culture to the level of universality that only the capitalist mode of production has enabled and which is precisely what interests Marx: that 'humans take the whole world as object of their activity'[24] is the description of a process where the empirical and Kantian notions of 'world' get mixed up and radically reformulated. Again, the problem of the difference between human and animal society is ignored, universality becomes a static, natural attribute of our species. Something that Benton, Singer, et al. can easily deny on an empirical level: after all, no human being has ever lived in a condition of actual, complete universalism.

Yet, the idea that every time we underline a difference between humans and animals we are perpetuating a speciesist view of nature is illogical. If such 'coherent', 'non-speciesist' definition of 'moral status' must obscure differences which are essential to understand the specificity of human society, it brings reactionary consequences. As we will see, it prevents us from understanding class relations and, as a consequence, it destroys the possibility of formulating a political theory of Animal Liberation. How could we ever understand and solve the problems of animal suffering *in general*, if human society were not driven by its own dynamic towards universalism?[25] Benton's criticism of the Marxian concept of 'human potential' seems to ignore the left-wing Hegelian universalism that influenced the *Manuscripts*. Human potential is not something that should be 'fulfilled',[26] but rather *produced* in the process of historical self-determination of humanity. Benton's argument seems to move from the supposition of an abstract and unhistorical Human Nature, as if Marx's 'species-being' had inherent potentialities that merely await disclosure. But this is *the right-wing interpretation of Hegel*, while Left-Hegelians like Marx insisted on the creative power of the human *Geist*. The contradiction that Benton derives from this, the antinomic nature of technological development ('the individual historical potential to deliver "mega-deaths" at the press of a button is dependent upon the realisation of the collective histor-

---

23   Benton 1993, p. 41.
24   Benton 1993, p. 39.
25   We will deal with this problem in Chapter 7.
26   Benton 1993, p. 39.

ical potential to construct hi-tech weaponry'[27]) is no objection to Marx, who never believed that the development of human potential was something good *in itself*: the idea that development *per se* is good, and the idea that we can judge something good from an abstract universalistic position, are both extraneous to historical materialism. For it is clear that the universality of human culture is a product of its inner *struggle*, the outcome of an *open* historical process, where the constructive and the destructive potential go hand-in-hand. It is precisely the way in which we face and solve our social contradictions (and our relation to nature) that defines the constructive or destructive attitude of human Society. This is not a theoretical issue that can be discussed from a general point of view. It is a concrete, political question. What is certain is that without the *apocalyptic* development of capitalist modernity, the very idea of a universal solution to the human/animal problem would have been inconceivable.

Luckily, Marx does not start with a moral prejudice in favour of humans. Nor is he interested in granting human beings some 'moral privilege'. What Marx wants is to describe the dynamism of human society: how its structures work, and how they can be modified. Since his focus is on the laws of social transformation, Marx has no interest in formulating an anthropocentric ethics or a political utopia grounded on any static anthropology (i.e. the description of some constant and transhistorical characteristics of 'the' human being). As a matter of fact, Marx is describing neither what the human being *is* (philosophical anthropology), nor what he *ought to be* (ethics), but how it *becomes* (political economy). For Marx, history is the arena where the human being *becomes what it is*: his rebuttal of ethics is grounded in his materialist assumption that there is *no opposition between the real and the ideal*. Thus, Marx and Engels considered communism not some sort of *ideal* that we should make real, but 'the *real* movement which abolishes the present state of things'.[28] If human reality did not embody the possibility of a society where production is realised for the common good, communism would be just an unreal abstraction: a moralistic sermon or a philanthropic dream. But since the human being is the animal that produces its own means of subsistence, communism is the real possibility to put such conditions under its control.

Of course, Animal Rights Theorists sometimes describe Marxism as a form of *communitarianism*, i.e. a moral theory in which the collective ontologically proceeds and exceeds the individual. The sociological ground for such ethics is *holism*. Yet, Marx is neither Durkheim, nor Parsons, nor obviously Luhmann.

---

27   Benton 1993, p. 40.
28   Marx and Engels 1969, p. 35.

The fact is that Marx never attempted to elaborate a *universal theory of society*, his aim being always the explanation of the *capitalist mode of production*.[29] History is relevant to him because the process of the formation of capitalism helps us to understand its essence, its potentiality and its limits. In this respect, Marx was surely a Hegelian, trying to understand how individual freedom made its way through the winding road of history. Often accused of being a totalitarian and anti-individualistic thinker, Hegel himself proposed a theoretical model that is at odds with holism and functionalism: according to Hegel, the objective structures of Spirit should be justified by the way they *enable* individual freedom; thus, history becomes the process where individual and collective freedom meet and become one without losing their dialectical reciprocity. This scheme works for Marx, too, although here the process is not determined *in advance*, being the result of several intertwined *conflicts*.

Having eradicated dialectics[30] and conflict from Hegel's thought, it is no accident that Singer interprets his philosophy of history in a *teleological* sense, and fails to understand the meaning of *social totality* in both Hegel and Marx. Singer's failure in understanding historical materialism is thus rooted in his incomprehension of Hegel: 'also like Hegel, Marx thought that history is a necessary process heading towards a discoverable goal'.[31] Yet, Marx radicalised Hegel's philosophy, emphasising the efforts by which humanity tries to

---

29   A critique of such misinterpretation of Marxism as a way to explain society or history 'in general' is offered by Lenin himself: 'Why does Marx speak of "modern" society, when all the economists who preceded him spoke of society in general? [...] Marx speaks of one "economic formation of society" only, the capitalist formation, that is, he says that he investigated the law of development of this formation only and of no other. [...] [F]rom the standpoint of the old [...] economists and sociologists, the concept of the economic formation of society is entirely superfluous: they talk of society in general, they argue with the Spencers about the nature of society in general, about the aim and essence of society in general, and so forth. In their reasonings, these subjective sociologists rely on arguments such as – the aim of society is to benefit all its members, that justice, therefore, demands such and such an organisation [...] It is obvious that Marx's basic idea that the development of the social-economic formations is a process of natural history cuts at the very root of this childish morality which lays claim to the title of sociology. [...] The gigantic step forward taken by Marx in this respect consisted precisely in that he discarded all these arguments about society and progress in general and produced a scientific analysis of one society and of one progress – capitalist' (Lenin 2001).

30   In his discussion of *Phenomenology*, for instance, Singer observes that the universal nature of words like 'This', 'Here' and 'Now' is a consequence of the fact that knowledge must be communicated (2001, pp. 71–3); Hegel's crucial intuition, though, is that the *reflection* on those universals which occurs through the phenomenon of language, dialectically *produces*, *performs*, a contradiction.

31   Singer 2000, p. 55.

make a 'collective agent'[32] out of historical contingency. The idea that history could *mean* something as a result of struggle, is alien to Singer; and so is the Hegelian and Marxian idea of 'objective reason'. Reason is, for Singer, either individual or absolute, either a mechanical calculus or a cosmic force.[33] From his nominalistic perspective, 'collective mind is a religious idea';[34] 'Universal mind' is nothing but 'a collective term for all the human minds'.[35] There is no mention of the *social mediation* which should link these two aspects of the Hegelian thought. Even when he quotes 'Hegel's social theory',[36] Singer never describes society as something that happens *between* individuals. For Singer, 'social' means either the banal idea of materially *being together*, or the intellectual phenomenon of *communication*. For Hegel, though, society is the making of reality through interaction, the historical process by which our activity on the world mirrors what we are, and helps us understand what we could be. Interestingly, for Benton, too, the concept of a 'universal human community'[37] is trapped between the false alternatives of nominalistic empiricism and Kantian idealism: i.e. society as it materially *is*, or as it *should be* from an ideal point of view. But, as we have seen, what interests Marx is precisely the relation *between* real and ideal, between the empirical state of society and its historical potentialities, i.e. the way in which concrete historical possibilities emerge from social interaction, thus becoming values and ideas that can orientate human praxis. Not surprisingly, for Singer, the definition of 'genuine human needs' is a matter of 'agreement',[38] not the result of material forces which seek to become self-conscious by determining their own conditions of existence. 'Universal Mind' is for Singer always a state, never a process. This is the reason why Singer imagines it to be 'harmonic', rather than conflictual.

This false assumption justifies his thesis that Marxian communism should be a sort of heaven on Earth. Of course, the abolition of class conflict does not imply the abolition of *every* kind of human conflict. This mistake is very similar to the confusion between violence and domination, which is typical of Animal Rightism: just as power relations become obfuscated in the generic concept of 'violence', so class oppression is mystified as one of several forms of conflicts. On one side, when we talk about 'domination' and 'classes' we talk

---

32   Korsgaard 2018, pp. 103–4.

33   Singer 2001, p. 89.

34   Singer 2001, p. 95.

35   Singer 2000, p. 20.

36   Singer 2001, p. 96.

37   Benton 1993, p. 15.

38   Singer 2001, p. 37.

about *structures* which produce *effects* on a more general level than 'violence' and 'conflicts'. On the other, and consequently, when we talk of the *abolition* of domination and classes, we talk of the end of specific power structures, not of an irenic state of things where all violence and conflicts magically disappear.[39]

In the section of the *Grundrisse* called 'Forms of Pre-capitalist Society', Marx describes how the relationships between individual and collective historically changes, how the very notions of 'individuality', 'community', and 'property' should be theorised in order not to lose their specificity.[40] Contrary to what many might expect, for instance, in *Capital* the concept of 'private property' is not opposed to that of commune or State Property, but to 'individual property'.[41] While private property is a typical bourgeois phenomenon – since it is intrinsically conflictual, related to a series of social and historical preconditions which are anything but 'natural' – communism is and can only be the social form where the potential freedom of *capitalism* is fully accomplished for *each* and for *all*. Only if this radical demand for freedom is completely met are we justified in considering communism an improvement over the capitalist mode of production, a stage of social progress where the conflict between individual labour and collective production has been overcome. Those who believe that in socialism such conflict has ceased to be because the State or Society are more important than its members, because individuals cannot desire anything which contradicts the social norm, are criticising a social model that had already been criticised by the young Marx: i.e. primitive communism.[42] Animal Rightism is blind to this kind of analysis. Francione's theory, for instance, only works within the modern, i.e. bourgeois framework of private property. This means that his attempt to put an end to the property status of animals accepts capitalism as its standard social model. Although he recognises that different theories and concepts of property exist, he decides not to discuss them.[43] The impolitic consequences of such a pragmatic move are obvious. First, the only kind of property that exists outside the domain of bourgeois economy seems to be State Property.[44] Since the State-form is here considered an eternal essence, statist bureaucratism is the only possible outcome of Marx's articulated and

---

39   This is the reason why I think that Wadiwel's use of the words 'violence' and 'war' (2016, p. 187 ff.), although framed in a Foucauldian context, can be confusing: they do not hit and deconstruct the theoretical loci which produce Animal Liberation Ideology. See, for instance, his defence of veganism as a form of 'desertion from war' (p. 205).

40   Marx 1983, p. 383 ff.

41   Marx 1962, p. 791.

42   Marx 1968, p. 534.

43   Francione 1995, p. 13.

44   Francione 1995, p. 45.

dialectical analysis.[45] Second, property is never discussed in its historicity: it has no genesis and, consequently, it knows no end. Yet, such omission is particularly relevant in an analysis of the human-animal relationship, since both Marx and Francione know that animal oppression is implied in the genesis of property as such: 'the domestication and ownership of animals are very closely related to the development of the very idea of property or money'.[46]

The idea that 'property' is not an eternal, Platonic essence, or that Marxism does not hold communities superior to individuals, are totally unintelligible to Francione.[47] Yet, according to Marx and Engels, this is precisely the case, since both 'individuality' and 'property' are socio-historical structures whose meaning is determined by a specific, dialectical context. 'Individuality' and 'property' change their meaning in a post-capitalist society, as they would be unrestrained by a particular, oppressive interest. If the abstraction we now call 'ethics' (the free determination of individual will according to universal ideas of Good and Evil) could make any sense, it would be in a libertarian communist society. But even then, ethics would rather be the *goal* of a liberated society than one of its premises. With the achievement of a truly free, rational and democratic society, in fact, 'choice' would be entirely a matter of self-determination, a process in which individuals mirror themselves in the social structures they create, in which institutions would no longer be opposed to them as an alien power.

3   The Role of Animals in Marxism

3.1   *Marx and Engels on Vegetarianism and Antivivisectionism*

So, what will be of animals in a society where class struggle is over and where the antagonism between the human being and nature – as the young Marx thought – is superseded? Do animals have any chance to live better than today? If we read what Marx and Engels had to say about vegetarianism and antivivisectionism, presumably not. Is Sztybel right in the end? Again: no. He is wrong because not only did he not rely on what Marx and Engels explicitly wrote about this and merely argues on the basis of misinterpreted passages, but also because Marx and Engels's *opinions* on this matter are not relevant, nor are they a necessary consequence of Marxist *theory* as such.

Sure, it must be said – and I will not deny it – that neither Marx nor Engels ever said that animals could play a different role in human society than that

---

45   See also McMullen 2016, pp. 145–6.

46   Francione 2005, p. 34.

47   Francione 1995, p. 35 and p. 293; 1996, p. 20; 2000, p. 208.

of victims, not even in communist society. If communism makes the division of labour obsolete, it does not necessarily abolish the productive activities of the former societies. Thus, the 'omnilateral man' of the future can go fishing even if the job of the fisher as such has been abolished: 'in communist society, where nobody has one exclusive sphere of activity but each can become accomplished in any branch he wishes, society regulates the general production and thus makes it possible for me to do one thing today and another tomorrow, to hunt in the morning, fish in the afternoon, rear cattle in the evening, criticise after dinner, just as I have a mind, without ever becoming hunter, fisherman, herdsman or critic'.[48] Even if we can agree with Marcuse on the ironic nature of such a passage, an explicit refusal of animal oppression in Marx's writings is impossible to find.[49]

It is important to underline that the protection of animals in England was often characterised by bourgeois contempt against the savageness of the lower classes:

> the gradual legislative protection of animals was shot through with class concerns, the blood sports of the lower classes, such as bull running and the baiting of various animals, condemned and suppressed in the early nineteenth century while fox hunting and shooting were permitted to continue into the twenty-first. Early nineteenth-century animal welfare activists were convinced that the lower classes were inherently more cruel in their treatment of animals.[50]

Major institutions like the Royal Society for the Prevention of Cruelty to Animals, founded in 1824, had an active role in passing this kind of legislation:

> Historians of the RSPCA (the 'Royal' prefix was added in 1840) and the early anti-cruelty legislation routinely invoke class in their explanations of why fox hunting was not targeted as cruel. Thus Brian Harrison has argued that in its early years the society 'was quite unashamed in focusing primarily on cruelty committed at the lower end of society, quite explicit in its belief that cruelty was more common there than elsewhere', while Robert Malcolmson contends that social control, rather than cruelty per se, was the real motivation for legislating against lower class sport. Sports

---

48   Marx and Engels 1969, p. 33.
49   Although this does not mean that Marx or Engels were, in any respect, 'animal-haters': Foster and Burkett 2016, pp. 43–4.
50   May 2013, p. 7.

such as bull running, cock or dog fighting, or badger baiting were condemned not merely for the cruelty they involved but for their presumed tendency to undermine social order. They kept the labouring classes from work, encouraging disorderly association and promoting gambling among them.[51]

Even if it is possible to articulate differently the relation between animal abuse and class struggle – for instance to, underline those situations in which members of the working class protested against animal oppression[52] – it is no wonder that Marx and Engels were sceptical about the class orientation of the major welfarist institutions of their times.

Along the same lines goes their references to meat consumption. Surely, Marx and Engels never discussed vegetarianism as a possible alternative to meat-eating; generally speaking, they described meat as a privilege of the wealthy classes, a privilege that ought to be extended to the rest of society. In England, a higher wage means that 'the worker eats more meat; he satisfies more needs'.[53] 'When the English worker is employed he is satisfied. And he can well be satisfied, at any rate the textile worker, if he compares his lot with the fate of his comrades in Germany and France. The worker there earns just enough to allow him to live on bread and potatoes; he is lucky if he can buy meat once a week'.[54] Engels was even convinced that meat-eating favoured our evolution and was keen to justify cannibalism as a necessary evil: 'With all due respect to the vegetarians the human being did not come into existence without a meat diet, and if the latter, among all peoples known to us, has led to cannibalism at some time or other (the forefathers of the Berliners, the Weletabians or Wilzians, used to eat their parents as late as the tenth century), that is of no consequence to us today'.[55] Engels was particularly harsh with vegetarianism and antivivisectionism, which he considered to be extraneous to 'scientific socialism'. He talks sarcastically of 'opponents of inoculation, supporters of abstemiousness, vegetarians, anti-vivisectionists, nature-healers, free-community preachers whose communities have fallen to pieces, authors of new theories on the origin of the universe, unsuccessful or unfortunate inventors'.[56]

51   May 2013, p. 63.
52   Adams 2010.
53   Marx 1967, p. 8.
54   Engels 1972b, p. 303.
55   Engels 1962c, pp. 449–50.
56   Engels 1972a, p. 455.

It must be said, though, that he was also the one who denounced our *violent domination* of nature, and foresaw the *revenge* that nature was going to take on us, foreshadowing the idea of a forthcoming harmony between society and nature. Engels explains how the unity of 'humanism and naturalism' proclaimed by the young Marx is to be intended:

> All the planned action of all animals has never succeeded in impressing the stamp of their will upon the earth. That was left for man. In short, the animal merely *uses* its environment, and brings about changes in it simply by its presence; the human being by his changes makes it serve his ends, *masters* it. This is the final, essential distinction between the human being and other animals, and once again it is labour that brings about this distinction. Let us not, however, flatter ourselves overmuch on account of our human victories over nature. For each such victory nature takes its revenge on us. Each victory, it is true, in the first place brings about the results we expected, but in the second and third places it has quite different, unforeseen effects which only too often cancel the first ... Thus at every step we are reminded that we by no means rule over nature like a conqueror over a foreign people, like someone standing outside nature – but that we, with flesh, blood and brain, belong to nature, and exist in its midst, and that all our mastery of it consists in the fact that we have the advantage over all other creatures of being able to learn its laws and apply them correctly ... But the more this progresses the more will men not only feel but also know their oneness with nature, and the more impossible will become the senseless and unnatural idea of a contrast between mind and matter, the human being and nature, soul and body, such as arose after the decline of classical antiquity in Europe and obtained its highest elaboration in Christianity.[57]

One may raise the question: will such 'oneness' imply some change in the relation between humans and animals? Judging from what we have seen so far, it is easy to suppose that Engels's answer would probably be: no. As a matter of fact, though, we do not know. Marx and Engels's opinions on the welfarist, vegetarian and antivivectionist societies of their times do not count as a definitive answer. Thus, let us not be scared by the sacred totem and let us ask: what is the correct and most coherent answer from a *Marxist* point of view?

---

57   Engels 1962c, pp. 451–3.

3.2   *What Are the Implications of Marx's Theory for Animal Liberation?*
Any serious attempt to see if Marxism could make room for animal liberation should see through Marx and Engels's explicit and contingent 'opinions' and seek out some organic connection at a 'theoretical' level. We must engage with the core of their thought. I assume that this will undoubtedly prove that, on this point, Marx and Engels's critique of animal welfarism does not imply a rejection of Animal Liberation. To make this clear, let us go back to the idea of a continuity between the human being and the other animals. As Filippi correctly writes, Marx admired Darwin: the latter's theory of evolution had finally shown that the human being was not a fallen angel, but an animal in all respects.

> If we accept such continuity between the human and the non-human animal (and for a genuine Communist there should be no reason to deny this), we should begin to ground our ethical principles not on ephemeral differences (like skin colour, the number of legs, the ability to speak English or to find mushrooms), but rather on the fact that we are all – humans and non-humans – living and conscious.[58]

Now, we already criticised the recourse to 'ethical principles' from a Marxist point of view. What we should understand is that, according to Marx, the difference between human and non-human animals is not 'ephemeral' but substantial. As we have seen, Marx would in fact define the human being not simply as something 'other' than the animal: humanity means 'becoming-other', our nature implies incessantly 'getting out' of the animal condition ('As men originally made their exit from the animal world – in the narrower sense of the term – so they made their entry into history'[59]). History is the *locus* where such 'getting out' actually takes place. History is itself an uncompleted gestation. But we can never understand such 'becoming-other-than-itself' if we do not place socially productive labour as the *proprium* of humanity: *Homo sapiens*' ability to radically modify his environment and, thus, his own development.

The other animals play a rather passive role in Marx's critique of political economy, since we have always seen them as productive factors. Historically, the human being used other animals

(a)   as food
(b)   as labouring-force

---

58   Filippi 2003.
59   Engels 1962b, p. 166.

(c)   as commodity

finally, but only in recent times,

(d)   as bodies for biomedical research.

Marxism has thus always considered animals as elements of social production. Now, if we look at Marx and Engels's theory, such use of animals was intended by them as a *historical necessity*. It is crucial to understand what this 'necessity' means, because it is here that animal liberation and Marxism seem to diverge. What I want to make clear is that Marx and Engels – in keeping with their anti-ethical position – always intended such necessity in a *logical* and *value-free* sense. Logical: because an activity which is the 'condition of possibility' of our existence in the present cannot be judged according to a set of moral values which is itself a historical consequence of those acts of the past. Value-free: not only because humankind has hitherto been driven by necessity (lack of physical and spiritual means, of resources, etc.), but also because individuals have always faced the alternative between social conformity and social exclusion. Moral verdicts are *a posteriori* assumptions: they forget that material struggles determine collective and individual existence more than ethical reasoning. Marx and Engels's moral indifference is appropriate for describing a world that is not at all ruled by moral principles. Every animal rights activist who may take offence at Marx and Engels's lack of understanding for animal sufferance should reflect on the fact that – according to them – *human slavery* obeys the same kind of historical necessity.

> It was slavery that first made possible the division of labour between agriculture and industry on a larger scale, and thereby also Hellenism, the flowering of the ancient world. Without slavery, no Greek state, no Greek art and science, without slavery, no Roman Empire. But without the basis laid by Hellenism and the Roman Empire, also no modern Europe. We should never forget that our whole economic, political and intellectual development presupposes a state of things in which slavery was as necessary as it was universally recognised. In this sense we are entitled to say: Without the slavery of antiquity no modern socialism.[60]

This does not mean, however, that they did not consider slavery something humanity should get rid of. They simply believed that only when economic development had made slavery objectively obsolete could the subjective request for 'universal freedom' become a moral necessity. Even capitalism is

---

60   Engels 1962b, p. 168.

not condemned as a moral aberration, but as a productive system whose historical necessity has already vanished. The individual capitalist is not to blame as a moral agent. Better: he is *not at all* to blame:

> I paint the capitalist and the landlord in no sense *couleur de rose*. But here individuals are dealt with only in so far as they are the personifications of economic categories, embodiments of particular class-relations and class-interests. My standpoint, from which the evolution of the economic formation of society is viewed as a process of natural history, can less than any other make the individual responsible for relations whose creature he socially remains, however much he may subjectively raise himself above them.[61]

Capitalists simply mirror a social mechanism that they unconsciously produce with their very existence *qua* elements of production. It would be pointless to ask them to be 'good' and not exploit workers, because this would simply mean they should disappear as capitalists.

Now, when Marx and Engels talk of 'historical necessity', they always mean a social condition that can be *superseded*, a state of things that changes according to social *progress*. As for animals' concern, such necessity is already superseded in both cases (b) and (c). The use of animals as (b) *labouring-force* – to be distinguished from the labouring-force produced by the human hand – is purely mechanical and has been gradually substituted by the use of machines: as is shown by 'the term "horse-power", which has survived to this day as an expression for mechanical force'.[62] Finally, the use of animals as *commodities* (cloths, entertainment, etc.) is accidental and secondary, subjected to historical fluctuations. Being an epiphenomenon of production, there is no Marxist reason why we should not substitute animal-based goods with synthetic goods.

A meat diet and vivisection apparently require more complex arguments, but the question is actually rather simple. Animals are here, too, considered elements of production, yet this happens in such an abstract and general way that it is easy to suggest that their exploitation will never end. We will discuss the economic nature of such an argument in the next chapter. It is true that Engels justified both carnivorism and vivisection with 'scientific' – rather than economic – arguments, but his arguments no longer stand up today from a 'scientific' point of view, and Engels himself would probably reject them. It is not

---

61   Marx 1962, p. 16.
62   Marx 1962, p. 397.

by using the rather positivist arguments of the *Dialectics of Nature* that a Marxist could argue against vegetarianism and antivivisectionism. Deprived of the scientific aura in which they were wrapped, the defences of meat-eating and animal testing are subject to historical change. Yet, even if Engels were right, this would not mean that the historical necessity of animal killing cannot be overcome. According to Engels's own arguments, it is rather clear that this is the case.

> The meat diet led to two new advances of decisive importance, the harnessing of fire and the domestication of animals. The first still further shortened the digestive process, as it provided the mouth with food already, as it were, half-digested; the second made meat more copious by opening up a new, more regular source of supply in addition to hunting, and moreover provided, in milk and its products, a new article of food at least as valuable as meat in its composition. Thus both these advances were, in themselves, new means for the emancipation of man. It would lead us too far afield to dwell here in detail on their indirect effects notwithstanding the great importance they have had for the development of the human being and society.[63]

It is evident that such a necessity is a contingent, historical one, bound to a process of evolution that has already taken place; Engels's argument itself implies that we do not need a meat diet now. As it would be stupid to use animals (or human beings) as *vis motrix* when the steam-machine could work more and better, the same could be said for meat-eating: once the natural struggle for survival that led to meat consumption is over, humankind could change its diet according to new, ecological and democratic values. In the end, what we need are 'proteins', not 'meat'. The slaughterhouse is not an ontological necessity.

4   The *Real* Problem: Animal Alienation

It is true that only the human being can dominate nature and all other living beings, but such speciesist domination presupposes the social domination on its peers. As we have seen, spiritualistic dualism must therefore be thought of as a consequence of an already developed and established social hierarchy. Marx's dialectical methodology is the only way to get the Animal Liberation

---

63   Engels 1962c, p. 450.

Movement out of its abstract, unhistorical and *ethological* understanding of the human-animal relation. What the human being does to the other species it does not as a member of a species, but as a social collective:

> it is of course easy to imagine a powerful, physically superior person, who first captures animals and them captures men in order to make them catch animals for him; in brief, one who uses the human being as a naturally occurring condition for his reproduction like any other living natural thing; his own labour being exhausted in the act of domination. But such a view is stupid, though it may be correct from the point of view of a given tribal or communal entity; for it takes the *isolated* the human being as its starting-point.[64]

Engels: 'Not everyone can make use of a slave. In order to be able to make use of a slave, one must possess two kinds of things: first, the instruments and material for his slave's labour; and secondly, the means of bare subsistence for him. Therefore, before slavery becomes possible, a certain level of production must already have been reached and a certain inequality of distribution must already have appeared'.[65] If domination is intrinsically a collective phenomenon, only society can overturn such domination of humans *and* nature.

As we will see in the next chapters, from all this it follows that Marx and Engels's explicit arguments against animal welfarism do not belong to the 'core' of their theory. Their attitude is also probably due to the bourgeois and sentimental nature of the Animal Rights Movement in the nineteenth century. Thus, it is a pity that Marx did not write a critical history of the human-animal relation, because he had something to say about it: 'it may here be incidentally observed, that Descartes, in defining animals as mere machines, saw with eyes of the manufacturing period, while to eyes of the middle ages, animals were assistants to man' (Marx 1962: 411n). In fact, as we will see, the inclusion of animals in the struggle for a liberated society does not imply a revision of Marx's materialistic understanding of history.

The real, structural problem is that, according to Marx and Engels, animal labour *does not produce alienation*. Only if animals were considered – at least *in potentia* – active members of the productive process and, therefore, could *benefit* from it could one speak of 'animal alienation'. Apparently there is no trace of this in Marx. In his short history of pre-capitalist societies,[66] Marx

---

64   Marx 1983, pp. 403–4.
65   Engels 1962b, p. 149.
66   Marx 1983.

starts from our direct appropriation of natural resources, as if this were ground zero of our social evolution. Animals are already there as 'resources' for us. But before animals became resources for us – not only in the form of domesticated animals, which is a rather later discovery, but also as hunted food – it took a very long time, according to evolutionary theory. Thus, it is important for Marxism that the prehistoric phases of human social evolution are taken into account, as Engels himself did, writing *Ursprung der Familie* and adding a note to the English edition of the *Communist Manifesto*, where he maintained that the expression 'All human history is history of class struggle' should be corrected as follows: 'All *written* human history is history of class struggle'.[67] As we will see in the next chapter, until the problem of 'natural history' (i.e. the relation between evolution and history) is discussed, the human-animal relation cannot but be defined by mere violence. Here is the circularity on which Sztybel tried to put his finger. Not that Marx grants human beings a speciesist privilege over other animals, but that our 'becoming human' in a communist society, although putting an end to the natural struggle for life, does not put an end to our war against the animal world. Yet, if human slavery was nothing but an inevitable phase in the construction of a free and liberated society, why should this not be the case for speciesism too?

67   Marx and Engels 1972.

CHAPTER 5

Marxism and the Repression of Nature

As we have seen, the main difficulty in unifying Marxism and Animal Liberation from a theoretical point of view is not that animal exploitation is considered by Marx and Engels as a historical necessity, since this judgement
involves human exploitation, too, and because several forms of animal exploitation are temporary phenomena that social progress has already made obsolete. The problem is that the animal enters into the Marxist scheme of social
reproduction always as an 'external' and 'passive' element: it does not take part
in its active construction. Therefore, according to Marx, animals are not even
essential to the understanding of economic structures and to the definition of
sociological categories.

At the same time, animals are often considered by Marx as general and
abstract elements of production to such a degree that it is tempting to consider their exploitation by humans as intrinsic to Marxism, almost an *a pri-*
ori presupposition of human society in general, something necessary in an
ontological sense. This is so taken for granted that Grundmann, in an attempt
to define the nature of ecological problems in the Marxist sense, assimilates
the extinction of species to the depletion of resources, despite the fact that
endangered species are infinitely more than those exploited by human societies.[1]

Marx writes that the animal 'appears as an integral part of the *original pro-*
duction fund' [*Bestandteil des ursprunglichen Produktionsfond*].[2] Yet, this 'original' background is an abstraction that should not be understood ontologically. Marx knew it so well that he often remembers how animals should be
considered, in turn, the *product* of human labour. Now, the thesis of animals
as 'original production fund' can only be theoretically justified as a necessary
presupposition of the scientific analysis of capital. As Marx himself writes,[3]
it is an abstraction that has an important methodological meaning: capitalist society can only be analysed by starting from its systemic presuppositions.

---

1   Grundmann 199, p. 105.
2   Marx 1983, p. 400.
3   Marx 1962, p, 192.

1   Animal and *Capital*

1.1   *The* Systemic *Analysis of Capital*
In the same way it is possible to justify other apparently arbitrary assumptions: in analysing the specific process of capital reproduction, for example,
it would be completely misleading to identify human and animal labour. Of
course, both humans and animals work, and both work for the capitalist.
Yet, there is a specific trait of human labour, a very specific position of the
worker in his/her relation to the capitalist that animals do not have. A different understanding of the role played by workers and animals inside the
capitalist machine is not a consequence of a speciesist prejudice: it is the
very structure of the capitalist mode of production which creates such distinction of roles and functions. By ignoring it, we would simply ignore the way
in which capitalism operates. Rosa Luxemburg, for example, criticises Adam
Smith for identifying workers and animals by labelling their activity as 'productive labour'. Since we know that Luxemburg was certainly not indifferent
to the suffering of non-humans, it is important to explain her objection to
Smith. Luxemburg is well aware that animal labour, just like human labour,
means 'expenditure of a certain quantity of muscles, nerves, brain'.[4] The problem is not here, it is not the generic production of *use values*; it is clear that
animals (no matter if autonomously or guided by the human hand) are able
to produce use value. The problem is rather this: what is the source of the
valorisation of capital? If one does not distinguish human labour under capitalism from animal labour, one fails to understand the specificity of the capitalist mode of production. This is the sense of Luxemburg's critique of 'Smith's
belief that the creation of value is a direct physiological property of labour, a
manifestation of the animal organism [...]. Just as the spider produces its web
from its own body, so labouring man produces value'.[5] Luxemburg speaks here
of 'physiocraticist' elements in Adam Smith, thereby pointing to the persistent belief that social wealth is produced by 'natural' processes. According to
the physiocrats, wealth could only consist of the increase of material wealth
and, since industry merely 'elaborates' materials that it receives from already-
existing forms of labour (agricultural products, extraction of raw materials), the
real source of such wealth can only be 'nature'.[6] Adam Smith himself proved
this way of reasoning to be wrong: labour is an essential part of value production as an activity exerted *on* nature. Marx developed this important insight

---

4   Marx 1962, p. 185.
5   Luxemburg 1951, p. 40.
6   Marx 1967, p. 12 ff.

of classical political economy, showing how value – in the dual form of use value and exchange value – is a product of the appropriation of surplus labour by capital. And yet, in order for this to happen, a 'free subject' is required to sell his own 'abstract labour-force' as a 'commodity'. Various conditions must then be respected for the money holder to find the labour force on the market. Among them: the *market* as a *universal* form of the exchange of goods and services, the bourgeois *legal system* and the *industrial revolution* with its specific level of production. The exchange of goods, in itself, does not include other kinds of relationships except for those implied in its own nature. In order to sell their own labour-force as a commodity, owners of the labour-force must dispose of it, therefore they must be free owners of their work capacity, free owners of their own persons. The second indispensable condition is that the possessor of the labour-force cannot sell other goods. Workers under capitalism, then, cannot objectify their working power on their own, but, on the contrary, are socially *forced* to sell it. Even if such power is a living force encapsulated in their bodies, they need someone else in order to make it work.[7]

Thus, capitalism is characterised by the free legal status of the wage earner, '*free* in the double sense, that as a free man he can dispose of his labour-power as his own commodity, and that on the other hand he has no other commodity for sale, is short of everything necessary for the realisation of his labour-power'.[8] Workers' entire existence is bound to the market where they sell their own labour power as a commodity in order to earn the wage needed to buy other goods. Everyone is formally, legally free. From a juridical point of view, the worker is no longer an *instrumentum* like the slave,[9] save for the time when the capitalist buys his generic labour power to invest it in the process of commodity production.

This presupposes a determined development of the productive forces: 'If the productivity of labour had reached only such a stage of development that a man's labour-time no more than sufficed to keep him alive, to produce and reproduce his own means of subsistence, then there would be no surplus-labour and no surplus-value, and there would be no difference at all between the value of labour-power and the value which it creates'.[10] Now, the generic labour power that is presupposed by the capitalist productive process is *not*

7   Marx 1962, pp. 182–3.
8   Marx 1962, p. 183.
9   Marx 1962, p. 210n.
10   Marx 1967, p. 19.

the 'animal labour force': it is a *social* force. Through the division of labour and technology, the human labour power has become *malleable*, i.e. applicable to an infinite number of highly *mediated* labour processes.

> Owing to the extensive use of machinery, and to the division of labour, the work of the proletarians has lost all individual character, and, consequently, all charm for the workman. He becomes an appendage of the machine, and it is only the most simple, most monotonous, and most easily acquired knack, that is required of him. [...] The less the skill and exertion of strength implied in manual labour, in other words, the more modern industry becomes developed, the more is the labour of men superseded by that of women. Differences of age and sex have no longer any distinctive social validity for the working class. All are instruments of labour, more or less expensive to use, according to their age and sex.[11]

Though animal labour power could still be compared – within certain limits – to that of the slave, 'general' labour power is of an utterly different kind. Wage earners are in fact mere *carriers of social labour power*, ready to fuel their individual energy into the social productive machine, into the several operations of this machine: such a process has nothing more to do with the individual-artisan labour process, which begins with, and ends in, *a* specific object. 'By nature unfitted to make anything independently, the manufacturing labourer develops productive activity as a mere appendage of the capitalist's workshop'.[12] What is 'productive labour' then? To answer this question, Marx necessarily takes the point of view of capitalism: 'productive labour' is here always bound to circumstances that characterise the capitalist mode of production. Thus, one must acknowledge that 'productive labour' is not even human labour *per se*: human labour is 'productive' only if labour power is exerted as a 'service' (i.e. against a wage), only if it *produces capital*. Human labour is productive only if it fits capital's cycle of self-valorisation.[13]

1.2   *The* Genetic *Analysis of Capital*

However, Marxian materialism also aims at a historical understanding of the rise of bourgeois society. Such historical understanding is not just an accessory or scholarly interest:

---

11   Marx and Engels 1972, pp. 468–9.
12   Marx 1962, p. 381.
13   Marx 1967, p. 122 ff.

The bourgeois economists who regard capital as an eternal and *natural* (not historical) form of production then attempt at the same time to legitimize it again by formulating the conditions of its becoming as the conditions of its contemporary realisation [i.e. the distinction between the 'free' wage-earner and the capitalist as a natural and systemic distinction, rather than the historical product of the dispossession of one part of society by the other, MM] ... On the other side, much more important for us is that our method indicates the points where historical investigation must enter in, or where bourgeois economy as a merely historical form of the production process points beyond itself to earlier historical modes of production. In order to develop the laws of bourgeois economy, therefore, it is not necessary to write the *real history of the relations of production*. But the correct observation and deduction of these laws, as having themselves become in history, always leads to primary equations – like the empirical numbers e.g. in natural science – which point towards a past lying behind this system. These indications [*Andeutung*], together with a correct grasp of the present, then also offer the key to the understanding of the past – a work in its own right which, it is to be hoped, we shall be able to undertake as well. This correct view likewise leads at the same time to the points at which the suspension of the present form of production relations gives signs of its becoming – foreshadowings of the future. Just as, on one side the pre-bourgeois phases appear as *merely historical*, i.e. suspended presuppositions, so do the contemporary conditions of production likewise appear as engaged in *suspending themselves* and hence in positing the *historic presuppositions* for a new state of society.[14]

Now, if we consider the actual history of the modes of production, animals can be considered something 'already given' only if we ignore previous historical phases which led, through domestication, to the first forms of class society. At any rate, if we want to understand the *development* of capitalism, we simply cannot ignore that. We have already seen that, in order to understand how capitalism structurally works, it is methodologically justified to sever capitalism from its historical becoming. Yet, this cannot mean erasing the process by which animals *become* part of our social reproduction, because this would mean to treat them as a sort of *ontological* trait of human society as such. In doing so, we would commit the mistake of bourgeois economists who, conceal-

---

14   Marx 1983, p. 373.

ing the historical origins of capitalist society and its presuppositions, eternalise the capitalist mode of production.

The fact that the exclusion of animals in Marxian theory is sometimes justified does not therefore mean that it is always justified. Though it is useful to take the role of animals for granted when we want to understand some aspects of the capitalist 'system', this could be a mistake if we intend to investigate its 'genesis' (and its possible overcoming). Severed from the *historical* dynamics that originated it, the human-animal relationship is fixed in the current form of domination: it is made into something unchanging and eternal, coextensive with the history of humanity and with the structure of human society. Here, the exclusion of the animal from the analysis of the exploitation process becomes problematic: the fact that animals are not 'exploited' according to capitalist laws does not imply that they are not exploited at all. Seeking to avoid an overlapping of these two definitions of exploitation, we risk obliterating animal oppression, as it was irrelevant to the genesis of capitalist society.

Such theoretical difficulty appears evident when Marx speaks of the 'relationship of domination' [*Herrschaftsverhältnis*], the master-servant relation in its juridical sense. Marx observes that the master-servant relation – a social relationship involving the unilateral appropriation of the means of production, i.e. of the social condition for the reproduction of life – is exercised on humans and *not* on animals. 'Basically the appropriation of animals, land etc. cannot take place in a master-servant relation, although the animal provides service. The presupposition of the master-servant relation is the appropriation of an alien *will*. Whatever has no will, e.g. the animal, may well provide a service, but does not thereby make its owner into a *master*'.[15] Here, again, it is important to underline that Marx does not deny in general the existence of animal will. He simply denies that such will can become part of 'social will'. On the contrary, the will of the slave – or, better, the remission of his will – is an integral moment of social production and therefore can also be the basis of its possible overthrow. In fact, the means of production 'forms a necessary ferment for the development and the decline and fall of all original relations of property and of production, just as it also expresses their limited nature'.[16] But if human slavery plays a role in this process of development and decline, we know nothing about animal slavery. The mere *description* of a state of fact – the effective and persistent exclusion of the animal from the process of reproduction of social life –

---

15   Marx 1983, p. 408.
16   Ibid.

has become a *justification* for a state of fact. It is as if, by adequately describing reality, we fail to *question* it: the accuracy of the description *misses* something crucial, just like the 'pure' description of 'free' market relations conceals the truth of capitalist oppression.

2   History and Natural History in Marx and Engels

To understand how Marx and Engels encouraged this *quid pro quo*, it is necessary to analyse their general conception of history and, therefore, to widen the field of our research. Let us for the moment leave Marx's economic writings aside and have a look at Engels's works on history and anthropology. The interest of the late Engels in anthropology and archaeology was aimed at establishing a bridge between 'natural history' and 'human history' (in other words: between evolution and history).[17] This was meant to prevent any form of 'biologism' in economic explanations (which would have led – as indeed happened with social Darwinism and, more recently, with sociobiology – to a justification of class oppression in terms of 'natural' conflicts) and to establish a correct relationship between animality and humanity. 'Historical materialism' must face a double, apparently contradictory, task. In order to be *materialistic*, it has to link human beings to the rest of the living world, drawing no rigid lines in nature, conceiving of life in terms of perpetual evolution; in order to be *historical*, it needs to explain the laws of movement of human society as *distinct* from those of animal societies. Not only did this entail a distinction between scientific domains and their specific methodologies, but it also implied a political bet on humankind, on its ability to determine its own destiny. In fact, where an 'animal' behaviour still dominates the scene, the 'conscious' element is reduced to a minimum and social changes can be described in merely statistical, environmental terms; humans never leave the narrow sphere of necessity, they do not form a 'collective agent' in a proper sense. Instead, where the organisational power of labour prevails, society becomes dynamical and its development, although still influenced by necessity and conflict, is already oriented towards the possibility of freedom (i.e. the conscious self-making of a humanity). Historical materialism attempts to hold these two modes of explanation together.

2.1   *Labour and Homination*
Engels's attempts to find a connection between nature and history, however, include assumptions that are no longer valid from a biological-evolutionary

---

17   Timpanaro 1975.

point of view. As we know, Engels came to conceive of *homination* as a product of human beings, according to the motto: 'work has created man'. The evolution of humans and their emergence from the animal world would have been conditioned, indeed even *produced*, by labour. Engels knew full well that the standing position and the opposable thumb – two preconditions of labour – are obviously still fully explainable in 'naturalistic' terms. Having become autonomous thanks to the new posture, however, the human hand 'could henceforth attain ever greater dexterity and skill, and the greater flexibility thus acquired was inherited and increased from generation to generation'.[18] Human action thus becomes human labour and this leads, through the natural sociability of the species, to the invention of language; this would have finally determined a cerebral development, which was also influenced by a meat-based diet. Today, it is easy to disagree with this Engelsian/Lamarckian narrative: scientific research no longer tries to explain the cerebral transformation of the first hominids as a consequence of hereditary traits acquired through habit.[19]

2.2   *Human Labour and Animal Activity*

The question from which we started is: to what extent should we consider dominion over nature a socio-historical progress in the Marxist sense? The first thing to do, however, is to distinguish the two phases of this process of enslavement of nature. If humans, in fact, succeed in imposing their will on the surrounding nature through the more or less contingent domestication of plants and animals, it is only with the birth of class societies that such power breaks free from its limits and accidentality and becomes a 'project' of domination. Marxist materialism finds here a key, from an economic point of view, to understanding the transition from natural history to human history. We will see, in fact, how a substantial mutation occurs in the transition from the first to the second phase, a transformation which reverberates in the very concept of human labour.

In a famous passage from *Capital*, Marx distinguishes human labour from animal activity, underlining how the first always begins as an intellectual process. 'What distinguishes the worst architect from the best of bees is this, that the architect raises his structure in imagination before he erects it in reality. At the end of every labour-process, we get a result that already existed in the imagination of the labourer at its commencement'.[20] Although this assump-

---

18   Engels 1962c, p. 445.
19   Yet, for a contemporary reprise of the meat thesis see Bonicelli 2006, p. 152; Stanford 1999, p. 58.
20   Marx 1962, p. 193.

tion can be questioned by ethology and zoosemiotics, it retains an undisputed value of truth as regards the relationship between individual labour and *social planning*. In what Marx calls 'the appropriation of natural substances to human requirements', there is indeed a first phase of symbiosis with the environment in which it is not possible to speak of 'labour' in the proper sense. That this 'immediate' relationship between humans and nature has been real sometimes in the past is undeniable, since humans originate from animals. Marx writes that 'those primitive instinctive forms of labour that remind us of the mere animal' are irrelevant for the understanding of capitalism, and relegates them to archaic, pre-historic ages. Here, humans begin to master the '*objective conditions* of their life' (earth, spontaneous products of nature, animals): 'the *real appropriation* through the labour process happens under these *presuppositions*, which are not themselves the *product* of labour, but appear as its natural or *divine* presuppositions'.[21] The final allusion to the 'divine' nature of these presuppositions refers to the fact that, as we shall see, our early 'economic dependence' from the natural context produces, on a cultural level, a parallel 'mystical dependence' from it, i.e. the divinisation of nature. But, in order to establish a complete transition from animal activity to human labour, two more preconditions are required: (1) a sufficient *symbolic articulation* and (2) the *specialisation* of labour, since properly human labour is always *socially productive*.

The first passage belongs to the history of *instrumental reason*. The production of tools is undoubtedly the first step towards the transformation of human living activity into labour. The very form in which the world gets appropriated assumes a new, eccentric fashion with respect to the animal world. But *not* for the use of the instrument itself – which is common to other species – but rather for its consequences for humans in terms of self-consciousness. As a form of mediation between humans and nature, tools make it possible for us to emerge from animal immediacy by treating nature as an 'object'.[22] But in this way, nature itself changes: from being mere means of subsistence, animals become means of labour: 'in the earliest period of human history domesticated animals, i.e., animals which have been bred for the purpose, and have undergone modifications by means of labour, play the chief part as instruments of labour along with specially prepared stones, wood, bones, and shells. The use and fabrication of instruments of labour, although existing in the germ among certain species of animals, is specifically characteristic of the human labour-process'.[23]

---

21   Marx 1983, pp. 384–5.
22   Pannekoek 1953, p. 61.
23   Marx 1962, p. 194; Grundmann 1991, p. 107.

Secondly, it must be remembered that human labour is also, and above all, social labour. It is interesting to note that, differently from the arguments proposed in *Dialectics of Nature*, Engels's *Origin of the Family* places the distinction between humans and apes at the level of social life, maintaining that our evolution would be inexplicable without our constitutive 'sociability'. It is precisely our specific way of socialising or, better, the way in which our natural sociability *declines*, that can explain 'man's development beyond the level of the animals'.[24] It is clear then that although certain human traits are the result of natural selection, the (self-)creative characteristic of human labour cannot be considered, according to the same Engelsian arguments, as individual-specific: they are properly social ('Man is isolated only through the historical process. Originally he presents himself as a *social, tribal, gregarious animal*'[25]).

Cooperation is therefore the natural basis of human activity. Yet, for cooperation to become proper human labour, a further, double precondition is still needed: from the one side, the differentiation in the relationship between humans and nature, and, from the other, the differentiation among humans. Such double process is at the same time cause and effect of the 'division of labour'. It is here that *the ideality embodied in the individual working process is mediated with the total social labour*. This is also the form in which such ideality becomes a proper form of *planning*, i.e. something which transcends natural, animal conditions. Reproduction of life in animals does not need to be socially mediated in such 'ideal' forms. This leads us to see the decisive passage from animals to humans, from natural history to human history: such transition is evident in sedentary societies through the domestication of plants and animals but, even more so, in *class* society. The organic unity of animal social life gets specified in human society through a series of leaps and ruptures: the organic *unity* of human social life can be defined 'higher' than the animal one, precisely because it presupposes such fractures. This is the paradox of human history: humans *break the immediacy* of animal life, what we experience as 'unity' and 'immediacy' is nothing but a process of 'reconstruction'. We were the one who produced that 'fragmentary' life in the first place, yet without those fractures there would be no synthesis. It is precisely this paradoxical structure that can be defined as 'human' according to Marx and Engels (whenever they talk of our 'exceptionality' with respect to animals).

The modern shape of human labour is the final phase of the whole process: if we fix our attention on its goal-oriented global structure, we fail to recognise

---

24   Engels 1962a, p. 41.
25   Marx 1983, p. 400. See also Marx and Engels 1969, p. 31.

the material cause of its intrinsic dynamism. Tools are necessary to the dialectic between idea and final product which, according to Marx, is typical of human labour. They introduce that 'mediation' between humans and nature which takes the form of 'distance' and 'objectification'. From the point of view of the object, however, as soon as individuals cease to produce only for themselves and start producing within a group (which happens very early: even the phenomenon of redistribution in hunter-gatherer societies can be considered a form of social production), the social character of the product is revealed. Hence, the phenomenon of 'social mediation' increasingly assumes the form of the 'division of labour'. These two parallel articulations of the relationship outside and inside society lead, through domestication and expropriation, to the reduction of animals and of humans to labouring tools.

Such reduction into slavery is, however, a precondition of human freedom, as Marx and Engels understand it. Of course, slavery could never be the premise of freedom if we understand freedom in a purely mechanical sense, as the ability to move 'freely' in an undetermined environment, or as the result of spontaneous free associations of an isolated mind. The point here is that the very concept and the very essence of freedom changes according to the material progress of human possibilities. That freedom cannot be conceived outside a social context simply means that the limits of what humans can do are only a result of their interaction. Rather than a crypto-authoritarian trait of communitarian thinking, such belief is a mere tautology: it belongs to the platitudes of social ontology that the results of small-scale activity are essentially different from what large-scale societies, or States, can do. The Hegelian twist in all this is that the objective growth of human possibilities feeds back on the subjective cognition of the Self. This also means that material contradictions end up being reflected in the human Self.

Thus, if it is true, as Marx says, that the specificity of human labour is the ability to imagine the outcome of production, 'for us the essential question is: in whose head is the result of the intended labour process anticipated?'[26] The growing division of labour causes the labouring activities to be ideally planned in the heads of individuals, though even such an individual process is in many ways mediated with the labour of others. Furthermore, it is only in class society that the division between intellectual and manual activities gives a *unitary form* to the overall social labour. At the beginning, of course, such unity is the mere 'mutual interdependence of the individuals', just as its planning, far from being 'universal', is in reality a mere ideology, a masking of particular interests;

---

26   Sohn-Rethel 1978, p. 85.

the overall social will is here opposed to the single worker as an 'alien power', a transcendent and coercive will.[27] However, it is precisely this transition, the imposition of class exploitation that allows the *productive and organisational leap* from which humans *really* start to produce the conditions of their own existence and, therefore, begin to differentiate themselves from animals. It is in this very specific and limited sense that we can agree with Barbara Noske when she writes that Marx and Engels considered hunter-gatherers as 'barely human'.[28]

3   From Primitive Communism to the Early States

3.1   *Progress and Class Struggle*

According to Marx and Engels, domination over nature and domination over workers seem to be both 'necessary' for the emergence of a 'properly human' existence and, therefore, for the transition from natural history to history in the narrow sense. The human project originates as a *project of domination* which produces a self-referential movement: it initially starts as a way to control and exploit nature, but finds its definitive fulfilment only as a project of domination over humans. That this is the case is demonstrated by what Engels himself writes about the birth of the State: he tries to describe such a historical transition – better: a transition that inaugurates 'History' – as a 'necessity'. The existence of the early States is justified from the point of view of a universal social evolution: therefore it includes the stage of animal domestication as a necessary premise of such progress. Yet, as we shall see immediately, the 'necessity' of domestication and the 'necessity' of class domination are not of the same kind.

First of all, let us note how the institute of the *gens* – which, according to Engels, immediately precedes the class system – is described by the author of *The Origin of the Family* in a rather sympathetic way. With no trace of exploitation, machismo, State and bureaucracy, the *gens* organisation produces a human type which, compared to the bourgeois one, is praised by Engels with touching words. Yet Engels is quick to add:

> let us not forget, however, that this organisation was devoted to failure ... Everything that was outside the tribe was out of the law. Where there was

---

27   Marx and Engels 1969, p. 34.
28   Noske 1989, p. 74.

not a peace treaty expressed the war between tribes and tribes reigned, conducted with the atrocity that distinguishes men from other animals and that only later will be mitigated by interest. The noble constitution, at the peak of its development, as we see it in America, presupposes a very limited production, consequently an extremely poor population on a territory of vast dimensions; therefore an almost complete subjection of the human being by the external nature, which rises before it, alien and unknown, which is reflected in the infantilism of religious ideas. The tribe remains the frontier of man, both towards the stranger and towards himself: the tribe, the *gens* and their institution were sacred and intangible, they were a superior power granted by nature, to which the individual remained unconditionally subject in his way of feeling, thinking and acting. Although the men of this age seem grandiose to us, they do not yet differ from each other, they are still attached, to put it with Marx, to the umbilical cord of the natural collectivity. The power of this natural community had to be broken – it was broken.[29]

Engels frames his own description of the end of this noble society with two pitiless judgements: it 'was devoted to failure' [*dem Untergang geweiht war*] and its power 'had to be broken' [*mußte gebrochen werden*].[30] These are, at the same time, *value* judgements and *factual* judgements, although in the Engelsian analysis these two aspects are not immediately distinguishable. The end of the tribal society is here recognised by Engels as necessary through an argument which starting from the *formulation of a law of development* ('it was devoted to failure') ends with the *explanation of a fact* ('it was broken'). If history's immanent dynamic prepares the possibility of a free human society, the end of the *gens* society is nothing but a case of such general process. It is a 'fact' that we subsume under a general 'law'. It is clear, however, that the concrete proceeding of the Engelsian analysis moves in the opposite direction to what is expressed here: the materialistic method can only move from the particular (the fact) and end up with the formulation of the law (development). However, what happens here is that the single fact analysed by Engels leads to the recognition of the emergence of class domination as necessary; at the same time, this developmental law does not work for the previous stage: hunter-gatherer societies are closed in a circle, as it were; they do not need any necessary trans-

---

29   Engels 1962a, p. 97.

30   In the *Manifesto* we read an analogous formulation about feudal relations: 'they had to be broken, and they were broken' [*Sie mußten gesprengt werden, sie wurden gesprengt*] (Marx and Engels 1972, p. 467).

ition to a 'superior' social form. The progression: (a) hunter-gatherer societies
→ (b) tribal-agricultural societies → (c) State is not *linear*, nor does it express in
itself any 'progress'. There is no law of development that can express the transition from hunter-gatherer societies to agricultural and pastoral societies and,
from these, to the early States. Not only does the transition from the first to
the second not obey any intrinsic necessity, but even when this passage takes
place, it is not at all *homogeneous* to that which marks the end of agricultural
and pastoral societies and the rise of the archaic States. We realise this if we
compare, in the description given by Engels, the passage from (a) to (b) with
that from (b) to (c).

It is interesting to see that although the passage from (a) to (b) is sketched
in the sense of a natural and almost spontaneous evolution, Engels gives *no
justification* for it. Neither in the *Anti-Dühring*, nor in *The Origin of the Family*, nor in the *Dialectics of Nature* is it explained why some populations leave
the state of hunting and gathering and begin to live in tribes devoted to breed-
ing and/or agriculture. In *The Origin of the Family* Engels states that humans
switched from vegetarian food to eating fish (which would imply the discovery of fire since 'fish becomes edible only by the use of fire') thus becoming
'independent of climate and locality'.[31] There is no mention of 'original scarcity',
although Engels is convinced that 'owing to the continual uncertainty of food
supplies, cannibalism seems to have arisen' and that only 'with the invention
of the bow and arrow, [...] game became a regular source of food, and hunting
a normal form of work'.[32] In the *Dialectics of Nature* Engels offers a description
of the different activities of the human being ('agriculture was added to hunting and cattle-breeding, then spinning, weaving, metal-working, pottery, and
navigation'[33]) and, although he certainly sees in them a progressive growth in
human *possibilities*, he does not bring arguments to justify this series as evolutionary. The reason is very simple: there is no intrinsic, immanent reason for
conceiving this series as a progression *in itself*. It did not exist at the time of
Engels and does not exist today. The reasons for the transition to agriculture are
still obscure and, analysed from a scientific point of view, the cost-benefit *ratio*
appears entirely in favour of the nomadic lifestyle of hunter-gatherers: agriculture drastically reduces the food base by selecting certain species, modifying
them and often impoverishing them (it increases the quantity at the expense of
their quality); as a consequence, farmers depend *more* on the whims of nature
and are thus exposed to famine. The diet of hunter-gatherers is manifold and

---

31   Engels 1962a, p. 31.
32   Ibid.
33   Engels 1962c, p. 450.

flexible. During a famine that forced the World Food Program to support 30 percent of the Botswana population, Bushman hunter-gatherers did not need any help: they even *helped* Herero and Tswana women to feed their families;[34] the increase and concentration of the population was at the same time the cause and effect of the transition to agriculture which, as Diamond made clear in his famous critical analysis of agriculture, determined an unhealthy environment and heavy consequences on social life.[35] However, we must not deal here with the debate on the 'historical causes' of agriculture. What really interests us here are the *political effects* of agriculture, for this is exactly the problem that intrigued Engels. The domestication of animals and plants is a characteristic feature of human societies that are evolving towards the *State-form*, thus abandoning their original equality of conditions and their passive attitude towards the natural environment.[36]

This becomes evident in the way Engels describes the passage from (b) to (c). To justify the necessity of the end of the *gens* system, Engels takes two elements into account: firstly, a structural-economic cause; secondly, a super-structural, ideological reason. To begin with, Engels cites the question of *wars among tribes*, a phenomenon that is almost unknown to hunter-gatherer societies.[37] Sedentary-agricultural and nomadic-pastoral societies, instead, are characterised by an intensification of struggles for the possession and exploitation of the land. This is due to the fact that the transition from hunter-gatherer societies to sedentary modes of production leads, contrary to what was once believed, to a *greater dependence on natural resources*. This necessarily implies an *increase in inter-tribal antagonism*. In a work that documents and describes in a more analytical way these Engelsian pages, Rosa Luxemburg wrote:

> The primitive state of agriculture at that time did not allow for any larger cultivation than that of a village mark, and for this reason presented strict limits to the solidarity of interests. And finally, it was the same inadequate development of labour productivity that also generated periodic conflicts of interest among the various social alliances, thereby making brute force the only means to solve such conflicts.

On the other hand, 'wherever agriculture was already sufficiently flourishing to nourish people well and securely, without taking up the entire labour force

---

34   Lee 1968, pp. 39–40.
35   Diamond 1987, pp. 64–6.
36   Engels 1962a, pp. 155–6; Engels 1962b, p. 166.
37   Service 1971.

and the entire lifetime of these individuals, there was also the foundation for a systematic exploitation of these peasants by foreign conquerors'.[38] It is therefore the very existence of a permanent 'social surplus product'[39] caused by the domestication of plants and animals which generates conflict, regardless of whether this product is scarce or abundant.

Even more interesting is the 'ideological' motivation offered by Engels for the end of tribal societies: a limited production implies a sort of intellectual *subjection to nature*. Under such circumstances the tribe marks a limit to the possibility of human evolution. The *gens* are limited not only in their domination and knowledge of nature, but also, and above all, of their own inner nature: this phase, thus, determines a obstacle to the development of human consciousness. Such limitation must be described in cognitive-universal terms (nature remains the opaque background of unknown forces) and practical-individual ones (social conditioning blocks the development of the individual). As we have already seen, economic dependence generates a parallel mystical deification of nature. This dependence exists in hunter-gatherer societies, too. Criticising Sahlins's concept of 'original affluent society', for instance, Archibald observes that the distinction between 'labour' and 'free time' in hunter-gatherer societies is incorrect, as it filters and interprets their social experience through bourgeois concepts.[40] In gathering and hunting societies, dependence on nature extends beyond strictly productive labour, involving all magical rites of everyday life, which, though not directly 'productive' in economic terms, are supposed to have an effect on hunting activities.

Yet, in 'Neolithic societies' such mystical and economic subjection to nature becomes all the more unbearable, since humans, although still objectively dependent on nature, begin to sever themselves subjectively from it. On the other hand, this subjective factor is certainly not the element that *drives* the whole process, even if it forms a fundamental part of it, the very basis of the human idea of freedom and autonomy. Freedom would have been impossible without the urge to break free from nature's all-encompassing embrace.

Hence, the historical 'necessity' of class domination arises from these two elements. But what has caused the social bond of the *gens* to be necessarily 'broken'? Engels's answer is lapidary and deserves to be read in its entirety:

> it was broken by influences which from the very start appear as a degradation, a fall from the simple moral greatness of the old gentile society. The

---

38   Luxemburg 2004, p. 79.
39   Mandel 1967.
40   Archibald 1989, pp. 182–3.

lowest interests – base greed, brutal appetites, sordid avarice, selfish rob-
bery of the common wealth – inaugurate the new, civilised, class society.
It is by the vilest means – theft, violence, fraud, treason – that the old
classless gentile society is undermined and overthrown.[41]

By the way, this is also a clear example of how little Marxism can be considered
a form of 'economic necessitarianism'.

   Theft, abuse, and violence can, however, be understood as *universal historical forces* and freed of the *contingency* that qualifies them, only if their arbitrary
character can be explained. But the only possible explanation for this lies precisely in the *unstable* nature of the order which follows the domestication of
plants and animals. It is the instability of Neolithic societies which turns such
irrational means into a rational force. The onset of internal social imbalances
and inter-tribal conflicts is not determined by the passage from the (imaginary) 'scarcity' of hunters-gatherer societies to the 'still insufficient' productivity
of agricultural societies: rather, it is due to the introduction of means of production which inaugurate in themselves a need for a growing control over natural resources. Indeed, it was the *imperfect control* over nature introduced by
domestication and agriculture which produced the need for a *totalitarian control* over human and non-human resources. From an ideological point of view,
the deep modification operated by Neolithic societies in our relationship with
nature breaks the eternal order of the magical culture of the hunter-gatherers
and inaugurates the dialectic that leads to the institution of patriarchal religions.

   Thus, the supposed 'progress' from hunter-gatherer societies to the early
States is *not* linear and is broken into two separate processes: domination over
nature and domination over humans. The first expresses our escape from natural history, the second the triumphal beginning of civilisation and written
history (History with capital H). It is thus only from the point of view of *domination*, of *systematic violence*, that the transition from hunter-gatherer societies
to Neolithic societies is *homogeneous* to the transition from Neolithic societies
to the early States. The arbitrariness and violence with which humans appropriated animals were destined to be denied by another arbitrary and violent act
of appropriation against humans themselves: the expropriators were expropri-
ated.

---

41   Engels 1962a, p. 97.

3.2 *Progress and Animal Exploitation*

Human evolution certainly takes place according to those two distinct drives that Engels set out to unify: natural history and human history. It is necessary at this point to understand that the use of the term 'progress' for both sides of this development is *equivocal*. One should actually speak of two different forms of progress that obey different laws: one properly evolutionary (blind-mechanical) and the other historical (based on human planning). Through domestication, hunter-gatherer societies slowly disappear and give birth to State economies based on *intensive farming*. But while the first passage may well have been the product of a more or less conscious rationalisation of resources (still internal to a situation in which the human animal adapts itself to the environment), the second step, though bound to particular environmental conditions, is certainly the result of the 'choices' made by the insurgent political-religious elite.

It is this passage from hunter-gatherer societies to the early States that must be described as *the passage from natural history to real history*, even if it is not identifiable and determinable in an exact way (nor as a uniform process for each human society). It is accomplished, on the one hand, as exploitation of nature, and, on the other, as exploitation of humans. *Instrumental reason* takes the needs of hunter-gatherer societies to a higher level yet without producing a qualitative alteration in their structure. It is only the intensive exploitation of natural and human resources, encouraged and administered by a political centre, which produces a new structure of social needs. The first *totalitarian* social order is also the first *truly human* order, the one which opens the possibility of a *conscious control* over production. Totality has both the power to exterminate the Other, and to elevate Being to the level of Universality.[42]

The 'progress', in a human-historical sense, therefore, implies the birth of the State, a division of functions and a more or less direct control of social labour. This is because, as we have already seen, in order to guarantee the existence of non-productive classes (craftsmen, public transport workers, merchants, officials, priests), there has to be an accumulation and distribution of

---

42   It is this Hegelo-Marxian conclusion that severs my approach from that of other political versions of antispeciesism, still too affected by methodological individualism or anarchist scepticism towards totality. Wrenn (2015), for instance, concedes that 'organization within movements is essential for mobilizing resources and efficiently utilizing those resources' (p. 31), yet she accepts Francione's concept of bottom-up radicalism. To me, the problem with Animal Rights Organisations is not a bureaucratic and administrative one: the problem is not that they reify the spontaneous radicalism of direct action, rather that they do not objectify it in the Hegelian sense, i.e. they do not truly elevate it to a universal level.

surplus resources.[43] Although there is no evolutionary necessity leading from hunter-gatherer societies to socialism, we can now say with Engels that without the overcoming of 'primitive communism', we could not fight for 'civilised communism'. This is not simply a lame tautology (without classes one could not fight for a class*less* society): the fact is that only the *historical, real development* of civilisation allows today a truly free and creative social organisation, qualitatively different from that offered by pre-Neolithic bands and tribes (still characterised by magical terror and embryonic forms of internal hierarchy). It is not an abstract metaphysics of progress, but the critical analysis of capital that unveils the genesis of class society and its historical limits: being something that has become, class society can be overcome. To understand this, however, it is not necessary to backdate this law of development to the Palaeolithic, nor to imagine that 'original scarcity' was the trigger which started the whole process. The illusion that arises from such a retrospective look considers every modification of the mode of production that results in an *increased capacity* of the human being to *control* and *dominate* the surrounding environment, as 'progress' and, *therefore*, a necessary and inevitable stage of historical development.

Yet, the needs of hunter-gatherer societies are in themselves fully *satisfied*. Their social (and demographic) equilibrium, their 'ideology', and their cognitive powers: everything here takes place in a dimension of immanence which may seem dull to us, but that does not require any process of 'overcoming'. If this happens, however, humans set the conditions for the development of civilisation as we know it: the domestication of plants and animals is the act by which the immanence of those societies can be disrupted and reorganised on a different level. In so far as it generates social and ideological *contradictions*, domestication is itself a historical drive, a force of progress, but only as it enables a class-oriented economic development of society. It is important to stress that productivity did not increase because of technology alone; productivity grew thanks to 'specialisation' combined with redistribution of the products by a 'coordinating centre'.[44] Thus, domestication did not *cause* the transition to class societies, although it did lay the foundations for its original accumulation: it can generate social differences, not classes. It is the *conditio sine qua non* of political history, but, precisely therefore, it remains on *this* side of social progress.

---

43   Childe 1950.
44   Service 1971.

4   Conclusion

Animal liberationists sometimes catch a glimpse of this ambiguity in Marx, but they have so far failed to define it: the problem with Marxism is not that humans are granted some speciesist privilege over animals, but that our 'becoming human' in communist society, our overcoming of the natural struggle for existence does not imply the end of animal exploitation. *Humans behave towards the other animals always as 'animals' and never as 'humans'*, in the sense of extending to them the hopes of liberation and justice that they see arising in their history.

Yet, there is no reason to deny the plausibility of this expansion. On the contrary, everything seems to push in that direction. If human slavery can be considered an inevitable transition in the construction of a free and equal society, the same could be said of animal slavery: in this perspective, we would be animals that *learn to put an end to their hostility* against the other animals. This conclusion in Marx and Engels is never explicitly drawn. Since Marx and Engels never really introduced animals as 'subjects' in their description of class history, Marxism always continued to see domestication as the obvious consequence of a historical necessity. In this way, even the systemic meaning of the animal in human society has been distorted, not to mention the more general relationship between socialist revolution and dominion over nature (as Marx affirms in the passage of the *Grundrisse* mentioned above, in fact, for a dynamic understanding of capitalism as a historical social formation, it is essential to identify that which 'transcends' such a formation).

The first act by which it is possible to introduce the animal in a Marxian theoretical framework is *pulling it out* of the confusion between natural and historical necessity (as we have tried to do here, analysing those works by Marx and Engels where animals are evoked, but not theorised from a political point of view). This is possible if the essence and the measure of progress is not seen as the appropriation of *specific goods*: 'Economic epochs are distinguished not by *what* is produced, but by *how*'.[45] Progress is the increased power of society in the satisfaction of needs, not the fact that our needs are satisfied in a *determined* way. It is therefore necessary to separate the general notion of progress from specific productive means. Although this may seem at first glance to be an unjustified abstraction, if one is reminded of the historical-universal process through which the bourgeois society progressively emancipates itself from the limits imposed by specific natural conditions, slowly becoming a global and

---

45   Marx 1962, pp. 194–5.

inter-cultural society, such a passage appears necessary. Considered from *this* point of view, which is the landing point of the entire historical process, the properly productive element of progress cannot be fixed to an *accidental* fact like the domestication of this or that animal or plant: social progress is rather bound to the *structure of class conflict*. 'Without antagonism there is no progress. This is the law that until today our civilisation has followed'.[46] If the study of social progress in its concrete and historical development is inseparable from certain means of production and goods, the progress of society as such – the 'universal history' (*Weltgeschichte*) – is not the mere sum of all these concrete historical processes, but rather their *qualitative redefinition*.[47] Socialist progress is *other* than bourgeois progress because it finally enables the conscious, free and collective action of the producers themselves: it produces different *goods* in a different *way*. From this point of view, the goods and the productive means of class society constitute only *phenomenal* aspects of a historical process which has its real *essence* in the internal struggle of classes and which finds its *raison d'être* in the possibility of its overcoming. The animal, whether reduced to commodity or enslaved as a means of production, is a gear in the class machinery. Like every other social aspect, it too awaits its own redefinition in a different socialist order. It is only at this point that we can *reintroduce* animals in the Marxian scheme and understand why their domestication meant for us more than just 'beef' or 'ivory': it implied domination over other humans. The subjugation of animals does mark a step in the evolution of human *freedom*, but only because is part of the history of our own *slavery*.

---

46 Marx 1972, pp. 91–2.

47 Nibert (2013) has recently argued that animal exploitation had destructive consequences on human society, and denounced as 'ideological' traditional accounts on the positive effect of domestication on human social progress. Although I agree with his critical attitude, I will here defend a dialectical concept of 'social progress' and a different account of the history of anthropocentrism. Of course, every specific use of animals could be dismissed as unnecessary and destructive in the last instance. Yet, I believe that the effect of domestication *in general* has produced decisive consequences on our social interactions. While the use of *this* or *that* animal is important for the particular development of a specific society, but is irrelevant from the point of view of 'universal history', the same cannot be said for the exploitation of nature as such. The problem of progress from the point of view of universal history will be treated in Chapter 7.

CHAPTER 6

The Dialectical Animal

A cross section of today's social structure would have to show the following: At the top, the feuding tycoons of the various capitalist power constellations. Below them, the lesser magnates, the large landowners and the entire staff of important co-workers. Below that, and in various layers, the large numbers of professionals, smaller employees, political stooges, the military and the professors, the engineers and heads of office down to the typists; even further down what is left of the independent, small existences, craftsmen, grocers, farmers *e tutti quanti*, then the proletarian, from the most highly paid, skilled workers down to the unskilled and the permanently unemployed, the poor, the aged and the sick. It is only below these that we encounter the actual foundation of misery on which this structure rises, for up to now we have been talking only of the highly developed capitalist countries whose entire existence is based on the horrible exploitation apparatus at work in the partly or wholly colonial territories, ie, in the far larger part of the world. [...] Below the spaces where the coolies of the earth perish by the millions, the indescribable, unimaginable suffering of the animals, the animal hell in human society, would have to be depicted, the sweat, blood, despair of the animals. [...] The basement of that house is a slaughterhouse, its roof a cathedral, but from the windows of the upper floors, it affords a really beautiful view of the starry heavens.[1]

1   Animality and Anthropopoiesis

With the publication of *Dialectic of Enlightenment* in 1944, Adorno and Horkheimer laid down the theoretical ground for what was later to become known as the 'Frankfurt School'. The book proposed a devastating critique of 'instrumental reason' and of human 'mastery of nature', a critique that – in Adorno and Horkheimer's intention – was directed against the industrial and scientific praxis of the manipulation of nature that was progressing in both the East and the West. Although not interested in a metaphysical critique of *Tech-*

---

1   Horkheimer 1985, pp. 379–80; 1978, pp. 66–7.

nik, Adorno and Horkheimer shared Heidegger's and Anders' opinion about the political neutrality of instrumental reason. In their view, the USA and the USSR were both building on a wrong premise: that nature is at our complete and arbitrary disposal. Even Marcuse, whose political commitment to revolutionary Socialism is well known, assumed a position against the idea of an unlimited exploitation of nature, and instead endorsed what was later to become the German Green Movement in the late 1970s.

With PETA's campaign 'Holocaust on your plate', even Adorno has gained some acknowledgement in the animal rights movement, PETA having taken some of his quotes alongside an endless list of 'famous personalities' who are either vegetarians or have something smart to say in favour of animals. Unfortunately, most animal rights activists prefer to read Adorno's carefully manufactured quote on the slaughterhouse than to engage in any serious reading of his difficult prose.[2] This is a shame, because – as I will try to show here – there is much more that Adorno (along with Horkheimer and Marcuse) could contribute toward a better understanding of our relationship with nature and to animal studies in general.

Herein I shall underscore that thanks to their dialectical and dynamic understanding of nature, Adorno, Horkheimer, and Marcuse have enabled us to escape the alternative between animal 'reductionism' and human 'exceptionalism'. These critical theorists neither establish an *absolute difference* between humans and non-humans (something that would sever us from the animal kingdom), nor preach some sort of *absolute identity* between them. The first option is typical of those who look for intrinsic qualities (such as reason, language, morality, soul, etc.) that could be described as specifically human, and can thereby justify the assumption of our uniqueness in nature. According to those who follow the second option, there would be *nothing* in human beings that could distinguish them from other animals; in short: we could (and should) therefore study humans according to the same ethological principles we apply to other animals.

It is clear that what is at stake in the most noble attempts to save our uniqueness from ethological reduction is a battle for freedom. From the other side, those who campaign against such attempts are guided by the moving intent to defend the defenceless; seeing in human exceptionalism a way to justify our alleged right to postpone the interests of other species in favour of our own,

---

2   See PETA's campaign *Holocaust on your Plate* that used, for purely agitatory ends, a sentence falsely attributed to Adorno (Patterson 2002, p. 51). For an antispeciesist critique of this misuse of Adorno, see Witt-Stahl (2003). For an analysis of the *reductio ad Hitlerum* implied in PETA's rethoric, see Meschiari (2019).

many animal rights activists are often tempted to welcome scientific findings
that explain human behaviour in terms of biologically programmed mechanisms. Singer's commitment to sociobiology is a telling example of this kind of
approach.[3] Is there a way out of this double bind that presents itself in the guise
of a ritual sacrifice? Must we choose, like Descartes,[4] between human freedom
and animal lives? I think the Frankfurt School teaches us that such an alternative is only apparent.

Critical Theory's vision of the animal could be defined as *anthropopoietic*:[5]
according to such a view, the animal is essential to the making of man, and
'man' is a product of a certain relationship to the 'animal'. This is not to be interpreted in merely Darwinian terms: we were indeed – as Rachels remembers –
'created from animals',[6] although such indisputable evidence does not explain
the specific role that our *differences* from the other animals plays in the making of the nature/culture opposition. At the same time, this role should not
be understood in merely *symbolic* terms.[7] Adorno and Horkehimer's conception, as we can derive from their critique of the Enlightenment [*Aufklärung*[8]],
understands such relationships in a very specific and concrete composition,
where both the evolutionist and the symbolic sides of the human/animal difference cooperate in a dialectical theory of animality. Here, 'human' is understood
as a *negation* of the animal. In the relationship between human and non-
human, this 'non' is conceived as a *generative otherness*; a process of making
of both the 'human' and the meaning of his human-like experience as human.
It is the human/animal relationship that produces the human *Self* through the
constant negation of its animal Other. As I shall henceforth propose, the pretext
for such *symbolic* and *real* negation of the animal is ultimately the domination
of nature.

Adorno and Horkheimer's theory is also dialectical since it tries to articulate
the relation between theory and praxis: it shows how the most noble and speculative ideas in human culture are deeply rooted in the domination of nature
and, therefore, have a practical, although hidden, trigger. At the same time, this
leads to the conclusion that theory itself *is* a form of praxis and that any attempt

---

3   Singer 1981, p. 1999.
4   See, for example, Descartes: 'if they [the non-human animals] thought as we do, they would
    have an immortal soul as we do' (Letter to the Marquis of Newcastle, in Decartes 2000, p. 277).
5   From the Greek *anthropos* (man) and *poiesis* (to make). The expression alludes to the pro-
    ductive role held by the other animals in the making of the human identity.
6   Rachels 1990.
7   As happens in 'zooanthropology': See Marchesini et al. 1999 and Tugnoli et al. 2003.
8   The German word *Aufklärung* does not simply cover the Enlightenment (*Lumière, Illumin-
    ismo*), since it describes the process of 'rationalisation' intrinsic to the history of civilisation.

to free ourselves and the rest of nature from oppression, necessarily means to start thinking differently, overturning the logic of domination, accepting alterity as the repressed and yet undeletable counterpart of reason.[9]

2   From the Institute for Social Research to the 'Frankfurt School'

Like many philosophical and cultural labels, it has often been discussed whether the expression 'Frankfurt School' has a univocal meaning. The authors usually held to be members of the school were, in some way, affiliated with the Institute for Social Research founded in Frankfurt am Main in 1923 by Felix Weil. Although originally oriented towards 'orthodox' Marxism, under the direction of Max Horkheimer the Institute rapidly broadened its theoretical horizons and became an interdisciplinary research centre. The *Zeitschrift für Sozialforschung* – the Institute's journal – hosted contributions by such diverse figures as Erich Fromm, Leo Löwenthal, Friedrich Pollock, Otto Kirchheimer and Franz Neumann. Also associated with the Institute were Walter Benjamin, Alfred Sohn-Rethel and Siegfried Kracauer. Because of the political positions and the Jewish origins of many of its members, the Institute was forced to emigrate during the Nazi era. It thus moved to the USA until 1951, when most of its members returned to Germany and the Institute was able to re-open under Pollock's directorship.

After World War II, as the popularity of some of the leading figures of the Institute increased, the expression 'Frankfurt School' became popular in the German sociological and philosophical debate. Admittedly, none of the members of the Institute had ever thought of themselves in such terms, although the phrase was eventually accepted by Adorno himself.[10]

If one assumes a strictly historical point of view, it is clear that no such thing as 'The Frankfurt School' exists. It is impossible to recollect all the philosophers, psychologists, economists, sociologists, literary critics, who were actually

---

9   Of course, there are differences among the various members of the Frankfurt School, but I believe that those differences mainly emerge from the consequences one derives from *Dialectic of Enlightenment*. I am myself pushing this theory in a political direction which probably would have not pleased these authors. At any rate, although I think my dialectical theory of nature is quite 'orthodox' in relation to the thought of Adorno, Horkheimer and Marcuse, I do not expect experts and scholars to accept my interpretation. What interests me here is the *use* I can make of *Dialectic of Enlightenment* for my purpose: to provide Marxism with a dialectical theory of animality.

10   Adorno 1997g, p. 351; 1976, p. 66.

members of or simply collaborators with the Institute under an indisputable and coherent label. Any attempt to outline such a philosophical *Weltanschauung* is destined to fail.

It is true that during the late 1920s and '30s, under the direction of Horkheimer, the Institute gave an important contribution to the analysis of capitalist society, working inside a theoretical frame that could be defined as a sort of 'scientific paradigm' *à la* Kuhn. Facing an international situation that could hardly be explained in purely Marxian terms – such as the impact of modern mass society in Europe, the growing influence of Fascism in Italy and Germany, and the dogmatic involution of Russian socialism – Horkheimer managed to direct the collective efforts of the Institute to update its original orthodox Marxist orientation. Instead of simply rejecting Marx, Horkheimer encouraged his colleagues to investigate both the objective and the subjective sides of social reality, the latter being usually dismissed as irrelevant by official communism. Concepts and analysis derived from 'bourgeois' thinkers like Nietzsche, Freud, Durkheim or Weber were taken into account, in an attempt to explain social phenomena in a more global and complex way.

What Horkheimer and the other members of the Institute understood as their general 'philosophy' during this time was called the 'Critical Theory of Society'. According to Horkheimer and Marcuse,[11] while 'traditional' theory relied on a contemplative and unilateral relation between subject and object, a 'critical' theory assumed a more practical and dialectical approach. This was a necessary premise of social science, since any attempt to consider the subject of knowledge independent from its object (society) would end up in that kind of subjectivism that Marx had criticised as ideological. At the same time, Critical Theory questions both the economic objectivism of orthodox Communism and Durkheim's conclusion about the impossibility for the subject of sociology to transcend its social environment. It rather believes that it is possible to *understand* society while trying to *change* it and that the only way to escape the alternative between hollow rationalism (the subject determines the object) and blind irrationalism (the object determines the subject) is to assume a reciprocal determination of the two poles. In this respect, although less optimistic about the revolutionary possibilities of the Proletariat in more advanced societies, Critical Theory still derived from Lukács's *History and Class Consciousness* the necessity of a 'unity of theory and praxis'.

It is usually remarked that the main theoretical innovation proposed by Critical Theory in the 1920s and '30s was the attempt to combine Freud's psy-

---

11   Horkheimer 1992; 1975; Marcuse 1965; 1988.

choanalysis with Marx's critique of political economy. As a matter of fact, some contributions to the *Zeitschrift für Sozialforschung* openly drew a parallel between Marx's dialectics between material basis and ideological superstructure of society and Freud's theory of an unresolved tension between the Id and the conscious activity of the individual. The Institute was thus actively working on a new concept of *ideology*, showing the role played by hidden libidinal drives in the organisation of modern rational societies: a clear attempt to explain why centuries of civil, moral and material progress could not prevent Europe from experiencing a catastrophic step back into irrationalism.

The idea of a parallel reading of Marx and Freud was not unique to the Institute of Social Research at the time (one need only think of the pioneering work of Wilhelm Reich), nor was it characteristic of all its members and collaborators: some of them, like Neumann, simply rejected it, while others, like Benjamin, never openly integrated Freudian concepts into their work. It should also be noted that even Erich Fromm – who had produced the most important contributions for the *Zeitschrift* in terms of such a parallel reading – eventually left the Institute and his personal attempt to integrate Marxism and psychoanalysis was then openly criticised by Horkheimer, Marcuse and Adorno. Thus, even the formula Marx+Freud could hardly be considered a trademark of the school.

In the end, although I do not think it is possible to use the expression 'Frankfurt School' to describe the thought of *all* the members and collaborators of the Institute during *all* its phases, I suggest it could still be used in its original meaning: it thus describes the theoretical frame of its leading figures during the 1950s and '60s, i.e. the work of Adorno, Horkheimer and Marcuse. In the following text, I will limit my analysis to these thinkers. In so doing, I am not simply selecting them because of their historical influence. I do believe that the way their work was received in the philosophical and sociological postwar debate was somewhat aware of what they had in common. I suggest that the crucial turning point in the theoretical history of the Institute is in fact the publication of *Dialectic of Enlightenment* with its new, dialectical concepts of reason and nature. It is not by chance that the book appeared after Adorno joined the Institute and begun his intellectual partnership with Horkheimer (while, in the previous years, Horkheimer had tried to outline, along with Marcuse, the broad philosophical vision of Critical Theory). The central thesis of the book – which I will try to articulate in the following pages – laid down the basis for the following years of interdisciplinary work at the Institute. Some of its longtime members, like Marcuse, recognised the great relevance of the book and, although not officially affiliated with the Institute after the emigration, worked on the theoretical path opened up by it. Others, like Fromm, did

not: they simply left the Institute and took a totally different route (it is sufficient, for instance, to read Fromm's *Escape from Freedom* – written in the same
years as *Dialectic of Enlightenment* and working on very similar themes – to see
how traditional, i.e. anthropocentric and undialectical, is Fromm's treatment of
nature). Some others, like Habermas, started as orthodox defenders of Adorno
and Horkheimer's theses, but ended up rejecting their innovative and scandal-
ous core.[12]

3   From Nature to Animals

In the present chapter, while trying to isolate the key elements of Adorno's,
Horkheimer's and Marcuse's theories of domination, I will provide the missing
links that could make their work fruitful for the animal liberation movement. In
its general terms, such theory denounces the reduction of *nature* to mere object
of manipulation, showing how its exploitation is strictly related to the oppression of humans. At the same time, these authors often expressed contempt for
our mistreatment of *other animals*, underlying the important role played by the
repression of animality in the construction of human identity. But how does
this open critique of our mastery of nature relate to the more specific sensibility shown by Adorno, Horkheimer and Marcuse for the violence committed
against animals?

   Although their comments on animal oppression are constant and sound in
their denunciation of anthropocentrism, it is clear that these authors never
focused on such a specific theme and it is the task of the reader to draw the line
between natural and animal oppressions. I will firstly describe the broad theory of domination as it was sketched by the authors themselves and then try to
specify the position of the animal in this general scheme. In doing so, I will rely
more on anthropological and historical details than *Dialectic of Enlightenment*
does. Such a brief excursus will prove helpful in explaining more concretely
how animals contributed to the making of civilisation, a process which essentially implies both their material and symbolic oppression (i.e. domestication
and anthropocentrism). In addition to this, I hope to show that the theory of
civilisation outlined in *Dialectic of Enlightenment* was sufficiently general to
survive more accurate archeological and anthropological research, and that it
was sufficiently rooted in historical and natural reality to be something more
than a vague, *a priori* philosophy of history.

---

12   Whitebook 1994, pp. 65–92.

Finally, a brief methodological remark. Some readers might find the following discussion lacking a clear definition of what Adorno, Horkheimer and Marcuse intended with the word 'nature'. Although it is usually better to help the reader with a preliminary definition of the technical terms used, I think it is not possible to do so in the present case. As a matter of fact, one of the central aims of this chapter is exactly to explain what Adorno, Horkheimer and Marcuse understand by that term. Their concept of nature must, therefore, be the conclusion and not the premise of the argumentation. This necessity derives from the structure of the object itself: the authors consider nature not as something static but rather as a process, a becoming. Accordingly, its essence must be described as a dynamic structure, involving phases, tensions between poles and even open possibilities. As a consequence, at the present stage, nature can only be defined negatively, i.e. by explaining what nature is *not*. According to Adorno, Horkheimer and Marcuse, nature is neither an external reality (they talk of inner and outer nature), nor is it simply identical to culture. As I will try to make clear, the opposition between nature and culture is both real *and* false, and the whole process of civilisation is a tragic attempt to come to terms with this paradox.[13]

4   The Structure of Domination

I think it is plausible to distinguish in Adorno and Horkheimer three main forms of domination:

1.   *Domination upon nature*, articulated in
     (a)   domination of 'external' nature (i.e. of *non-human* nature);
     (b)   domination of 'internal' nature (i.e. of human sensibility).
2.   Domination over 'man' itself in terms of *class domination*.
3.   The *hierarchical distinction* between spiritual/intellectual labour and physical labour.[14]

---

13   As I hope to show, it is impossible to read the dialectical structure of *Dialectic of Enlightenment* as a form of 'culturalism'. Morover, as we will see, the fact that the Frankfurt School does not rely on 'ecological science' (Foster 2000, p. 245) is a consequence of its innovative *dialectical materialism* which defines a form of *dynamic ontology* that cannot be reduced to a mere 'ecological critique' of modernity.

14   A more accurate understanding of the structure of domination would imply taking into account the oppression of the individual by collective (the so-called process of 'socialisation', *Vergesellschaftung*) and gender oppression. For the sake of brevity, we will not discuss them here.

In the first chapter of *Dialectic of Enlightenment*, Adorno and Horkheimer suggest that all these forms of oppression, although relatively autonomous and independent, work according to a similar logic. As Hegel pointed out in his *Phänomenologie des Geistes*, the relation of domination [*Herrschaft*] implies a hierarchical and oppositional distinction between its terms.[15] Being opposite poles of a mutual relation, the two elements cannot be defined outside it but only exist once the relation itself is established. The dominating pole defines itself as the negation of the dominated one and *vice versa*. According to Adorno and Horkheimer, all the aforementioned forms of domination converge and intertwine in the capitalist mode of production, which can be described as the perfect heir of an ancient history of sufferance and exploitation which involves the human body and soul, as well as nature as a whole. While 'violence' is a contingent relation between otherwise autonomous beings, 'domination' implies a structural, material and symbolic relation, where the opposite poles are reciprocally determined and cannot exist as such outside their practical relation. Much of the theoretical and practical nonsense produced by the Animal Rights Movement in the last decades comes from the incapacity to *distinguish between violence and domination*.[16]

Dialectic of Enlightenment thus marks an amazing attempt to understand the entire history of civilisation as a history of domination. Since the book is an attempt to understand the remote causes of the self-destruction of Modernity – it is, in a sense, a *genealogy of Fascism* – the focus of the authors is on the development of *Western* civilisation. At the same time, their use of the word civilisation [*Zivilisation*] still holds something of the general meaning that was typical of nineteenth-century anthropology: it thus indicates, in opposition to 'barbarism', the 'evolution' from nomadic to sedentary cultures and the birth of written history and cumulative knowledge. Adorno and Horkheimer were, in a way, foreshadowing Lévi-Strauss's distinction between 'hot' and 'cold' societies: 'the former seeking, by the institutions they give themselves, to annul the possible effects of historical factors on their equilibrium and continuity in a quasi-automatic fashion; the latter resolutely internalising the historical process and

---

15   Hegel 1977.
16   See for instance Regan, asking himself during a march against the Vietnam War, 'was my fork, like napalm, a weapon of violence?' (2003, p. 3; 2004, p. 31). Or Melanie Joy discussing the 'adaptive' or 'maladaptive' nature of 'psychic numbing' according to its function in terms of 'violence' (2010, p. 19). With such a vague concept of 'violence', it becomes impossible to distinguish between different *structures of power*. No wonder that human society is often seen as a global enterprise of meaningless 'violence' which can find its final redemption only through *ahimsa*. Contrary to such a mystical approach, political veganism should be understood as a *critique of domestication*.

making it the moving power of their development'.[17] Cold societies try to avoid oppositions and conflicts both inside and outside human society: their relation towards nature is respectful and 'mimetic'. Hot societies, on the contrary, live through inner and outer conflicts: they tend to consider nature an object of exploitation and something exterior to the human spirit. While humanity once lived in what Adorno and Horkheimer called the mimetic stage, some cultures slowly realised the oppositional way of life characteristic of hot societies. In *Dialectic of Enlightenment* such a move is sometimes evoked through the expression 'mythical stage'.

In a sense, Adorno and Horkheimer describe the way a particular hot society had become the hottest of all, choosing development for development's sake as its golden rule. At the same time, they suggest that such a move in the direction of a purely historical and cultural evolution is merely *apparent*. The height of Western civilisation shows human history moving in a *circle*: far from being a sequence of unpredictable events, history is nothing but the perpetual repetition – under different phenomenal forms – of those domination relationships upon which the entire structure of human society is built. As we shall see, the same radical opposition between nature and culture – which is one of the driving forces in the development of Western society – is denounced by Adorno and Horkheimer as a terrible *quid pro quo*.

5   The Specific Role of Animals in the General Scheme of Domination

A vast amount of time stretches between what Adorno and Horkheimer called the mimetic and the mythical phases of society, i.e. between animistic nomadism and the birth of primitive centralised States and hierarchical religions. I think one can identify such a long period of time with the passage from the Neolithic to the Bronze Age. For sure, the transition from nomadic to sedentary society did not produce in itself the reduction of nature to mere matter (it takes a long time to 'forget' that animals and plants were once worshipped as quasi-divine entities), yet it did provide its *material basis*. Although 'Neolithic culture'[18] did not conceive of itself as totally superior to a disqualified

---

17   Lévi-Strauss 1966, pp. 233–4; 1976, p. 312 ff.

18   Some social anthropologists have borrowed from archaeology the expression 'Neolithic revolution' assuming that the peculiar combination of nature exploitation and social stratification that took place in ancient Mesopotamia is not typical of Western history but is a more general phenomenon. Lévi-Strauss, for instance, considered the 'Neolithic revolution' the necessary (although not sufficient) precondition for the existence of 'hot' soci-

nature, the material side of our domination of nature began with the *domest-ication of animals* and *agriculture*: thanks to these, nomadic hunter-gatherer societies – economically characterised by simple reproduction – 'evolved' into sedentary societies, starting to exert a growing *control* over natural resources. Domination is not a mere act of violence directed against another being: it implies submission and a loss of independence on the part of the weak member of the relationship. One could describe in terms of domination every kind of regulation of the biological cycles of other species on behalf of our exclusive interest. Such enslavement of non-human nature is the *condition sine qua non* of speciesism, i.e. the material basis by which humans can consider themselves 'masters'. At the end of such a process, we find hierarchical societies where class division is established and a centralised, anthropomorphic religion preaches the superiority of a force that is not immanent to nature (*mana*), but rather controls it from above: the spirit [*Geist*].[19]

As a matter of fact, such sort of domination of external nature is insepar-able from an analogous control exerted over human nature; what we above designated as internal nature. Although these two processes are somewhat independent from one another, it is clear that the labour *discipline* imposed on those humans that moved from hunter-gatherer economies to primitive state systems is only possible when a *psychological mechanism* of control and repres-sion of the instinctual drives is at work. Parallel to the economic transformation of human society, a *political* change takes place: with the birth of a political and religious elite (i.e. of social strata not directly committed with material produc-tion), social relationships begin to be defined in hierarchical terms.

How all this happened is still not clear. Although imbued with deep his-torical knowledge, *Dialectic of Enlightenment* does not describe the making of Western civilisation *historically*. Thus, it is not always easy to understand

---

eties (Lévi-Strauss 1966). Anyway, since Adorno and Horkheimer focused themselves on Western civilisation, I am here speaking of the Neolithic in archaeological terms, although it could be an interesting task to see how their theory could describe a dynamic intrinsic to human social organisation as such.

19   In the following pages, the words 'spirit', 'spiritualistic' and 'spiritualism' imply a dualistic, transcendent conception of religion. They all refer to a discorporate power that is sup-posed to control nature from the outside. In this respect, any true animistic notion is not 'spiritualistic', since it does not articulate such opposition. It must be noted that the ter-minology in use among the Institute for Social Research is Hegelian: thus, the opposition between nature and spirit is dialectical and not static. Hegel supposed that the divide between spirit and nature was apparent, since nature is nothing but the unconscious activ-ity of the spirit itself. According to Adorno, Horkheimer and Marcuse, the contrary is true: all culture, including its spiritual sublimation, is nothing but natural activity.

which are the 'causes' and which are the 'effects' in the process of civilisation. The authors are more interested in describing how the different phases of Western civilisation articulated the several layers of domination. When they talk of a mimetic or mythical stage, they are clearly talking of a particular constellation of diverse elements such as the dialectic between culture and nature, reason and sensibility, labour-direction and labour-force, etc. Adorno and Horkheimer, however, underline the central position assumed by the exploitation of nature in the making of the entire mechanism of domination. Since this layer of violence and oppression of the non-human other reaches its peak at the height of civilisation, Adorno and Horkheimer believe that it can help us to reconstruct *a posteriori* its secret trigger. Of course, this does not mean that the exploitation of nature is the direct and exclusive cause of human oppression, but it is surely one of its *conditions of possibility*. In other words, it is the necessary (although not sufficient) precondition of it.

This is what Horkheimer likely contemplated when he wrote: 'Domination of nature involves domination of man. Each subject not only has to take part in the subjugation of external nature, human and non-human, but in order to do so must subjugate nature in himself. Domination becomes "internalized" for domination's sake'.[20] The structure of domination is essentially *circular* and *spiral-like*: it is true that our domination of nature made possible the accumulation of social surplus necessary for the birth of political hierarchy and slavery. Alternately, it was the social division of labour (between spiritual/intellectual activities and physical labour) that made possible the elaboration of the knowledge necessary to cement the *exploitation of nature*.

Although spiritual activity and intellectual labour are not synonymous, *Dialectic of Enlightenment* suggests that their respective spheres evolved according to the same logic (i.e. by distinguishing what is superior to what is inferior and by giving the first the role of commanding the second) and were often intertwined. They can be therefore considered moments of one and the same process of differentiation and refinement inside human society and the human soul. In such process we see the inferior side of the opposition (be it the body in relation to the soul, the senses in relation to the intellect, slaves or workers in relation to the ruling classes) symbolically marked as natural or animal-like. At the same time, it is precisely such societal, spiritual and intellectual cleavage that increases the power of accumulation of society as a whole, thus reinforcing the exploitation rate of animals and plants.

---

20   Horkheimer 2013, p. 66.

I think we can see all these elements at work in what anthropologists today call 'chiefdom', a social organisation more developed than a tribe but less complex than a state, where a central authority – which is often religious and political at the same time – organises the distribution of economic resources. According to some social anthropologists, if the chiefdom is successful in establishing the rule of alienated labour, its religious and political elite can eventually make the leap and give birth to a primitive State. If this corresponds to what really happened, Adorno and Horkheimer's distinction between the mimetic and the mythical phases of civilisation would be historically correct.

Alienation [*Entäusserung*] *from* nature, and domination *upon* nature were thus two sides of one and the same process ('Human beings purchase the increase in their power with estrangement from that over which it is exerted'[21]): the *cognitive structure of objectivity* arises as the logical and conceptual counterpart of class relations. 'The distance of subject from object, the presupposition of abstraction, is founded on the distance from things which the ruler attains by means of the ruled'.[22]

It is clear that, according to Adorno and Horkheimer's explicative model, human history knows no fall from grace: instrumental reason, labour constriction, spiritualisation and alienation from nature are intertwined phenomena and one could hardly put his/her finger on the moment when 'everything went wrong'. Yet, one cannot deny that such history knows a qualitative leap with the decline of the hunter-gatherer economy – enclosed in a magic and mimetic world, where humans still feel their unity with nature and the numinous power (*mana*) that embrace them – and the dawn of primitive states and patriarchal religions, where the divine eventually loses its nocturnal and maternal shape, and the domination of man and nature is justified as the work of an autonomous and superior spirit.

According to Adorno, a real, emphatic concept of society should properly be applied to those societal forms in which individual life is fully determined by such process of 'socialisation' [*Vergesellschaftung*].[23]

> In the first stages of nomadism the members of the tribe still played an independent part in influencing the course of nature. [...] In that order the world was already divided into zones of power and of the profane. The course of natural events as an emanation of *mana* had already been

---

21   Adorno and Horkheimer 1997, p. 25; 2002, p. 6.
22   Adorno and Horkheimer 1997, p. 25; 2002, p. 9.
23   Adorno 2003, p. 54 ff.; 2000, p. 29 ff.

elevated to a norm demanding submission. But if the nomadic savage, despite his subjection, could still participate in the magic which defined the limits of that world, and could disguise himself as his quarry in order to stalk it, in later periods the intercourse with spirits and the subjection were assigned to different classes of humanity: power to one side, obedience to the other.[24]

It could be said that the magic and nomadic world is characterised by *horizontal* relations both within and without society: its economic and political egalitarianism has no room for class rule and its organic exchange with outer nature prevents the subordination of other species' biological cycles to unilateral satisfaction of human needs. All this is clearly expressed on a symbolic level: the spiritual element is still fused and transfused in an animated and living nature, where edges are blurred and every transformation of a substance into another is possible. Human symbiosis with the animal is total and real, the hunter experiences a sort of mystical identification with it. Humanity cannot dominate the-other-than-itself if such symbolic otherness cannot be conceived.

It is precisely the symbolic genesis of such an 'other' that was made possible by the Neolithic culture, which inaugurates permanent mechanisms of control over nature, paving the way to class society. At the end of the Neolithic transition we find, at every level, relationships that can be defined, as opposed to what has been observed so far, as *vertical* and *hierarchical*. Primitive class societies, thus elaborated early mythologies and institutional religions, which symbolically reflected a force operating in natural and social relationships, bringing forth an ontological and hierarchical divide. The split between humans and animals, alongside their mutual contradiction, ideologically reflects the division and polarisation that has its basis in the real domination over natural processes, and the progressive hierarchisation of social relations.

6   The Dialectical Animal

6.1   'The Triumph of Culture and Its Failure'

The domination of nature and man is thus imposed as the *natural* law of society, and individuals are forced to align to it, under the threat of exclusion from the human community. The image of the dominating man becomes the idol

---

24   Adorno and Horkheimer 1997, pp. 37–8; 2002, pp. 15–16.

to which everything is sacrificed: the relationship with nature, with others and with oneself. The 'taming' of a human being according to societal rules is the *conditio sine qua non* of his/her social being, premise and consequence of that dominion that human society as a whole exercises on its natural other.

> Not only is domination paid for with the estrangement of human beings from the dominated objects, but the relationships of human beings, including the relationship of individuals to themselves, have themselves been bewitched by the objectification of mind. [...] For civilisation, purely natural existence, both animal and vegetative, was the absolute danger. Mimetic, mythical, and metaphysical forms of behavior were success-ively regarded as stages of world history which had been left behind, and the idea of reverting to them held the terror that the self would be changed back into the mere nature from which it had extricated itself with unspeakable exertions and which for that reason filled it with unspeakable dread. Over the millennia the living memory of prehistory of its nomadic period and even more of the truly prepatriarchal stages, has been expunged from human consciousness with the most terrible pun-ishments. [...] Humanity had to inflict terrible injuries on itself before the self – the identical, purpose-directed, masculine character of human beings – was created, and something of this process is repeated in every childhood.[25]

Reification [*Verdinglichung*], i.e. the reduction of living relations to 'things', to objects at one's disposal, to matter for manipulation, includes *our relation to the animals that we are*. The reification of the Self is a process that under-lines the entire history of civilisation, propelling and fastening its destructive potential towards nature. According to Adorno and Horkheimer, the corner-stone of Self-Reification is the violence exerted on the animal. In particular, the underpinnings are constituted by a form of implicit violence against the human animal. Adorno dramatised the function of such violence in a vibrant passage of his *Negative Dialectics*: 'A child, fond of an innkeeper named Adam, watched him club the rats pouring out of holes in the courtyard; it was in his image that the child made its own image of the first man. That this has been forgotten, that we no longer know what we used to feel before the dogcatcher's van, is both the triumph of culture and its failure'.[26]

25   Adorno and Horkheimer 1997, pp. 45–50; 2002, pp. 21–6.
26   Adorno 1997b, p. 359; 2007, p. 366.

It is important to stress the dialectical, antinomical nature of a process that can therefore only be expressed in contradictory terms: the affirmation of the Self is determined by the negation of the other-than-itself and such an onto-genetic and phylogenetic process should be read as the triumph *and* failure of culture. Whereas civilised humanity accomplishes a complete extirpation of its natural origin, we celebrate our victory over nature. At the same time, repressing and forgetting the memory of what we nevertheless *are*, we fatally miss our goal: the realisation of a 'humane', i.e. not 'bestial', society. Our destructive attitude towards (human and non-human) animality becomes the shibboleth that eventually denounces our illusions, unmasking the 'bestiality' of our society in the face of our ideological celebration of the superior and eternal values of civilisation as opposed to the blind violence and greed of nature.

6.2   *The False Alternatives of Civilisation*

It is through such an interpretation of the history of civilisation that one can fully appreciate Adorno and Horkheimer's words on the human-animal relation:

> Throughout European history the idea of the human being has been expressed in contradistinction to the animal. The latter's lack of reason is the proof of human dignity. So insistently and unanimously has this antithesis been recited by all the earliest precursors of bourgeois thought, the ancient Jews, the Stoics, and the Early Fathers, and then through the Middle Ages to modern times that few other ideas are so fundamental to Western anthropology.[27]

It is possible to understand the whole history of civilisation according to this conceptual polarisation because it is not only an exterior scheme, but it derives from historical and objective structures of domination that originated through the evolutionary process and that *still* determine the political, economical and cultural forms of human society. According to Adorno and Horkheimer, it is in fact the present level of violence that we exert against nature that allows us to read the entire past history as a history of domination.

When Adorno and Horkheimer describe the analogy between vivisection and ritual sacrifice[28] they are not speaking metaphorically: both are an expression of our desire to put *all living reality under control*. The aseptic truth of science, along with the rigid distinction between subject and object in any

---

27   Adorno and Horkheimer 1997, p. 283; 2002, p. 203.
28   Adorno and Horkheimer 1997, p. 283; 2002, pp. 203–4.

experiment, is just another way to express the alienation between human and non-human nature, the ideological quintessence of their hierarchical polarisation. The core of such control does not change even if it is no longer exercised by the priest on behalf of a transcendent deity, but it is now totally in the hands of the man-scientist who considers himself – to add insult to injury – a fully *natural* being, driven by a *materialistic* world view, *emancipated* from theological beliefs etc. Yet, such 'immanentisation' of dominion upon nature not only repeats the violence of all time, it strengthens it: the false consciousness of a neutral and selfless knowledge casts all scruples away and makes it harder to reveal the continuity between traditional-irrational and modern-rational forms of oppression.

> Magic implies specific representation. What is done to the spear, the hair, the name of the enemy, is also to befall his person; the sacrificial animal is slain in place of the god. [...] Science puts an end to this. In it there is no specific representation: something which is a sacrificial animal cannot be a god. Representation gives way to universal fungibility. An atom is smashed not as a representative but as a specimen of matter, and the rabbit suffering the torment of the laboratory is seen not as a representative but, mistakenly, as a mere exemplar.[29]

The mind [*Geist*], and all that is good in its origins and existence, is hopelessly implicated in this horror.[30]

One point should be clear: the defeat of magical enchantment by conceptual distinction, the affirmation of the Self etc. are certainly forms of progress which Adorno and Horkheimer do not intend to give up, nor did they ever abstractly equate magic and science, thus rebutting the very idea of progress in the field of natural knowledge. Yet, if stressing the difference between magic and science is necessary, this does not imply one has to blind oneself to the destructive potential hidden in their common origin. What *Dialectic of Enlightenment* put into question is the *philosophy of history*[31] implicit in the *ideology of progress*; namely the idea that the hierarchical relations among humans and between humans and the other animals are philosophically *justified* in the name of a metaphysics by which historical time is linearly oriented 'for the better'. Adorno

---

29   Adorno and Horkheimer 1997, p. 26; 2002, pp. 6–7.
30   Adorno and Horkheimer 1997, p. 254; 2002, p. 185.
31   See the note entitled 'On the Critique of the Philosophy of History' (Adorno and Horkheimer 1997, pp. 253–6; 2002, pp. 184–7).

and Horkheimer do not deny such linearity actually *exists*. They write of the 'circularity of history', *Kreisähnlichkeit der Geschichte*,[32] which is, in fact, the effect of the *spiral mechanism* we have already examined: all societies grounded on the domination of human and non-human nature tend to expand and broaden their power. The point is precisely to scrutinise such a process in its premise and consequences to see if civilisation effectively moves inexorably toward the best. It is the very notion of the hidden mechanism at work in the process of civilisation that allows them to rebut its official ideology of civilisation: 'No universal history leads from savagery to humanitarianism, but there is one leading from the slingshot to the megaton bomb.'[33]

Adorno and Horkheimer are often criticised for their unilateral and pessimistic view of History. Further, their efforts to denounce instrumental reason are attacked as contradictory.[34] The problem is that much of such criticism works with a static and likewise unilateral concept of reason, whereas the Frankfurt School articulates the relationship between reason and nature, trying to disclose their historical entanglement. The contradiction here is objective, not subjective: it is a historical mechanism, not a logical shortcoming, thus it cannot be attributed to those who seek to master it conceptually. The charge of irrationalism aimed at the Frankfurt School is itself part of the social and ideological mechanism that both Adorno and Horkheimer try to criticise. Being a historical product, rationality is a fully objective process, although such objectivity does not at all mean it cannot be put into question. The intrinsic logic of such unstoppable historical force (in the face of whom individuals are utterly powerless) is, in fact, entirely *binary*: yes/no, reason/madness, progress/reaction, science/magic. Those who hesitate in front of these alternatives, those who try to question the genesis of such options are automatically excommunicated and expelled from the circle of reasonable people.

From the other side, Adorno and Horkheimer's dialectical reason is destined to evoke the scepticism of 'primitivists' *à la* John Zerzan who see in civilisation nothing but a Fall from the golden age of hunter-gatherer societies, rather than an ongoing process that expresses, even through its lacerations and its horror, a potential for hope. This kind of primitivist vision is one of false alternatives (culture *or* nature). It therefore embodies the same logic of civilisation which it claims to criticise. This logic of abstract negation – in Hegelian terms – represents a unilateral refusal that fails to understand that intrinsic law of devel-

---

32   Adorno and Horkheimer 1997, p. 52; 2002, p. 27.
33   Adorno 1997b, p. 324; 2007, p. 320.
34   Habermas 1987.

opment of civilisation that we have tried to articulate so far. Since the 1940s, Adorno and Horkheimer had clearly in mind that such 'inevitable' alternatives were actually part of the problem they were facing: 'the fronts are clearly drawn; anyone who opposes Hearst and Göring is on the side of Pavlov and vivisection; anyone who hesitates between the two is fair game for both.'[35] Only a correct understanding of the dialectics of civilisation can save the empathy for animals from the charge of being sentimentalist, while at the same time avoiding any collusion with the Nazi love for uncontaminated nature: 'In this world liberated from appearance in which human beings having forfeited reflection, have become once more the cleverest animals, which subjugate the rest of the universe when they happen not to be tearing themselves apart – to show concern for animals is considered no longer merely sentimental but a betrayal of progress. In the best reactionary tradition Göring linked animal protection to racial hatred, the Lutheran-Germanic joys of the happy murderer with the genteel fair play of the aristocratic hunter'.[36]

7   Materialistic Solidarity

Dialectic of Enlightenment was intended as a materialist theory of culture, an attempt to bring the false alternatives and ideological oppositions of civilisation to their real base, i.e. the exploitation of the human and non-human life. The scientific ideology of progress is thus denounced as the other side of traditional metaphysical thinking as it shares with it the idea of independence of thought from its social and natural substrate.

'The establishment of total rationality as the supreme objective principle of mankind', writes Adorno, 'spell the continuation of that blind domination of nature whose most obvious and tangible expression was to be found in the exploitation and maltreatment of animals'.[37] The animal here is the shibboleth of supremacist spiritualism: 'animals play for the idealistic system virtually the same role as the Jews for fascism'.[38] This link is so deep that it can be proved *e contrario*. As we have already seen, the mechanism of racial hatred seems to need the symbolic negation of the animal in order to be psychologically triggered.

35   Adorno and Horkheimer 1997, pp. 291–2; 2002, p. 211.
36   Adorno and Horkheimer 1997, pp. 291–2; 2002, p. 211.
37   Adorno 1996, p. 215; 2001, p. 145.
38   Adorno 1993, p. 123; 1998, p. 80.

Perhaps the social schematisation of perception in anti-Semites is such that they do not see Jews as human beings at all. The constantly encountered assertion that savages, blacks, Japanese are like animals, monkeys for example, is the key to the pogrom. The possibility of pogroms is decided in the moment when the gaze of a fatally-wounded animal falls on a human being. The defiance with which he repels this gaze – 'after all, it is only an animal' – reappears irresistibly in cruelties done to human beings, the perpetrators having again and again to reassure themselves that it is 'only an animal', because they could never fully believe this even of animals.[39]

As a consequence, a characteristic feature of Adorno's, Horkheimer's and Marcuse's materialism is their declared intention to make room for other animals in the project of human liberation. Such approach distinguishes Critical Theory both from positivist naturalism (which recognises the animality of man, but without expanding the circle of ethical consideration to non-human animals) and spiritualism (which, even if it shows 'compassion' towards other animals, it denies the animal nature of man himself). It is only by recognising their *mediating* role in the relationship between man and nature that animals help us to put the dialectic of civilisation in the right context. If this does not happen, our look on civilisation will be out of focus, and our answers to the problems raised by our control over nature will be mislead by bad conscience and self-justification. It is no coincidence, then, that Critical Theory has been so often misunderstood and rejected, simultaneously accused from opposite sides of irrationalism and rationalism, materialism and idealism.

Even among Marxists there were misunderstandings. Although Adorno, Horkheimer and Marcuse still considered Marx the only possible ground for a critical analysis of capitalist *economy*, their critique of Western civilisation went far beyond Marx. For the Frankfurt School, it was only via a different relationship with the animal – based on compassion and solidarity with the 'damaged life' – that it was possible to see and denounce the hidden idealistic sides of Marxist materialism. Surely Marx could not imagine the alienating and destructive development that the domination of man over nature would bring in the twentieth century. Yet, Marx and Engels's unshakable belief in the goodness and rationality of such domination reveals an inability to conceive a *limit* in our appropriation of nature, a limit that would have forced them to accord nature the status of the *subject*.

---

39   Adorno 1997a, p. 116; 2005a, p. 105.

Marx and Engels could not accept this, since they believed that man could free himself only by breaking the *mystical* connection, the 'umbilical cord'[40] with nature, something that 'primitive' cultures symbolically and ideologically express through a series of anthropomorphic projections. As shown in *Dialectic of Enlightenment*, although being an important phase in the historical process of human emancipation, the disqualification of the animal and its reduction to an object turns against humans, since such *de-anthropomorphisation* of the world ends up in a state of absolute *inhumanity*: the Nazi barbarism, totalitarianism and the 'administered world'. Along with the idea of an endless domination over nature, Marx and Engels have passively accepted the above mentioned circularity of progress that characterises the history of civilisation. In so doing, they betrayed the materialistic inspiration of their thinking.[41] The limit that humans meet in their transformative praxis is not constitutive of nature qua *object*, but of nature qua *subject*. It is therefore a limit that can only be traced once humans re-discover *the nature that they are*. It is not a question of finding such a limit as an external force compelling us (as happens in Malthus and in most contemporary ecological discourse), it rather means to empathically trace it as *our own limit*. Only by seeing ourselves as nature do we see in nature a limit to our desire to dominate. Since we did – or began to – emancipate ourselves from nature and yet we are still and completely nature, we can learn to listen to a will which is not our own, although it surely speaks through us. Experiencing empathy toward nature, we hear nature asking us to lay down our weapons. This happen, however, only *through the animal*. It is important to stress that such a reconciliation ideal is not to be understood here – as happens in Ernst Bloch – in the sense of an 'absolute Subject which mediates itself with itself',[42] but rather in the sense of an encounter *between individuals*. This is possible only by giving back animals their repressed subjectivity, recognising them as alter egos of the human subject. Critical Theory is not an updated version of romantic *Naturphilosophie*: Adorno, Horkheimer and Marcuse do not start from a self-generating 'principle of being'[43] but from a Darwinian understanding of nature. Here, through random clashes and competitive encounters, human subjectivity discovers itself alienated in non-human nature.

No matter how paradoxical this may sound, Critical Theory believes that Marx's refusal to acknowledge the *subjectivity* of nature as a limit to human expansionism produced a *flaw* in his materialist vision. In an attempt to correct

---

40   Engels 1962a, p. 97.
41   Marcuse 1972, pp. 68–9.
42   Schmidt 1971, p. 159.
43   Marcuse 1972, p. 68. See Noske 1989, p. 191n.

the idealistic consequences of such premises, Marcuse wrote: 'no free society is imaginable which does not, under its 'regulative idea of reason', make the concerted effort to reduce consistently the suffering which man imposes on the animal world'.[44] Such an act of solidarity would supersede the idealism implicit in our global praxis and, by closing the circle of materialism, would open up new relationships with non-human nature.

Apparently, Marx and Engels wrote something very similar: 'The identity of nature and man appears in such a way that the restricted relation of men to nature determines their restricted relation to one another, and their restricted relation to one another determines men's restricted relation to nature.' All this 'just because nature is as yet hardly modified historically'.[45] Still, the decisive move is missing: the route back *from man to nature* that would help to overcome our narrow and egoistic look and break the circularity of domination. By seeing nature as a mere *substrate* of domination, refusing to see it as a subject (i.e. something *active, vital*, with whom we can engage in a relationship of mutual *understanding*), Marx and Engels betrayed their materialist dialectic, forgetting,[46] among other things, Hegel's key lesson on the master-servant relation. Commenting on this famous passage in Hegel's *Phenomenology*, Georges Bataille came very close to some insights expressed by Adorno and Horkheimer in *Dialectic of Enlightenment*: 'To subordinate is not only to alter the subordin-

---

44   Marcuse 1972, p. 68. Schmidt hopes we 'will learn to a far greater degree to practise solidarity with the oppressed animal world, and that in the true society the protection of animals will no longer be regarded as a kind of private fad' (1971, p. 113). Adorno, too, spoke of a 'cranky idea' when dealing with Schopenhauer's defence of animals, but added: 'my own view is that a tremendous amount can be learnt from such crankiness' (Adorno 1996, p. 215; 2001, p. 145). The important treatment of moral philosophy in *Negative Dialectics* ends up with a critique of Kant's indifference towards animality: 'the individual is left with no more than the morality for which Kantian ethics – which accords affection, not respect, to animals – can muster only disdain: to try to live so that one may believe himself to have been a good animal' (Adorno 1997b, p. 294; 2007, p. 299). See also the aphorism '*Sur l'eau*' in *Minima Moralia* (Adorno 1997b, pp. 176–7; 2005a, pp. 155–7).

45   Marx and Engels 2004, p. 51.

46   It is no accident that, according to Hegel, 'the absolute right of appropriation which human beings have over all "things"' is the factual proof of Idealism and the practical confutation of both realism and Kantianism: 'The so-called "philosophy" which attributes reality in the sense of self-subsistence and genuine being-for-and-within-itself [*Für- und Insichsein*] to unmediated single things, to the non-personal, is directly contradicted by the free will's attitude to these things. The same is true of the other philosophy which assures us that the mind cannot apprehend the truth or know the nature of the thing-in-itself. While so-called "external" things have a semblance [*Schein*] of self-subsistence for consciousness, intuition, and representational thinking, the free will idealizes such actuality and so is its truth' (Hegel 2008, p. 60).

ated element but to be altered oneself. [...] Nature becomes man's property but it ceases to be immanent to him. It is his on condition that it is closed to him'.[47]

The Italian Marxist Sebastiano Timpanaro wrote in his famous essay *On Materialism*: 'materialism is much more than a gnoseological theory.[48] Materialism entails also the recognition of man's animality (superseded *only in part* by his species-specific sociality); it is also the radical negation of anthropocentrism and providentialism of any kind, and it is absolute atheism. Thus it represents a *prise de position* with regard to man's place in the world, with regard to the present and future 'balance of power' between man and nature, and with regard to man's needs and his drive for happiness'.[49] Curiously, Timpanaro does not draw any *practical* consequence from the observation of our animality and does not question the fact that the relationship between species is always declining according to *our* needs and *our* happiness. The Frankfurt School has, in turn, underscored how a materialistic ethic should ground itself in the *solidarity* between beings who share suffering, pain and death. As Horkheimer wrote in *Materialism and Morality*:

> Human beings may [...] struggle in concert against their own pains and maladies what medicine will achieve, once it is freed from its present social fetters, is not to be foreseen although suffering and death will continue to hold sway in nature. The solidarity of human beings, however, is a part of the solidarity of life in general. Progress in the realisation of the former will also strengthen our sense of the latter. Animals need human beings.[50]

In 1933, he suggested the well-known metaphor of the skyscraper to describe the structure of the capitalist society which is quoted at the beginning of this chapter. One could say that, even when they acknowledge our animality, Timpanaro and all those Marxists who do not see the inherently idealist/spiritualist structure of dominion, remain comfortably seated in the cathedral. They never plan to descend into the depths of the animal horror. Hence the narrowness and contradiction of their materialistic point of view: a unilateral vision that does not investigate the *genesis* of the alterity between human and nonhumans, but only asserts it as an undisputed fact.

---

47   Bataille 1989, p. 41.
48   Theory of Knowledge. From the Greek *gnosis* (knowledge) and *logos* (discourse).
49   Timpanaro 1975, p. 249.
50   Horkheimer 1993, p. 36.

8   A New 'Dialectics of Nature'

Critical theorists pushed their *dialectics of nature* far beyond Engels, who acknowledged humans as part and parcel of a wider natural order, but could only conceive of our action in terms of desire for *power* and *control* over non-humans. Let us re-read the important passage where Engels foreshadows the end of the opposition between humanity and nature:

> At every step we are reminded that we by no means rule over nature like a conqueror over a foreign people, like someone standing outside nature – but that we, with flesh, blood and brain, belong to nature, and exist in its midst, and that all our mastery of it consists in the fact that we have the advantage over all other creatures of being able to learn its laws and apply them correctly. [...] But the more this progresses the more will men not only feel but also know their oneness with nature, and the more impossible will become the senseless and unnatural idea of a contrast between mind and matter, man and nature, soul and body, such as arose after the decline of classical antiquity in Europe and obtained its highest elaboration in Christianity.[51]

Adorno, Horkheimer and Marcuse more radically argue that it is by opening up the possibility of a different relationship with nature that humanity will reveal nature as intrinsically *dialectical*. Engels and Marx believed – long before reading Darwin – that a true materialist interpretation of the universe should see nature as becoming, history. This is the reason why they constantly attacked the restricted view they labeled 'vulgar' materialism. It was the landmark of such reductionist materialism to conceive nature as a static and unchanging (i.e. non-dialectical) order. Yet, when it comes to our relationship with non-human nature, Engels assumes that natural history is destined to endlessly repeat itself. According to such a perspective, a liberated society cannot but be 'a vast joint-stock company for the exploitation of nature'.[52] The Frankfurt School, on the contrary, makes it clear that a *different* relationship with the environment and the animals is possible. Recognising itself as part of natural history, human culture would in fact produce a radical turn that could deny the necessity of violence and interrupt the eternal perpetuation of dominion (what Adorno called *das Immergleiche*, always-the-same).

---

51   Engels 1962c, p. 453.
52   Adorno 1996, p. 216; 2001, p. 145.

8.1   *Nature as Remembrance*

The return of the identical in the history of civilisation, the repetition that makes progress move in a circle, *is nature itself*. Conceiving of the history of civilisation as a *continuation* of natural history, in fact, human culture is unmasked as *doubly false*, as it claims to be 'other' than a purely natural mechanism of violence. As a matter of fact, it is this very blind violence that human culture inherits from nature. 'The whole ingenious machinery of modern industrial society', write Adorno and Horkheimer, 'is no more than nature dismembering itself'.[53] The point is not to *imitate* an imaginary, idyllic nature – a move made by the Nazis and that resulted in mere 'anti-intellectualism, lies, bestiality' – but to let the 'remembrance of nature'[54] come to surface as the suffering counterpart of reason. Contrary to the Nazi myth of origin, the function of such memory would not be regressive: 'recollection [...] is not remembrance of a Golden Past (which never existed), of childhood innocence, primitive man, et cetera. Recollection as epistemological faculty rather is synthesis, reassembling the bits and fragments which can be found in the distorted humanity and distorted nature'.[55] The memory of nature is the memory of the 'brutality' hidden in the mechanism of civilisation. Only through the remembrance of its natural origin could the human spirit solve its intrinsic antagonisms and recede from its ontological battle against the rest of the living world. 'In mind's self-recognition as nature divided from itself, nature [...] is calling to itself'.[56] This is because 'the world of nature is a world of oppression, cruelty and pain, as is the human world; like the latter, it awaits its liberation'.[57]

8.2   *The Liberation of Nature*

The liberation *of* nature is at the heart of the dialectic of nature taught by the Frankfurt School. It should, however, be understood in both senses of the genitive (subjective and objective) and thus seen as (1) emancipation of humans *from nature* and (2) emancipation *of nature itself*.

8.2.1   The Emancipation *from* Nature

In the first sense, one could speak of the emancipation of humans from nature, i.e. from natural relations understood as blind necessity, as the realisation of what human civilisation has always promised through the spirit (justice, unity,

---

53   Adorno and Horkheimer 1997, p. 292; 2002, pp. 210–12.
54   Adorno and Horkheimer 1997, p. 292; 2002, pp. 210–12.
55   Marcuse 1972, p. 70.
56   Adorno and Horkheimer 1997, p. 57; 2002, p. 47.
57   Marcuse 1998, p. 166.

harmony, etc.) and never really achieved. In the first instance, the redemption of nature would be the liberation of human culture from the yoke of natural selfishness. All the binary schemes, all the false alternatives of civilisation that we mentioned before are symbolical reworkings of that very mechanism of violence that the human animal learns from the natural struggle for existence. 'The world controlled by *mana*, and even the worlds of Indian and Greek myth, are issueless and eternally the same. All birth is paid for with death, all fortune with misfortune'.[58] Such mythical image is nothing but a mimetic and symbolic response to 'natural conditions', an unchanging order of cycles which human beings must accept *as it is*. The horror of death is not only the sublimation of the flight instinct, but also the awareness of an evil that is inherent in things: cruelty, suffering, disease. The redemption of humanity would be in the first instance its redemption *from* nature: the metamorphosis of a natural being that could empathise with the *universal suffering* in a way that other animals do not know. This does not mean that there are no instances of ethical behavior or respect for others in the animal kingdom, but they do not take the form of *universality*, which is characteristic of the concept.

Justice, spirit, freedom and all concepts belonging to the spiritualist tradition indicate therefore an otherness from nature that still *has to be realised*. This leads to a redefinition of both reason and nature. If reason would *help* rather than oppress nature, through this very act it would break the circle of crude necessity and thus be *born* as reason, thereby performing a qualitative leap (which, as we will see, is a transformation in/of nature itself). In this regard, in his *One-dimensional Man* Marcuse wrote that 'the ill-treatment of animals [is] the work of a human society whose rationality is still the irrational'.[59] It is only in dialectical relationship with nature that reason (the form that the principle of self-conservation assumes in human culture) can be determined as rational or irrational.

A free human-animal relationship becomes here the shibboleth of reason, i.e. of a rational attitude that has emancipated itself from violence and oppression, since it is only the *radical impotence* of non-human animals that could move reason to make a *step back*. Such empathic withdrawal would in fact realise the *distance* from the Other, the separation necessary to make such an Other appear and manifest itself in its otherness. It is thus from this possible relationship with the Other that the essence of humanity is both *realised* and *superseded*: it is only from a changed relationship with the animal that our otherness

---

58   Adorno and Horkheimer 1997, pp. 32–3; 2002, pp. 11–12.

59   Marcuse 2002, p. 242.

from the context of natural violence would finally *be real* and the jump from the *realm of necessity* to the *realm of freedom* would be accomplished. Such an act of solidarity would show the falsity of the spiritualist illusion while meeting its broken promises: the history of solidarity with nature would belie the history of the domination of nature, realising that Alterity that there never was. This critical awareness organically changes the *whole* constellation reason/nature and sets the dialectical overturn that allows us to speak of redemption of nature as a work *of nature itself*.

8.2.2   The Emancipation *of* Nature

In the second sense of the expression 'liberation of nature', in fact, one can speak of emancipation *of* nature itself from *animal selfhood* (which in the human animal ends up absurdly with the dream of a totalitarian control over the rest of the living world). In the very moment in which a free human order would make room for such long repressed and annihilated alterity, its qualitative leap would not be something that happens to nature, but *in* nature. Such human change would lead to a path of *cooperation* and *solidarity* between species far beyond what the selective mechanisms may have produced in the course of evolution. Nature itself would thus inaugurate, through the humility of humans, a concept of universal peace.

The image of nature as 'stepmother' is in fact the ideological image of an *alien* reality that opposes humans and threatens them. Yet, as Adorno emphasises, this image is nothing but the grim face of humanity itself, as it counteracts other living beings in the struggle for life; once the war mask is abandoned, nature too would appear to us as an order in which justice is *finally possible*. If, as we have seen, reason, even humanity, *have never been*, since they remain unrealised potentials (historical suffering is, so to speak, the only negative track and hope for such possibility), then *nature* itself awaits for its realisation and calls humanity for relationships with the Other made of care, listening and respect.

Human history is, therefore, a rope between the animal terror – the fear of a return to the undifferentiated – and the state of conciliation among different species. It is in such an order – the result of a millenary process, made of violence and domination but also of untapped possibilities – that the relationship between identity and difference could find its own equilibrium and reconciliation.

9   The Reconciliation of Nature

It is clear that Adorno, Horkheimer and Marcuse think of nature not in terms of *substance*, but *relation*. The relational essence of nature is evident in the phenomenon of *empathy* and it is based on *mimesis*. This is why our relationship with the other animals needs to be articulated at the level of *expression* and not of that of *intentionality* (i.e. as intersubjectivity, not as object-relation). Adorno outlined a cosmic-historical vision in which the dialectic of nature includes the emancipation of nature itself in his analysis of natural beauty. In his last, unfinished work, *Aesthetic Theory*, Adorno writes not only that Man, but that nature itself *does not yet exist*.

> The image of what is oldest in nature reverses dialectically into the cipher of the not-yet-existing, the possible [...] The boundary established against fetishism of nature – the pantheistic subterfuge that would amount to nothing but an affirmative mask appended to an endlessly repetitive fate – is drawn by the fact that nature, as it stirs mortally and tenderly in its beauty, does not yet exist. [...] Vis-à-vis a ruling principle, vis-à-vis a merely diffuse juxtaposition, the beauty of nature is an other; what is reconciled would resemble it.[60]

This means that nature, as we know it, embodies potentialities still waiting to be unleashed. Human liberation and liberation of nature are thus moments of the same process, a process, however, not to be intended – *à la* Rousseau – as a liberation of some pristine nature oppressed by civilisation, since – as mentioned above – civilisation is nothing more than 'nature dismembering itself, nature that is tearing apart itself.' Nature appears to us as 'memory', a 'lost dream' because it evokes in us the image of what we could achieve by listening to his suffering voice. In the first case we have a pantheistic runaway, i.e. the negation of the natural history of man as a mere mistake; in the second, we read such history as an attempt – a terrible, hallucinatory attempt – to heal the pain of the world.

Only in a *reconciled*, pacified order, i.e. in an order that has *dialectically overcome* the antithesis between nature and culture, can the human/non-human relation be articulated beyond the false choice between mere identity (biological reductionism) and absolute difference (spiritualism). 'Peace', writes Adorno, 'is the state of differentiation without domination, with the differen-

---

60   Adorno 1997d, p. 115; 1997e, p. 73.

tiated participating in each other'.[61] The 'differentiated' is what eludes both the 'principle that dominates' (the same) and the 'widespread fragmentation' (the difference): it manifests itself only when identity and difference open up and leave room to otherness in the form of mutual communication and understanding. Such a state presupposes the entire history of civilisation but at the same time it denies it by realising its promise of happiness.

If the relationship between human and non-human, between reason and nature cannot be defined in abstract, static, biological and ontological terms but only *in practice*, as the *relationship* between subjectivities, the whole bioethical question of reductionism appears to us in a different light. The man-animal relationship is in fact destined to remain a mere speculative question and we are forced to choose between false alternatives if it is treated on a purely 'scientific' level. The Frankfurt School teaches us to think such a relationship as *real*, avoiding the simple answers of both flat naturalism and metaphysical transcendence. Adorno, Horkheimer and Marcuse teach us that it is only by an *act of solidarity* that humans can decide what happens to them and their Other. In other words, it is only in *praxis* that the question of what the human being 'is' can be decided.*

---

61   Adorno 1997c, p. 746; 2005b, p. 247.
*   This chapter was previously published as: "The Dialectical Animal: Nature and Philosophy of History in Adorno, Horkheimer and Marcuse", *in Journal for Critical Animal Studies*, 10, no. 1 (2012).

PART 3

Conclusion: Beyond Nature

.·.

CHAPTER 7

Towards a Post-Neolithic Society

1   Materialism and *Technē*

A materialist overview of history and society need not rely on a static concept of nature. Differently from what happens in physics, the reduction of any social process to individual intentions and actions (methodological individualism) is a form of subjective idealism. Sociological materialism is the opposite of sociological atomism. This apparently leads us in the direction of holism and functionalism, but it is not necessarily so: as we have seen, Marx's stress on 'conflict' and 'contradictions' makes room for *agency* and political *transformation*, rather than prioritising the interest of totality. Sure, materialistic explanations of human behaviour which ignore how the *meaning* of our actions is socially constructed are not materialist *enough*. Materialism should leave such a static concept of 'nature' behind. Yet, the point is not to abandon the concept of 'nature' altogether; rather, materialism should go *beyond* 'nature' in order to grasp nature as a *relational process*. Again, though, this has nothing to do with constructivism and postmodernism either.[1] It is the concrete and historical *dialectics of animality* hitherto described, which helps us not to slip into this kind of subjectivism. Marxism offers a solid theoretical basis to understand nature in such terms, while avoiding ontological mystifications (biologism and subjectivism), and methodological bias (social atomism and holism).

Inspired by Feuerbach's materialism and Hegel's concept of a dynamic totality, Marx believed that the human essence could never be revealed by any biological or statically sociological explanation. The nature of human 'nature' is dialectical precisely because it articulates the relationships between our physical constitution and the complex web of intersubjective exchanges (what Hegel called 'objective spirit'). The whole point of an antispeciesist under-

---

1   Rather than denouncing 'binarism' as the source of all evil, celebrating the Nietzschean joys of 'post-humanism' and the dream of pure 'alterity', the theoretical perspective proposed here follows Adorno's negative dialectics: it seeks to materially abolish class and species hierarchies, rather than 'deconstruct' them (Maurizi 2018); furthermore, since 'the first access path to a nonhuman is necessarily anthropocentric and thus anthropomorphic' (Wolf 2018, p. 172), it belies both the idolatry of the Animal Other, and the sterile defamation of universalism and humanism as mere instruments of power.

standing of Marx is to unveil the role played by animals in such a historical articulation of biology and society.

Sure, Darwinism can help us in overcoming the dualism of the Christian-Platonic tradition: but not through an *animalisation of humanity*. This is the limit of Singer's attempt to reform the Left in accordance with evolutionary theory.[2] It is important to remember the subterranean ideological conflict which has crossed the field of biology in recent decades. From one side, Neo-Darwinism attempted to reduce both human and animal behaviour to DNA-driven mechanisms, denying or strongly reducing the importance of free agency and self-determination. From the other side, ethology and environmental sciences have challenged the old mechanistic view of nature, discovering how rich and complex animal behaviour can be.[3] While the first model turns both animals and humans into machines, whose desires are nothing but epiphenomena of hidden, unconscious and mechanical causes, the second model shortens the distance between animals and humans, underscoring the psychological and social negotiations which produce meaning in the animal world. Both models negate the spiritualistic divide between humanity and nature. Their political implications, though, are not the same. It is no wonder that left-oriented biologists like Lewontin, Gould and Rose have contested the ideological dangers of Neo-Darwinism.[4] Singer quotes Lewontin's objections to Neo-Darwinism and sociobiology but dismisses them as a mere example of 'historical materialism'.[5]

---

2   Singer 1999.
3   In turn, this has changed the very way we should understand ethological interactions with animals: see Acampora 2006, p. 2010.
4   Lewontin 1996; 2000; Gould and Lewontin 2010; Rose 2010.
5   Singer 1999, p. 30. The problem with Singer's 'universals' is not only that they tend to justify sexism, xeonophobia and social hierarchies (1999, pp. 36–7). This is surely a troubling *practical* consequence of his insistence on biological 'constants' of human behaviour. Even if Singer avoids 'naturalistic fallacies', in fact, the idea that such phenomena are *natural* means that their interpretation in sociological and historical terms should be considered derivative, superficial and not pertinent in the last instance. Yet, as we have already underlined, even if it was possible to formulate a biological 'scheme' behind our actions, this would not imply that our social *interactions* could be derived from such a scheme (and, consequently, neither the *social* meaning of that kind of individual behaviour). The real, *theoretical* problem, thus, is that Singer's 'universals' are simply generalisations from empirical history. Singer is convinced that such universals might be proven by biological research and become 'facts' that the Left should take into account. But what often happens is that this kind of research formulates its concepts in such an abstract way that the supposed biological explanation of human behaviour becomes meaningless from a sociological point of view. It is the very essence of *social* facts that makes them utterly different from facts that can be described in purely biological terms. Not surprisingly, though, Singer ends up with a celebration of the virtues of the free

Understanding materialism as a form of coexistence between species means rethinking our relation to nature. At the same time, it is only by changing our practical attitude towards nature that such a cultural shift can actually take place. In other words, it is only by *fulfilling* the ideological hopes of spiritual-istic culture that materialism can turn its back on that history of never-ending oppression. This raises the problem of *technology*, a problem whose inner dia-lectic gets obfuscated by both reductionist physicalism and holistic and anim-istic fantasies. As we have seen, *Dialectic of Enlightenment* denounces the secret alliance between science and magic, vulgar materialism and spiritualism. Both take part in oppression, both can be refuted only by a practical choice in favour of liberation. The problem of technique will not be answered either by the cynical reduction of humans and animals to objects of manipulation, or by restoring the sentimental Soul of nature in a hopeless dream of universal love.

Animal rights activists and primitivists who argue against technological ali-enation fail to see the contradictory structure of instrumental reason.[6] Animal Liberationists are keen to understand the use of tools as a process of estrange-ment of the first hominids from nature and vegetarianism; it is what Adams calls 'implemental violence':

> Hunting is the second stage of meat eating. When meat is obtained through killing animals who are not domesticated, there is little reliance on feminised protein. With the second stage, implemental violence is introduced, as well as the selection of some members of a community to be hunters. Distance from the animal is achieved through the imple-ments used to kill the animal as well as from the division of a culture into hunters and nonhunters.[7]

Primitivism assumes the hunter-gatherer way of life as the only natural form of technology: 'As the Paleolithic Age gave way to the Neolithic arrival of agri-culture and civilisation-production, private property, written language, gov-ernment and religion-culture could be seen more fully as spiritual decline via division of labour, though global specialisation and a mechanistic technology

---

market and a neo-Darwinian justification for Clintonism and Blairism as politics which give a Left-wing twist to the natural, innate principle: 'Never ask a person to act against his own self-interest'. According to Singer, 'the current economic fashion for privatising enterprises and introducing competition into areas that were previously state monopolies is consonant with this way of thinking' (1999, p. 41).

6   For a different but sympathetic treatment of *technē* see Benvegnù (2018, p. 111 ff.).

7   Adams 2010, p. 114.

did not prevail until the late Iron Age'.[8] Whereas the first thesis rejects hunting and meat consumption, the second abhors agriculture and vegetarianism: both argue from the point of view of a fixed, natural relation between humans and technology. It should be clear now that no such static/harmonic relation exists. Technology is intertwined with social and historical progress; it expresses, so to speak, the law of transformation of social energy. Technology knows no *intention* and no favourite *victims*: it can both oppress and liberate humans and animals. As Adorno and Horkheimer clearly saw, it is the very *indifference* of technology to its objects which turns it into an instrument of domination.

Thus, a proper treatment of technology should deal with both class struggle *and* the human-animal contradiction. From this perspective, the idea that technology is but a neutral method, something that simply improves the conditions of humanity, is doubly false. If we fail to articulate the problem of technology in one of its sides, it is easy to consider human *technē* as the main 'cause' or even the 'essence' of oppression, and consequently slip into reactionary or technophobic positions.

On the one hand, the interests defended and expanded by technology are those of the ruling classes, there are no *general* interests of humanity behind the historical development of technology; any other neutral account of the history of technology would be affected by teleology: it is only *a posteriori*, as a result of human struggles, that the underclass and the exploited can make sense of such development, turning it into a *universal* process of self-liberation.

On the other, the very needs that have been historically satisfied by such development are distorted by the spiritualistic dualism of human and nature. The shape of those needs is in itself contradictory. Even the idea of living longer, eating more, being healthy etc. has no fixed, objective measure in nature. The question of 'how' one lives is essential to determine the content of those needs and their satisfaction. This question includes the social and natural relations in their historical and dialectical development.

The first pole of this technological contradiction leads us to understand the global process of civilisation in terms of universal history. The second will lead us to question the reified way in which we understand our needs and their relation to the non-human world.

---

8   Zerzan 1988, p. 65.

2   Universal History as a Catastrophe

The contrast between advocates and denigrators of progress can now find a solution that transcends the original opposition. This is possible because we have seen the pivotal role played by the animal question in the context of human historicity. The field of theoretical positions now becomes clearer. For critics of progress, the idea of a radical *discontinuity* between nature and history is central; in the anarcho-primitivist construction of Zerzan, this leap is identifiable in the transition from hunter-gatherer society to agriculture and sedentarism. History can be fully explained, starting from a single event – the birth of sedentary societies and the domination of nature – and the task of revolutionary action would be to delete this event and restore a lost equilibrium. Restoring nature means deleting history.

In metaphysical-bourgeois evolutionism, on the contrary, there is absolute *continuity* between nature and history. This continuity can be understood in the sense of vulgar materialism (history is a mere continuation of natural evolution, spiritual facts must be traced back to blind laws of nature[9]), or spiritualism (evolution is the preparation of history as the history of *Geist*, whose final goal is the self-recognition of a spiritual, universal Mind[10]). Historical action here is never revolutionary, it knows no ruptures, but always moves within the framework of given (natural or spiritual) laws.

In the Marxist tradition – and especially in the Frankfurt School – *continuity and discontinuity are interrelated*. There is continuity between history and nature (humans are animals) but history inaugurates structures that are peculiar to humankind, structures which are, in other words, human creations. Thus, we have a leap outside the natural dimension (humans are no longer animals), but a leap which, however, cannot really be accomplished, until humans come to *dominate* their own creation. This is also a justification of revolutionary action, whose goal is to ensure that such a leap becomes fully conscious. To what extent, in fact, can humans recognise themselves in such creations? As long as the social antagonism and the mere continuation of the natural struggle dominate the historical horizon, it is not possible to say that the human being is the subject of history and that such creations are truly human. They are still and will always be the result of contradictory and blind forces.

Bourgeois ideologists consider capitalism the supreme stage of evolution, the final, universal goal of human hopes. In *A Contribution to the Critique*

---

9   Wilson 1975; Wilson 1978.
10   De Chardin 1959.

of Political Economy Marx writes: 'universal history [*Weltgeschichte*] has not always existed; history as a universal history is a result'.[11] This sentence only apparently approves the self-evaluation of bourgeois society. For Marx, this meant that universal history was *becoming real* thanks to the unifying power of capitalism: little by little the whole of humanity will be subjected to its course. Universal history therefore has not been real since the beginning (when there were different, parallel, irreducible histories, so to say), but rather becomes real as a result of the historical action of human beings. Marx was obviously convinced that communism, not capitalism, would have the right to present itself as heir and executor of bourgeois universal history.[12] Communism is the solution to the riddle of history.

One hundred years later, in the middle of the Cold War and with the world threatened by a nuclear apocalypse, Adorno reflected on the significance of universal history. 'The concept of universal history [...] became all the more problematical, the closer the unified world came to being a total process'.[13] The unified world of industrial and post-industrial societies is characterised by absolute control, repression, self-destructive drives; it is difficult to conceive of it as a 'triumph of reason'. Bourgeois universal history, which emphasises a substantial continuity between history and nature, has no means to interpret such outcome, if not by seeing the germ of all evil in human nature; as we have seen, a specific feature of Marxism is to see in the transition from nature to history a leap which, however, is neither a mere degradation (as in anarcho-primitivism) nor a celebration of the human being as a sovereign bearer of a divine spirit. 'Discontinuity and universal history must be conceived together'.[14] However, this is possible only if we do not forget the radical and violent process that has made universal history possible: domination over nature. Only if this fact is not forgotten does universal history make sense. As a consequence, though, the concept of universal history becomes dialectical:

> Universal history must be construed and denied. After the catastrophes that have happened, and in view of catastrophes to come, it would be cynical to say that a plan for a better world is manifested in history and unifies it. Not to be denied for that reason, however, is the unity that cements the discontinuous, chaotically splintered moments and phases

---

11   Marx 1971, p. 636.
12   Marx and Engels 1969, pp. 34 ff.
13   Adorno 1997b, p. 313; 2007, p. 319.
14   Adorno 1997b, p. 324; 2007, p. 319.

of history – the unity of the control of nature, progressing to rule over men, and finally to that over men's inner nature.[15]

If the bourgeois ideologist fails to see that the destructiveness of capitalism is a product of class domination, speciesist Marxism cannot see that the destruct-iveness of civilisation is the product of domination over nature. Capitalism can be disclosed as a universal catastrophe only if we criticise the blind necessity that keeps humans and animals under the same yoke, in a complex and strati-fied power structure that envelops and disfigures them both.

The concept of *catastrophe* must here be understood in a *qualitative* and *retrospective* sense. It does not indicate a prognosis of a future collapse, but the ability to perceive a catastrophe which has already happened. History is not rational, but it can be understood *because of its irrationality*: its unity, its laws of development are those of domination. Under current circumstances, unity *is* contradiction, the *meaning* of history its *madness*. The catastrophe at the beginning of history is the self-negation of human animality which reduces our identity to a totalitarian, paranoid mechanism of exclusion of the Other. Universal history is thus the totality of not-freedom, the kingdom of neces-sity that we need to leave behind if we want to experience real freedom, if we want history to really begin. The history of the class struggle is the history of the struggle for freedom versus the blind necessity of natural processes. If we see human slavery as a necessary historical stage for the liberation of human beings, animal slavery could be understood in a similar way. But to do this, the animal should also be considered a *beneficiary* of human society, and not just its victim. Animal domestication could be considered part of human social pro-gress only if it is seen as a process through which humans manage to *articulate their relationship with animality*: both their own repressed animality and the animality of other living beings. By freeing themselves from the chain of dom-ination, humans should also free the other animals. These two acts of eman-cipation would be moments of the same dialectical process. As we have seen, in fact, changing our attitude towards animals would paradoxically suppress the consequences of anthropocentrism, while at the same time, retroactively, confirming its premises. Human exceptionalism would only be true if we tried to prove it wrong. The paradox lies in the *performative* nature of our relation-ship to animals and the fact that we usually think of history (and philosophy of history) in a *linear* way: 'what is unthinkable within this horizon of linear historical evolution is the notion of a choice/act which retroactively opens up

15   Adorno 1997b, p. 324; 2007, p. 320.

its own possibility: the idea that the emergence of something radically New retroactively changes the past'.[16] The universal catastrophe of history can be seen only from the point of view of the animal, as Best correctly writes.[17] It is, though, a more difficult task than Best believes. Because once we recognise the dialectical nature of the human/animal relation, it is impossible to find this point of view 'outside'. The look of the dying animal is always, at the same time, a look that concerns *me*, where I am *involved* as an *animal*. Let us recall Rosa Luxemburg and the buffalo: in their tears there is a moment of epiphany, 'the whole glorious war passed in front of my eyes'. It is from this radical point of view, in which the abolition of human and animal exploitation is one and the same, that we not only change history as we know it (i.e. the global meaning of history as class and species oppression), but at the same time produce new historical possibilities. This point of view, though, is not a comfortable spot from which we should contemplate a world in ruins. As usual: the point is not to 'interpret the world in various ways'. The point is to change it.

3   The Universal Human Being and the Enlarged Animal Society

We have already seen that the abolition of animal exploitation does not represent a problem for Marxist theory. The idea of animal liberation is usually opposed by leftists because it seems at odds with the current form of existence and reproduction of human society. As if this could not change. As if animal slavery were a natural necessity that cannot be overthrown. The opposition to the idea of animal liberation usually takes the form of an immediate response: starting from the effect that the abolition of animal exploitation would have on our current habits and lifestyles, it is judged undesirable or impossible. In this way, however, we commit the individualistic fallacy that is the trademark of all bourgeois thought. Although it may sound plausible to our ears, in fact, an argument that moves from the current preferences of human beings to define the future needs of humanity is irrelevant from a strictly Marxist point of view. It is easy to show how the various uses of animals that define our current lifestyle are historically determined and, consequently, accidental and transitory. Although animal killing can be somehow defined as a 'universal' characteristic of the human species, no human being conducts a lifestyle based on the exploitation of *animals in general*. Humans have never had rela-

---

16   Zizek 2008, p. 459.
17   Best 2014.

tions with animals in general: until now. A Spectre is in fact haunting globalised, capitalistic Humanity: The Spectre of Animality. And, as it should be clear now, it is the Spectre *of our own Animality*. The relationship of symbiosis, exploitation and domination between humans and animals has always been specific, socially, geographically and historically determined. Different practices and species have been hunted and tamed in the Americas, Europe or Asia over millennia; different uses, different needs and ways of satisfying them have been elaborated. One cannot speak, if not abstractly, of an intrinsic human need to exploit *the* animal. The human-animal contradiction is, in fact, a product of history that reaches its apex with capitalism. It is precisely here that the relationship of exploitation of nature loses any environmental specificity and becomes *universal*. It is precisely in capitalism that humans exploit *the* animal: modes of production get standardised and, with them, the self-representations, habits, and food specificities of human cultures.

Faced with this process of homogenisation, Marxism has two possibilities: to accept the current outcomes of this globalised culture or to reject it. In the moment in which it seeks to revolutionise the structure of global capitalism, subverting its productive relationships, Marxism must also ask itself the question: what will be of the actual needs? Since they are part and parcel of the blind exploitation of humans and nature, since they are connected to human oppression and ecological disaster, they cannot be accepted as such. Nor is it possible to go back to times when cultures, habits and customs were not globalised, to act as if global capitalism had never happened. Humanity has lost its specific relationship with the environment, has definitively broken the umbilical cord that bound it to determinate ecosystems. Once it has inherited from capitalism the frontal opposition between humanity and animality in this abstract and violent form, Marxism must choose whether to continue on the path of self-estrangement from nature (which has been hitherto a landmark of class societies) or to put an end to it. It is our planetary tyranny, with its reduction of life to disqualified matter, that produces 'the Animal' as a monstrous 'general singular'.[18] Perhaps, 'the Animal' is actually an inverted image of the Human in search for itself.[19] An image of nature searching for itself. Thus, by becoming 'spectral', animal existence unmasks civilisation as a sort of 'mirror phase' of humanity.[20] In the expulsion of the animal outside and in the enslavement of natural life, the human being is producing its own practical self-definition as

---

18   Derrida 2008.
19   Žižek 2013.
20   Timofeeva 2018.

universal animal.[21] The animal that we face as an abstract and universal thing is a secret image of ourselves.[22]

The overcoming of our estrangement from nature strongly pushes in the direction of a self-recognition as universal, dialectical animals. The communist society, solving the human/nature contradiction, leaving every form of dualism and spiritualism behind, could thus only be conceived as an *enlarged animal society*. The reintroduction of the animal in Marxist social theory, from which it was idealistically expelled, means the possibility of thinking animals as effective members of human society, even if the consequences of such inclusion are impossible to fully understand in the present.

4   *Rien faire comme une bête*

What about the needs of current society? How should we deal with our traditional 'need' to exploit animals? If needs must be historicised, how should they be judged? As we have seen, human needs emerge from history only in a mutilated and ideological form. There is always something *inhuman* and *oppressive* in them. Not only are these needs expression of our repressed animal nature, but we also know that such repression has always been a direct function of class domination. Individual needs are always social needs: this was true in Neolithic societies and will also be true in a communist one. In loosening this knot, 'the theory of need is faced with considerable difficulties'.[23] As soon as the social character of need is recognised, we accept 'the satisfaction of needs in their most immediate and concrete form' and, in this sense, 'we cannot lay claim *a priori* to any distinction between good and bad, genuine and created, right [*richtig*] and wrong [*falsch*] needs. However, it must also recognise that existing needs are themselves, in their present form, produced by class society. No neat distinction can be made between a need proper to humanity and one that would be a consequence of repression'.[24] It is this impossibility that determines

---

21   Marx 1968, pp. 516–17; Pannekoek 1953, p. 16.
22   It is only at *this point*, having developed the full dialectics of the human/animal relation, that I can agree with Best's insight: 'one is tempted to say, paraphrasing Marx, that the animal standpoint, not class analysis and communism, is "the solution to the riddle of history". The animal standpoint casts a brilliant light on problems that one cannot even see or identify through the opaque lens of humanism or its theoretical offshoots' (Best 2014, p. 18).
23   Adorno 2017, p. 103.
24   Adorno 2017, p. 103.

the fallacy of Animal Rights theories that abstract from the concrete history of humanity. Being the result of an historical praxis, needs can only be modified by action.

In the *Grundrisse*, Marx's analysis of the pre-capitalist modes of production ends with the description of bourgeois society as a form of organisation which serves as a prelude to the flourishing of human potentiality in communism.

> Thus the ancient conception, in which man always appears (in however narrowly national, religious, or political a definition) as the aim of production, seems very much more exalted than the modern world, in which production is the aim of man and wealth the aim of production. In fact, however, when the narrow bourgeois form has been peeled away, what is wealth, if not the universality of needs, capacities, enjoyments, productive powers etc., of individuals, produced in universal exchange? What, if not the full development of human control over the forces of nature – those of his own nature as well as those of so-called 'nature'? What, if not the absolute elaboration of his creative dispositions, without any preconditions other than antecedent historical evolution which make the totality of this evolution – i.e., the evolution of all human powers as such, unmeasured by any *previously established* yardstick – an end in itself? What is this, if not a situation where man does not reproduce in any determined form, but produces his totality? Where he does not seek to remain something formed by the past, but is in the absolute movement of becoming? In bourgeois political economy – and in the epoch of production to which it corresponds – this complete elaboration of what lies within man, appears as the total alienation, and the destruction of all fixed, one-sided purposes as the sacrifice of the end in itself to a wholly external compulsion. Hence in one way the childlike world of the ancients appears to be superior; and this is so, insofar as we seek for closed shape, form and established limitation. The ancients provide a narrow satisfaction, whereas the modern world leaves us unsatisfied, or, where it appears to be satisfied, with itself, is *vulgar* and *mean* [*gemein*].[25]

Yet, as we have seen, what characterises communism as a form of social fulfilment of needs has nothing to do with the *content* of production, but rather its *form*. The capitalist disruption of traditions, its struggle against pre-modern ways of fulfilling needs anticipates communism: by dissolving the limits of pro-

---

25   Marx 1983.

duction, capitalism paves the way to a universal state of things where the self-organisation of humanity is described by Marx in terms of 'absolute becoming'. Such a state of things, i.e. communism, is therefore not a 'state', but the continuous reassessing of social possibilities in an ongoing redefinition of relationships among humans and between humans and nature. Production, thus, must not be judged according to its specific, historical content ('what' we produce): social progress means the possibility to change life according to human needs, in a democratic, horizontal way ('how' we produce). Of course, overcoming the undialectical, spiritualistic dualism of human and non-human nature implies that the liberation of human needs cannot but be the liberation of those needs from the reactionary consequences of such dualism.

Now, if 'Animism denotes a view where the world is in constant flux',[26] a process of perpetual change where no fixed boundary exists between things, persons and landscape, such description could match the Marxian hypothesis of realised communism as absolute becoming. Communism as the immanent abolition of class society was intended by Marx and Engels as a way to get out of what they called 'prehistory', i.e. the history of class struggle or civilisation. Of course, Marx and Engels wanted prehistory to end, because they believed that history could *begin*, because they believed that necessity could make room for freedom, that a more rational relation between individuals, community, and nature was possible. If civilisation is the negation of the primordial state of mystical confusion and dependence from nature, communism is the *negation of negation*: the flux which characterised Palaeolithic animism (with its stress on horizontal relations, sharing, respect for ecosystems) would be restored, enriched by the potentiality of civilisation, by its concrete universalism, i.e. its ability to produce both *difference and unity*. The dialectic of civilisation has, thus, produced a decisive shift from local unification to universal differentiation. Contrary to animism, reciprocal respect between humans and nature would not be caused by a fundamental *indistinctness* between us and the other species: it would flourish from our ability to perceive and appreciate *difference*.

The so-called raising of the level of life between the Palaeolithic and the Neolithic has implied, as we have seen, a quantitative and qualitative intensification of the working processes.[27] Division of labour, class antagonism, sexual repression and religious alienation are only the subjective counterparts of human and animal exploitation. The dialectical overcoming of class society cannot take place leaving this relationship of domination unaltered: it cannot

---

26   Fuglestvedt 2014.

27   Godelier 1977.

remove the contradiction in the subject (the class struggle, social alienation), without removing it from the object (the struggle between humans and animals, natural alienation). As the end of class society does not restore 'primitive communism', so the end of animal oppression does not restore some primitive conditions of existence: it rather admits the possibility of *a post-Neolithic society*.

It would be a leap beyond the horizon of totalitarian functionalisation, towards a society in which the system of needs is not indifferent to the suffering of nature. Such a system would cultivate mimetic compassion towards animals and, at the same time, would finally give voice to human animality in all those forms that are currently censored because considered inferior (the body), dangerous (the unconscious and sexuality) or useless (art). In a society freed from the need: 'to be useless [*unnütz*] will then no longer be shameful'.[28] The useless, the non-functional, what is unbearable for the current scheme of domination and control, is a reminder of the primitive anguish, of the animal terror. The fixation on 'increased production is itself a piece of that bourgeois outlook which permits development in only one direction because, integrated into a totality, dominated by quantification, it is hostile to qualitative difference'.[29] Closed in the circle of total domination, theory can barely imagine what a different world would look like.

> If we imagine emancipated society as emancipation from precisely such totality, then vanishing-lines come into view that have little in common with increased production and its human reflections. [... A] society rid of its fetters might arrive at the thought that even the forces of production are not the deepest substratum of man, but represent his historical form adapted to the production of commodities. Perhaps the true society will grow tired of development and, out of freedom, leave possibilities unused, instead of storming under a confused compulsion to the conquest of strange stars. A mankind which no longer knows want will begin to have an inkling of the delusory, futile nature of all the arrangements hitherto made in order to escape want, which used wealth to reproduce want on a larger scale. Enjoyment itself would be affected, just as its present framework is inseparable from operating, planning, having one's way, subjugating. *Rien faire comme une bête*.[30]

---

28   Adorno 1997 f., p. 396; 2013, p. 104; see also Marcuse 1998, pp. 172 ff.
29   Adorno 1997a, p. 176; 2005a, p. 156.
30   Adorno 1997a, pp. 176–7; 2005a, pp. 156–7. Translation modified.

The idea of a *liberation of labour* which is also, in the perspective outlined here by Adorno, a *liberation from labour*, inversely implies the idea that the liberation from need in a communist society is, to a large extent, a liberation of needs. If the end of class society means the abolition of the appropriation of labour, it also means the possibility of a redefinition of needs in a totally new, open, creative sense.[31]

It is impossible to say how this redefinition would transform needs once animals have become subjects of a true political debate. Although it is impossible to imagine what will be of animals in a post-capitalist society, it is certain that all the uses in which the animal is reduced to a mere appendage of human need (from food to scientific experimentation, passing through all the forms of its commodification) would be criticised. It is hard to believe that human needs will completely change, while organised animal extermination will not. Human sensibility, reshaped in terms of a different perception of the self, could easily imagine forms of co-existence that are different from those inherited from a millennial system of exclusion and negation of the other.

---

31   Marcuse 1978, pp. 236–7.

CHAPTER 8

The Aporetic Nature of the Theory/Praxis Opposition

The analysis conducted so far has attempted to define the meaning of the reason/nature constellation in the thought of Marx, Engels, Adorno, Horkheimer and Marcuse. I consider these last three authors representatives of a precise stage in the history of the Institute for Social Research: essentially, the three decades following the publication of *Dialectic of Enlightenment*, which roughly correspond to the consolidation of the label 'Frankfurt School' in the German sociological debate of those years. The problematic relation between the 'Frankfurt School' and 'Orthodox Marxism' is well known: Adorno and Horkheimer, in particular, were accused by students in 1968 of having totally abandoned the perspective of revolutionary praxis. I shall now try to briefly address some unresolved issues from both the theoretical and the practical point of view. These are aspects which, as we have seen, cannot be rigidly separated, although for the sake of clarity I will try to avoid overlapping them. First, we will see what problems arise from the idea of a dialectical conception of nature (and reason), especially regarding our relationship with other animals and the way in which humankind must understand animal liberation. Secondly, we shall refer to the notion of praxis as understood by the Frankfurt School, outlining the problems it poses in itself and to the animal liberation movement.

As we have seen, according to Adorno, Horkheimer and Marcuse, it is only by fighting against the domination of (external and internal) nature and class oppression that the permanent threat to civilisation might find an end. If any of these aspects is not put into question, then the entire mechanism of *Herrschaft* is destined to perpetuate itself. It is undeniable that the understanding of nature implied in such theory (particularly in Adorno's most subtle passages) is rather difficult. Many interpreters have therefore considered it obscure, if not entirely contradictory. First of all, the idea that reason and nature are poles of a dialectical relation means that it is not possible to consider reason as a purely exterior power that violates nature. Contrary to a common cliché, far from supporting an anti-civilisation impulse, the Franfkurt School's critique of Enlightenment is an attempt to accomplish the traditional stances of civilisation itself. According to Adorno, Horkheimer and Marcuse, even in a social order where the exploitation of human and non-human nature has come to an end, it will not be possible to abolish technique altogether and the repression of instincts, since this would mean to deny the positive achievements of civilisation (or, at least, its unexpressed potential for freedom, creativity and satisfaction). It seems then impossible for these authors to separate clearly the good from evil in the history of civilisation. Even thinkers who appreciated the global vision of *Dialectic of Enlightenment* – like Murray Bookchin, for instance[1] – had criticised such a position. According to them, only if we distinguish the destructive side of reason from the constructive one is it possible to logically articulate a critical theory of domination.[2]

It must be recognised that such a risk in reading the works of the Frankfurt School is real. When, for example, Horkheimer writes 'reification is a process that can be traced back to the beginnings of organised society and the use of tools',[3] it is tempting to conclude that there is no way out of the disease that afflicts reason. However, though it may sound overly abstract and speculative, I think that the path outlined by Adorno, Horkheimer and Marcuse goes in another, more intriguing direction.

Firstly, as we have already seen, these authors assume that domination did not *happen* at some point in history, nor was it something that happened *to reason*. The urge to manipulate and control the other, on the contrary, dwells within the deeper layers of reason itself.

> From the time when reason became the instrument for domination of human and extra-human nature by man – that is to say, from its very beginnings – it has been frustrated in its own intention of discovering the truth. This is due to the very fact that it made nature a mere object, and that it failed to discover the trace of itself in such objectivisation, in the concepts of matter and things not less than in those of gods and spirit. One might say that the collective madness that rages today, from the concentration camps to the seemingly most harmless mass-culture reactions, was already present in germ in primitive objectivisation, in the first man's calculating contemplation of the world as a prey. Paranoia, the madness that builds logically constructed theories of persecution, is not merely a parody of reason, but is somehow present in any form of reason that consists in the mere pursuit of aims.[4]

---

1 Bookchin 1982, p. 283.
2 Marcuse was probably more inclined to follow such a line of reasoning, particularly in *Eros and Civilisation*, a work that was not welcomed by Adorno and Horkheimer.
3 Horkheimer 2005, p. 28.
4 Horkheimer 2005, p. 119.

This seems to be at odds with the idea of a mimetic world that does not oppress nature or consider itself superior to it. Yet, as *Dialectic of Enlightenment* suggests, magic had a manipulative side too, and it was also an attempt to control and, in some way, dominate the external world. The difference is the way it did so and the limited effects such an urge to control had on internal and external nature. Thus, magic did not produce the split between the human and the non-human, although it was the beginning of the historical process that led to it. It did not produce such a split because magic works through the *law of similarity*: as Marcel Mauss put it, the principle of magic is: 'one is all, all is one', 'nature triumphs over nature'.[5] Magic implies the idea of an invisible force, hidden behind the nature we see: it is this force that explains natural phenomena and makes it possible for the magician to work with them. It is the beginning of the spiritual illusion, but it was also the beginning of an *explanation* of nature, since magic was religion, art and science at the same time. So, contrary to the idea expressed by Lévy-Bruhl, according to which the 'savages' were unable to think logically, instrumental reason is part of the mimetic culture, although here it does not have the preeminence it gains in later civilisation.

If magic did not create the split between our self-consciousness and the rest of the natural world, it was anyway the first *expression* of a split that had already taken place. Such a split seems to be a characteristic of culture as such, the principal cause of all ambiguities that anthropologists observe in rites and myths. It is as if no symbolic system could do without *signalling its alterity from the rest of nature*. It is in fact the crucial task of rituals to annul the difference between culture and nature while, with the same gesture, reproducing it over and over. The ambiguity of magic systems does not end with the dawn of spiritualistic cultures. On the contrary, its paradoxical traits grow exponentially. Yet, according to Adorno, Horkheimer and Marcuse, while taking human culture's ambiguity towards nature to the extreme, the process of civilisation is also a frightening attempt to solve it.

It is true that, differently from the mimetic world, civilisation produces a *negative image* of what it oppresses (nature, the lower classes, the body) and this image serves to justify the rule of a disincarnated *logos*. Reason must understand nature as its opposite, projecting negative, destructive qualities on it, in order to enthrone itself. As a matter of fact, though, the mechanism of domination produces exactly the violence and chaos that it pretends to deny: nothing is more destructive of civilisation as these fantasises of being the opposite of nature. But, as we have seen, civilisation is not just a lie. Its values and goals

---

5   Mauss 2001, p. 92.

are not false in themselves, although they become untrue as soon as we use them to exploit nature or we believe that only by oppressing nature can they be achieved. The point is not to deny justice, equality and freedom, but to realise them. So, civilisation is nature and human culture – with all its ambiguous and contradictory tensions – is the specifically human way of relating to oneself and the Other. The question is: what would it mean for civilisation if a change in its egoistic attitude towards the rest of the living were to take place? If we stopped oppressing the non-human world, if we gave up our stereotypes of nature being a monstrous otherness, we would fully realise the ideals of civilisation while rejecting their basic assumption, namely, that they exist to counteract the violence of nature. Their lies would become truth. This is because the violence we experience in nature and that we use to justify our domination is also real. In a sense, civilisation has exponentially multiplied all the horrors and wonders of nature. From one side, it does nothing but perpetuate violence, oppression and death as can be found in all the living world; from the other side, its universal ideas of justice, liberty and care (foreshadowed by the religious idea of a peaceful life after death) are a clear protest against them. I believe this is the point where the Frankfurt School meets the demands of the animal liberation movement, providing an interesting philosophy of history that can explain the origin and the goal of the fight against speciesism.

It is probably no accident that the antispeciesist movement, carrying attitudes of empathy toward *all* suffering life, took its first steps in the wake of the Western tradition.[6] It is true that feelings of benevolence towards other suffering species can be found amongst other animals and in so-called 'primitive' cultures. In any case, non-human nature and 'primitive' human societies are anchored at a local level: this means that their violence cannot be compared with the devastating violence perpetuated by Western civilisation; at the same time (and for the same reason), by overcoming such localism, civilisation pro-

---

6   It is true that Buddhism and Jainism could, within certain limits, be regarded as ancient philosophies that anticipate antispeciesism in their professed respect for all beings. At the same time, antispeciesism emerges as a completion of Western universalism and a specific tradition of affirmation of rights; in a word, it is essentially a secular and immanent theory (though, of course, people can always personally be antispeciesists and embrace a particular religion). In addition to this, one could emphasise how the non-violence expressed by those religions arose from a highly developed and hierarchical civilisation and – as suggested by Marvin Harris – it was probably the product of a reaction against a violent and unjust social order (Harris 1998, p. 47 ff.). Thus, the birth of Buddhism and Jainism might show interesting historical analogies with the present idea of antispeciesism being a dialectical overturn of Western civilisation.

duces the idea and practice of a global and interspecies solidarity.[7] Just because non-human nature and 'primitive' human societies experience empathy and violence on a minor scale, they cannot conceive of a universal non-violent way of life like contemporary antispeciesism does.

The question of human exceptionalism, too, needs to be reconsidered in a new light. According to a sound antispeciesist critique, an ethical problem arises not when one identifies some psychological or social trait that is specifically human, but when such exceptionality becomes the pretext of domination, excluding from ethical consideration all those beings that do not possess such characteristics. But what would happen if this exception consisted in care for universal suffering? When Horkheimer writes that the very aim of civilisation is not the repression of nature but its conciliation and that to dominate non-human nature is a false and tragic attempt to transcend it,[8] his vision introduces us to the possibility of transcending nature without negating or disqualifying it. Though antispeciesism was yet to come, I think the animal liberation movement is the closest thing to the social and natural utopia envisioned by the Frankfurt School. In fact, it could be considered a way to transcend nature in the very moment we discover ourselves to be totally part of it. To *transcend* it, because we face *all* its violence, decay and death and still do not accept it as the last word, but rather we learn to listen to the voice of those who suffer, regardless of their species. But this will never be possible unless we admit that we are *part of it*. To put it simply, while mimetic cultures think of themselves as part of nature without being able to articulate their transcendence from it, and spiritualistic societies push such transcendence too far, forgetting to be part of nature, an antispeciesist culture could realise the synthesis between the two.[9]

---

7 In a sense, the privilege of 'universality' traditionally accorded to Western civilisation is real, although it does not prove its 'superiority' nor that it carries intrinsic philosophical qualities not to be found in other cultures. It simply means that its power growth globalises its horizon (along with that of all those cultures obliged to take part in its political and economic expansion), making it possible to face other cultures and nature itself as global phenomena.

8 Horkheimer 2004, p. 64.

9 Does this mean that humanity should force the lion to sleep with the lamb? With this objection we face a possible charge of anthropocentrism. Humanity would end up imposing its ethical rule on the rest of the living, a task that is both totalitarian (it would limit the freedom of, say, the lion to eat the lamb) and factually impossible. We would project on nature our idyllic image of it, thus falling back into anthropocentrism. I think this last objection is superseded by the dialectical argument we have developed before. By learning from the struggle for life to pull back from such struggle, to choose to listen to the suffering rather than pursuing self-preservation at any cost, humanity would act as an internal force of nature. Humanity *is* part of nature, so everything that happens in its conscience is itself part of natural history, an inner development of it. If ethical concern is part of nature, then the idea

Finally, some brief remarks on the question of praxis. Since the animal liberation movement was still at a primordial stage of development, it is clear that Adorno, Horkheimer and Marcuse never got the chance to seriously engage with its theory and action. Although they perceived and denounced the horror of slaughterhouses, they also criticised vegetarianism for being sectarian[10] and 'pre-mature'.[11] Thus, it is not what they wrote about the animal advocacy of their time that is interesting today for us, so much as the implications of their theories. Throughout Chapter 6, I have constantly tried to extend the range of their thoughts and see if and how they could support the Animal Liberation perspective.

It must be noted that what the Frankfurt School understand with the word 'praxis' is something more general than what is commonly accepted by contemporary political groups (including the Animal Liberation movement). Although the question of political commitment has been interpreted differently by Adorno, Horkheimer and Marcuse, they agreed on one point: namely that praxis, i.e. the transformation of social reality, should take account of the domination of nature. No transformative praxis could ever really change the world if it does not also put an end to the exploitation of nature. The importance given to praxis by Critical Theory, however, did not mean that any form of activism aimed at the transformation of reality should be accepted as such. Since the problem that needs to be addressed in the context of domination is the paranoid need to manipulate and control (i.e. the characteristics of instrumental reason), if political action does not contradict this logic, its results will most likely perpetuate it. This happens, for example, when political activity

of a universal solidarity is nothing but a coherent evolution of it. If, on the contrary, ethical concern is *not* a natural phenomenon (since being part of nature means to accept violence, decay and death), then it should be explained how such an idea came into existence in the human mind in the first place (and why other animals can show empathy for members of other species). Secondly, even if the idea of feeding the lion with synthetic proteins would probably be acceptable to both the lamb and the lion, this is not necessarily the conclusion that must be drawn from what I have said. Since my intention here was only to outline the overall vision of the dialectic of civilisation, I can be content to define the regulative ideal (in the Kantian sense) that follows from it and check if such an idea is consistent with the antispeciesist perspective. But it is clear that the idea of a universal solidarity can find more moderate applications, in addition to attempts to impose our own ethics on all living creatures. And since a dialectical theory of civilisation does not dismiss technique as 'evil', it is possible to imagine scientific developments that could make it easier for humanity to pursue such brotherhood with all other species, while saving their freedom.

10   Adorno and Hokheimer 1997, p. 272; 2002, p. 197.
11   Marcuse 1972, p. 68.

overshadows its goals and overestimates the organisational level (a problem that typically plagued traditional leftist groups). Even direct action, however, is not exempt from such risks. Although Adorno, Horkheimer and Marcuse had slightly different positions on the question of violence,[12] they all criticised the idea that liberation could be realised through violent means. They criticised the ideology of those groups that pursued action for action's sake, denouncing their impatience as a product of frustration and impotence. Adorno used the expression 'pseudo-activity' to underline how such actions could not transcend the *status quo*, but only reinforce it.[13] This does not mean, however, that *all* organisations and *all* direct actions are to be condemned as such. What Adorno, Horkheimer and Marcuse underline is that only if organisational efforts and direct actions are consistent with the idea of human and non-human liberation can they hope to trigger the epochal change they dream of. Yet, to be consistent with such an idea, as we have seen, implies that the entire structure of civilisation is put into question. How can political groups and single activists coordinate such a task with their everyday activity, amid the urgency of economic and ecological crisis, while facing the horrors of human and non-human exploitation?

Some critics attacked this position, considering it defeatist and elitist. It can be assumed that after the disappointments of the 1920s (when the Socialist revolution failed to seize power in Europe and Russia experienced the Stalinist regression), Adorno and Horkheimer gradually lost faith in the possibilities of a successful revolution. From this point of view, it is certain that the thought of Marcuse provides more footholds for revolutionary politics than that of his friends (although in *Counterrevolution and Revolt* and in his later essays on aesthetics, the differences with Adorno and Horkheimer seem to dwindle). However, I would emphasise that the apparent impossibility of conceiving of action on the part of Adorno and Horkheimer probably reflects the focal point of their theory of civilisation. A point that needs to be carefully taken into consideration.

Although, as we have seen, Critical Theory differs from traditional theory insofar as it aspires to change its object rather than taking a speculative attitude, on the other hand, it must be noted that traditional theory is by no means purely speculative. The traditional theory of knowledge (as it was developed by Greek philosophy and modern science) thinks the subject as an independent,

---

12   Adorno 1997c, pp. 759–82; 2005b, pp. 259–78; Marcuse 1966, pp. 133–47; Marcuse 2005, pp. 57–75.

13   Adorno 1997c, p. 771; 2005b, p. 269.

autonomous reality. Although the metaphysical subject and the subject of science are profoundly different and even opposite in some ways,[14] both are based on the domination of nature. In either case the foundation of knowledge is the estrangement from nature. With metaphysical reason, such alienation implies the belief that the subject dwells somewhere 'above' nature: it belongs to a spiritual kingdom destined to dominate the body and external reality. With scientific reason, such estrangement does not simply disappear, but rather turns into a formal method of investigation (mathematics and experiment) which denies the existence of a spiritual reality but not the need to control and manipulate nature (which is reduced to mere matter). The social need to dominate non-human reality is thus the basis of knowledge and its fundamental and hidden drive. If this is true, the abstract subject of traditional theory is only the mask of a concrete interest in the exploitation of the living world. It shows a speculative attitude because this reinforces its *distance* and its *power* over the object. The position of Critical Theory on this point is exactly the opposite. It openly admits to being *involved* with the object; it aspires to *change* society along with our relationship with the environment and other animals. Thus, its subject does not consider itself a separate and independent reality: it sees itself as part of the entire transformation process. It aspires to realise that ability to observe without intervening that the traditional subject (of both metaphysics and science) could only pretend to be. Traditional thinking claims to be free but it is a slave of necessity, a servant of the war that humanity has declared on non-human nature. In traditional theory, freedom of thought is a precondition: it means freedom *from* nature, namely freedom of the master over the servant. In Critical Theory, freedom of thought is the ultimate goal. It means freedom *of* nature, the freedom of a relationship between equals. Absurd and shocking as it may seem, the idea of praxis advocated by the Frankfurt School seeks to articulate such a demand. Effective political action must correspond to this need to overturn the logic of domination. In a way, it reverses the eleventh thesis on Feuerbach: humans so far have only changed the world, in various ways; the point is to contemplate it.[15] A difficult task indeed, as we have seen, one that only those who free themselves from the idea that the exploitation of non-human nature is necessary to human existence can consistently conceive, and hopefully realise. Veganism is thus the necessary, although not sufficient,

---

14   Horkheimer 2004: pp. 3–40.

15   This does not mean a retreat into aestheticism, although art and poetry show a different
       way to look at animals (Oerlemans 2018) and anticipate, in a way, a liberated world. The
       point is to change our attitude in such a way that even not-doing, waiting or listening to
       the needs of other species can became part of our social praxis.

step towards a proper understanding of what a free relation between natural individuals means, a step that Adorno, Horkheimer and Marcuse did not make themselves. But in order to make the vision of interspecies solidarity real, we must learn from them that only a different organisation of *society* can put an end to the history of domination and necessity and let the epoch of freedom begin: if social totality is wrong, no individual engagement, no matter how intense and altruistic, can be true.[16]

---

16   Adorno 1997a, p. 43; 2005, p. 39.

Antispeciesism and Anticapitalism

> The class struggle for the liberation of animals is the struggle for the
> liberation of the proletariat.
>
> Bündnis Marxismus und Tierbefreiung (2018)

∴

The thesis of this book can be summarised in the following Kant-inspired
motto: *animal liberation without human liberation is blind, human liberation
without animal liberation is empty.*

On the one hand, this means that those who wish to realise animal liberation without overthrowing the current economic system are simply deluding
themselves. No matter how 'radical' or 'aware' you think you are, no matter how
much you feel an 'alien' in the capitalist system: you are still a part of it. The
planetary economic, political, social and cultural system which we call 'capitalism' continues and will continue to destroy life on the planet, turning human
and non-human into slaves, massacring them until it is necessary to extract
profit from them. And all this will happen until we realise that the only way to
put an end to its logic is to attack its fundamental mechanism: i.e. the law of
profit, the valorisation of capital. By growing on itself, becoming abstract and
disembodied as financial capital, the power of self-valorisation travels at the
speed of light around the globe, attacking with its concentrated and pervasive
power the life of nations, threatening the existence of entire ecosystems. How
can we think of *freeing* the animals in a world where humans are still *slaves*?
Only by fighting this struggle against capital, by opposing its power to shape the
world in its image and likeness, can we hope to transform our individual commitment to animal rights, in a shared social project, in the construction of an
open, democratic, solidaristic society. Only by fighting for a more just society
will it be possible to fight for a more just humanity, which looks at the non-
human animal as a brother and not as a slave. In a society that treats humans
'like animals', the animal will never be a 'brother', no matter how serious our
individual fight against speciesism is. We must understand that the levers of
our misery and those of the other animals are partly the same: we must begin to
struggle here, and in the first person, but only by joining others can we achieve

our goals. Yes, 'with others', even with those who have not yet understood the centrality of the fight against speciesism. Because the construction of a true democratic society is something that affects all of us: workers, women, immigrants, children, the elderly, the sick.[1]

Today, many animal rights activists live in their little niche, celebrating their 'purity' while screaming their sorrow and their anger against the world, as if the suffering and death out there were something we 'deserve'. In the end, they say, humans destroy animal lives and therefore they deserve to suffer. Yet, 'Man' is nothing but a mask of Capital. Everything is done in the name of 'human' interest. 'Humanitarian' wars and 'human' rights serve to cover the interests of imperialism. The famous 'freedom of Man' is sacrosanct: above all the freedom of 'enterprise' and 'exploitation' to which all other freedoms are subordinated. And it is always in favour of 'human' well-being that technology is implemented, even if it is used for profit or to improve police control over our lives. Animal Rights Activists who identify 'Humanity' with the cause of the ills of the planet are victims of the ideology of the ruling class. Current society does not defend human rights more than it defends animal rights. In his passionate defence of Animal Rights, Francione is undisturbed by the fact that non-human entities like corporations are *persons*, while animals are not.[2]

It is time to abandon the misanthropy of Animal Rights and stop considering our 'speciesist' neighbour as an enemy, the mere 'object' of my praxis, someone who will be part of my struggle only if we 'convert' him/her to veganism. The enemy is elsewhere. It is an oppressive system centred on capital's self-valorisation. It is more important to struggle together with all the oppressed subjectivities to build a horizontal, plural society, in which power belongs to everyone, in which new, free relations are built, in which life is invented together. Such struggle must be carried forward day by day, everywhere, from the bottom up, in our daily existence, at home, in workplaces, in the ghettos, to the upper floors where decisions are taken, where the ruling class regulates our lives, to the international scenarios where we fight a planetary class struggle that still today massacres, bombs, destroys millions of humans and non-humans. Animal Liberation without human liberation is 'blind' because in order to see *what* is the target we want to strike next, it is necessary to recover the unity of the oppressed and exploited, to find where capital hides and dictates our existence. The Animal Liberation Movement should change

---

1 Although I understand the theoretical strategy of most post-structuralist Animal Rightists, I do not subscribe to its rhetoric of 'precarity' and 'indeterminacy' (Pyke 2019, pp. 52–3). For a problematisation of the 'precarity talk' in the neoliberal era, see Shukin 2018.

2 Francione 1995, p. 35; see Benton 1993, pp. 128 ff.

its strategy and tactics, defining its goals not in terms of liberation of individuals animals, or animals in general, but in the direction of a new social model, where the needs of human and non-human societies are balanced according to egalitarian criteria. Everything else can make us feel better, cleanse our conscience, but it will not change the world out there.

At the same time, and conversely, human liberation without Animal Liberation is 'empty'. For different reasons. First of all, because if what we are looking for is really a different mode of production, the consequences can only be radical. Anticapitalist politics, though finding in the *form* of production its guiding light, faces the problem of what *content* a different kind of social organisation would express. Though such content cannot be predetermined *a priori*, it is crucial that the socialist organisation of production envisages the end of the opposition between humanism and naturalism. It is impossible to foresee how a liberated, self-reflective form of socialisation will mediate the particularism and universalism of material production in a globalised context. Still, the theoretical and practical anticipation of such mediation cannot be merely postponed to future arrangements. Capitalism sets the problem of a universal form of production. What universal content corresponds to it? An answer to that question can only be formulated in abstract terms; it can only be expressed as an objective tendency. Antispeciesism and ecosocialism express the necessity of such a 'regulative ideal'.

To think of achieving an egalitarian society without putting an end to the extermination of other living species, through a hyper-productivist, expansive, selfish, violent and dominating mode of production, is a contradiction in terms. It rather implies a redefinition of our relation with the Other, in all its forms. Rethinking life, sharing life, can only mean opening oneself to the needs of the other lives on the planet, inventing different ways of living together: it can only mean interpenetration, attention, care, search for peaceful coexistence. I do not want to minimise the objective difficulty that this project may involve. But it is a process that will have to start, sooner or later.

Secondly, it is not possible to think that the education of a liberated humanity, a humanity finally freed from the anxiety to control everything, to crush the weak, from the necessity of *mors tua vita mea* [*my life, your death*], will be insensitive to the terrified look of the animal. We imagine a liberated society as one in which the blind violence of consumerism has been replaced by a conscious, reflective, autonomous culture; a culture which is open to dialogue, to confrontation, in which propaganda has been replaced by free information, in which the awareness of universal suffering shapes our ethical choices. Even today, in a violent, racist and selfish society, the rise of a new sensibility towards nature is apparent. Antispecism is the vanguard of such sensibility. Why should a society in which life is the result of cooperation and mutual respect not take a step further? Freeing the human from the system of organised selfishness is the necessary step for a new sensibility to be configured and developed, a new culture of freedom that includes the non-human living. A liberated society would not be really 'free' if science and technology were not finally freed from profit which turns them into instruments of oppression and reification. Science and technology should become instruments of liberation. Perhaps a day will come when the laboratories in which today animals are used for research will be places where we forge instruments of peaceful coexistence on our Planet.

Finally, it is not possible to think that capitalism, the last incarnation of hierarchical, classist, patriarchal and dominating societies, will disappear without uprooting the spiritualistic mechanism that sees 'Man' as 'son of God', which puts humans at the centre of the universe, lords and masters of the cosmos. Human liberation is also the liberation of the human animal, liberation from the cage of a civilisation built on this delusion of omnipotence, on the premise of our ontological difference from the rest of the living: an illusion that Darwin has destroyed, but unfortunately only on a theoretical level. It is time to make Darwinism real, but in the opposite direction of social Darwinism and Singer. We should neither animalise humanity, nor humanise animals: rather dissolve their static opposition, establishing a new social and natural dialectics.

That contemporary society, after having left behind such anthropocentric and spiritualist illusions, can still practice this dominion over the rest of nature means that it continues to act as if that verdict on the 'supremacy' of our species were still valid. Every scientist who acts as if nature were brute matter at his/her service is secretly a priest. Every vulgar materialist who practices domination over the rest of the living world is secretly a spiritualist: be it an avid capitalist or a communist convinced that the Earth 'belongs' to humans. To be a materialist today means knowing that we are *not* masters, and we must stop behaving as if we were.

Being an Animal Liberationist means taking materialism seriously; it means being aware that we are here on Earth *together* with other species, not *against* them. And although nature itself produces competitive mechanisms, this is not a law that has an absolute value: those who accepted nature as a moral standard, the social Darwinists, have set up extermination camps, killed the old and the disabled, sterilised defenceless people, used humans in horrorific experiments. There is violence in nature, of course: it is up to us to choose how to respond to such violence. The route we have taken so far has implied exerting *more* violence, threatening to wipe out all life on the planet, but we could instead lay down our weapons and imagine different relationships between us and all other living beings. It is up to us to build a society that rests on fundamentals different from the current ones. Our commitment as ecosocialist and antispeciesist militants is to overthrow a system that is based on iniquity, isolation and violence, and to replace it with a network of relationships based on solidarity, sharing, respect, and peace. For the humans and the other animals.

References

Acampora, Ralph R. 2006, *Corporal Compassion: Animal Ethics and Philosophy of Body*, Pittsburgh: University of Pittsburgh Press.

Acampora, Ralph R. 2010, 'Off the Ark: Restoring Biophilia', in *Metamorphoses of the Zoo: Animal Encounter after Noah*, edited by Ralph R. Acampora, Lanham: Lexington Books.

Adams, Carol J. 2010, *The Sexual Politics of Meat: A Feminist-Vegetarian Critical Theory*, New York: Continuum.

Adams, Carol J. 2018, *Neither Man Nor Beast: Feminism and the Defense of Animals*, New York: Bloomsbury Academic.

Adorno, Theodor W. 1976, *The Positivist Dispute in German Sociology*, translated by Glyn Adey and David Frisby, New York: Harper & Row.

Adorno, Theodor W. 1993, *Beethoven. Philosophie der Musik*, Frankfurt: Suhrkamp.

Adorno, Theodor W. 1996, *Probleme der Moralphilosophie*, Frankfurt: Suhrkamp.

Adorno, Theodor W. 1997a, *Minima Moralia*, in *Gesammelte Schriften*, Vol. 4, Frankfurt: Suhrkamp.

Adorno, Theodor W. 1997b, *Negative Dialektik*, in *Gesammelte Schriften*, Vol. 6, Frankfurt: Suhrkamp.

Adorno, Theodor W. 1997c, *Stichworte*, in *Gesammelte Schriften*, Vol. 10/1, Frankfurt: Suhrkamp.

Adorno, Theodor W. 1997d, *Ästhetische Theorie*, in *Gesammelte Schriften*, Vol. 7, Frankfurt: Suhrkamp.

Adorno, Theodor W. 1997e, *Aesthetic Theory*, translated by Robert Hullot-Kentor, Minneapolis: University of Minnesota Press.

Adorno, Theodor W. 1997f., *Thesen über Bedürfnis*, in *Gesammelte Schriften*, Vol. 8, Frankfurt: Suhrkamp.

Adorno, Theodor W. 1997g, 'Einleitung zum *Positivismusstreit in der deutschen Soziologie*', in *Soziologische Schriften 1*, in *Gesammelte Schriften*, Vol. 8, Frankfurt: Suhrkamp.

Adorno, Theodor W. 1998, *Beethoven: The Philosophy of Music: Fragments and Texts*, translated by Edmund Jephcott, Stanford: Stanford University Press.

Adorno, Theodor W. 2000, *Introduction to Sociology*, translated by Edmund Jephcott, Stanford: Stanford University Press.

Adorno, Theodor W. 2001, *Problems of Moral Philosophy*, translated by Rodney Livingstone, Stanford: Stanford University Press.

Adorno, Theodor W. 2003, *Einleitung in die Soziologie*, Suhrkamp: Frankfurt a.M.

Adorno, Theodor W. 2005a, *Minima Moralia*, tranlsated by Edmund Jephcott, London: Verso.

Adorno, Theodor W. 2005b, *Critical Models: Interventions and Catchwords*, translated by Henry W. Pickford, New York: Columbia University Press.

Adorno, Theodor W. 2007, *Negative Dialectics*, translated by E.B. Ashton, New York: Continuum.

Adorno, Theodor W. 2017, 'Theses on Needs', translated by M. Schuster and Iain Macdonald, *Adorno Studies*, 1, no. 1.

Adorno, Theodor W., and Max Horkheimer 1997, *Dialektik der Aufklärung*, in *Gesammelte Schriften*, Vol. 3, Frankfurt: Suhrkamp.

Adorno, Theodor W., and Max Horkheimer 2002, *Dialectic of Enlightenment*, translated by Edmund Jephcott, Stanford: Stanford University Press.

Adorno, Theodor W., and Walter Dirks 1956, *Soziologische Exkurse nach Vorträgen und Diskussionen*, Frankfurt: Europäische Verlagsanstalt.

Allen, Kieran 2011, *Marx and the Alternative to Capitalism*, London: Pluto Press.

Anders, Günther 1968, *Die Antiquiertheit des Menschen*, München: Beck.

Angus, Ian 2016, *Facing the Anthropocene: Fossil Capitalism and the Crisis of the Earth System*, New York: Monthly Review Press.

Antagonism and Practical History 1999, *Beasts of Burden: Capitalism, Animals, Communism*, on http://www.redtexts.org

Archibald, W. Peter 1989, *Marx and the Missing Link: 'Human Nature'*, London: Macmillan.

Assoziation Dämmerung 2013, *One Step Beyond Animal Liberation: An Interview With Assoziation Dämmerung*, http://www.asinusnovus.net

Bahro, Rudolf 1982, *Socialism and Survival*, London: Heretic Books.

Balluch, Martin 2005, *Die Kontinuität von Bewusstsein: das naturwissenschaftliche Argument für Tierrrechte*, Wien: Guthmann-Peterson.

Balluch, Martin 2008, *Abolitionism versus Reformism, or which type of campaign will lead to animal rights eventually*, http://vgt.at/publikationen/texte/artikel/20080325 Abolitionism/index_en.php

Banaji, Jarius 2011, *Theory as History: Essays on Modes of Production and Exploitation*, Chicago: Haymarket Books.

Bataille, Georges 1989, *Theory of Religion*, New York: Zone Books.

Baudrillard, Jean 2016, *Symbolic Exchange and Death*, London: Sage.

Beirne, Piers 2018, *Murdering Animals: Writings on Theriocide, Homicide and Nonspeciesist Criminology*, London: Palgrave Studies in Green Criminology.

Bell, Aaron 2011, 'The Dialectic of Anthropocentrism', in *Critical Theory and Animal Liberation*, edited by J. Sanbonmatsu, Plymouth: Rowman & Littlefield.

Benton, Ted 1988, 'Humanism = Speciesism? Marx on Humans and Animals', *Radical Philosophy* 50, Autumn, 4–18.

Benton, Ted 1989, 'Marxism and Natural Limits: An Ecological Critique and Reconstruction', *New Left Review* I/178, November–December.

Benton, Ted 1992, 'Ecology, Socialism and the Mastery of Nature: A Reply to Reiner Grundmann', *New Left Review* I/194, 55–74.

Benton, Ted 1993, *Natural Relations: Ecology, Animal Rights and Social Justice*, London: Verso.

Benton, Ted 1996, *The Greening of Marxism*, New York: Guilford Press.

Benton, Ted 2003, 'Marxism and the Moral Status of Animals', *Society and Animals*, 11, no. 1.

Benton, Ted, and Simon Redfearn 1996, 'The Politics of Animal Rights – Where is the Left?', *New Left Review* I/215, January–February.

Benvegnù, Damiano 2018, *Animals and Animality in Primo Levi's Work*, Basingstoke: Palgrave Macmillan.

Best, Steven 2014, *The Politics of Total Liberation: Revolution for the 21st Century*, Basingstoke: Palgrave Macmillan.

Best, Steven, and Anthony J. Nocella 2004, *Terrorists or Freedom Fighters? Reflection on the Liberation of Animals*, New York: Lanten Books.

Bocquet-Appel, Jean-Pierre, and Ofer Bar-Yosef (eds) 2008, *The Neolithic Demographic Transition and its Consequences*, Berlin: Springer.

Boggs, Carl 2011, 'Corporate Power, Ecological Crisis, and Animal Rights', in *Critical Theory and Animal Liberation*, edited by J. Sanbonmatsu, Plymouth: Rowman & Littlefield.

Bonicelli, Edoardo 2006, *Le forme della vita*, Torino: Einaudi.

Bookchin, Murray 1982, *The Ecology of Freedom: The Emergence and Dissolution of Hierarchy*, Palo Alto: Cheshire Books.

Bradley, Richard 1998, *The Significance of Monuments: On the Shaping of Human Experience in Neolithic and Bronze Age Europe*, London: Routledge.

Brightman, Marc, Vanessa E. Grotti, and Olga Ulturgasheva 2012, 'Animism and Invisible Worlds: The Place of Non-humans in Indigenous Ontologies', in *Animism in Rainforest and Tundra: Personhood, Animals, Plants and Things in Contemporary Amazonia and Siberia*, edited by Marc Brightman, Vanessa Elisa Grotti, and Olga Ulturgasheva, Oxford: Berghahn Books.

Bujok, Melanie, and Birgit Mütherich 2015, *Das Mensch-Tier-Verhältnis: Eine sozialwissenschaftliche Einführung*, Berlin: Springer.

Bündnis Marxismus und Tierbefreiung 2018, '18 Theses on Marxism and Animal Liberation', *Monthly Review On Line*, https://mronline.org/2018/08/28/18-theses-on-marxism-and-animal-liberation/

Burkett, Paul 1998, 'A Critique of Neo-Malthusian Marxism: Society, Nature, and Population', *Historical Materialism*, 2, Summer, 118–42.

Burkett, Paul 1999, *Marx and Nature: A Red and Green Perspective*, New York: St. Martin's Press.

Burkett, Paul 2009, *Marxism and Ecological Economics: Toward a Red and Green Political Economy*, Chicago: Haymarket Books.

C. Alain 2004, *John Zerzan and the Primitive Confusion*, London: Chronos Publications.

Cachel, Susan, and J.W.K. Harris 1998, 'The Lifeways of Homo erectus Inferred from Archaeology and Evolutionary Ecology: A Perspective from East Africa', in *Behaviour in Global Context: The Rise and Diversity of the Lower Palaeolithic Record*, edited by M.D. Petraglia and R. Korisettar, London: Routledge.

Cannon, Aubrey 2014, *Structured Worlds: The Archaeology of Hunter-Gatherer Thought and Action*, New York: Routledge.

Cauvin, Jacques 2002, 'The Symbolic Foundations of the Neolithic Revolution in the Near East', in *Life in Neolithic Farming Communities: Social Organisation, Identity, and Differentiation*, edited by I. Kuijt, Dordrecht: Kluwer Academic Publishers.

Calarco, Matthew 2016, 'Reorienting Strategies for Animal Justice', in *Philosophy and the Politics of Animal Liberation*, edited by Paola Cavalieri, New York: Palgrave Macmillan.

Cavalieri, Paola 2001, *The Animal Question: Why Nonhuman Animals Deserve Human Rights*, Oxford: Oxford University Press.

Cavalieri, Paola 2016, *Philosophy and the Politics of Animal Liberation*, New York: Palgrave Macmillan.

Chan, S. 2018, 'Good for Whom? Differences between Human and Animal Enhancement', in *Are We Pushing Animals to Their Biological Limits? Welfare and Ethical Implications*, edited by Temple Grandin and Martin Whiting, Boston: CABI.

Charlton, Anna E., Sue Coe, and Gary Francione 1993, 'The American Left Should Support Animal Rights: A Manifesto', *Animals' Agenda*, 1, January/February.

Cherry, Elizabeth, Veganism as a Cultural Movement: A Relational Approach, in Social movement studies. Vol.5(2), p.155–170.

Childe, V. Gordon 1936, *Man Makes Himself*, London: Watts and Co.

Childe, V. Gordon 1950, *The Urban Revolution*, Liverpool: Town Planning Review.

Childe, V. Gordon 1975, *What Happened in History*, London: Penguin.

Cohen, Yoram 2013, *Wisdom from the Late Bronze Age*, Atlanta: Society of Biblical Literature.

Cortez, Amanda Daniela, and Agustín Fuentes 2018, 'Of Primates' Bodies: Forms of Human-Other Primate Intercorporeality', in *Exploring Animal Encounters: Philosophical, Cultural, and Historical Perspectives*, edited by Dominik Ohrem and Matthew Calarco, London: Palgrave Macmillan.

De Chardin, Pierre Teilhard 1959, *The Phenomenon of Man*, London: William Collins.

Derrida, Jacques 2008, *The Animal That Therefore I Am*, translated by David Wills, New York: Fordham University Press.

Descartes, René 2000, *Philosophical Essays and Correspondence*, Indianapolis: Hackett Publishing.

Diamond, Jared 1987, 'The Worst Mistake in the History of the Human Race', *Discover*, May.

Diamond, Jared 1997, *Guns, Germs and Steel: The Fates of Human Societies*, New York: W.W. Norton & Company.

Dickens, Peter 1996, *Reconstructing Nature: Alienation, Emancipation and the Division of Labour*, London: Routledge.

Dickens, Peter 2003, 'The Labour Process: How the Underdog is Kept Under', *Society and Animals*, 11, no. 1.

Donaldson, Sue, and Kymlicka, Willy 2016, 'Make It So: Envisioning a Zoopolitical Revolution', in *Philosophy and the Politics of Animal Liberation*, edited by Paola Cavalieri, New York: Palgrave Macmillan.

Donovan, Josephine, and Adams, Carol J. 1996, *Beyond Animal Rights: A Feminist Caring Ethic for the Treatment of Animals*, New York: Continuum.

Drennan, Robert D., and Christian E. Peterson 2008, 'Centralized Communities, Population, and Social Complexity After Sedentarisation', in *The Neolithic Demographic Transition and its Consequences*, edited by Jean-Pierre Bocquet-Appel and Omar Bar-Yosef, Berlin: Springer.

Dunayer, Joan 2004, *Speciesism*, Derwood, MD: Ryce Publishing.

Eliade, Mircea 1978, *A History of Religious Ideas, Vol. 1*, translated by Willard R. Trask, Chicago: University of Chicago Press.

Empson, Martin 2014, *Land and Labour: Marxism, Ecology and Human History*, London: Bookmarks.

Engels, Friedrich 1962a, *Der Ursprung der Familie, des Privateigentums und des Staats*, in *Marx-Engels Werke* [MEW], Bd. 21.

Engels, Friedrich 1962b, *Antidühring*, in MEW, Bd. 20.

Engels, Friedrich 1962c, *Dialektik der Natur*, in MEW, Bd. 20.

Engels, Friedrich 1972a, *Zur Geschichte des Urchristentums*, in MEW, Bd. 22.

Engels, Friedrich 1972b, *Die Lage der arbeitenden Klasse in England*, in MEW, Bd. 2.

Engels, Friedrich 1973, *Die Entwicklung des Sozialismus von der Utopie zur Wissenschaft*, in MEW, Bd. 19.

Ferrari, Arianna, and Klaus Petrus 2015, *Lexikon der Mensch-Tier-Beziehungen*, Beilefeld: Transcript.

Filippi, Massimo 2003, 'Può un non vegetariano dirsi comunista?', *Rinascita Animalista. Officina della theoria*, http://www.liberazioni.org/ra/ra/officina004.html

Finsen, Susan 1988, 'Sinking the Research Lifeboat', *Journal of Medicine and Philosophy*, 13, no. 2: 197–212.

Foster, John Bellamy 2000, *Marx's Ecology: Materialism and Nature*, New York: Monthly Review Press.

Foster, John Bellamy, and Paul Burkett 2016, *Marx and the Earth: An Anti-Critique*, Leiden: Brill.

Francione, Gary L. 1995, *Animals, Property, and the Law*, Philadelphia: Temple University Press.

Francione, Gary L. 1996, *Rain without Thunder: The Ideology of the Animal Rights Movement*, Philadelphia: Temple University Press.

Francione, Gary L. 2000, *Introduction to Animal Rights: Your Child or the Dog?* Philadelphia: Temple University Press.

Francione, Gary L. 2009, 'More on Violence and Animal Rights', https://www.abolitionis tapproach.com/more-on-violence-and-animal-rights/

Francione, Gary L. 2010, 'On Violence', http://www.abolitionistapproach.com/on-violen ce/

Freud, Sigmund 2009, *Totem and Taboo*, translated by Abraham A. Brill, New York: Cosimo.

Fromm, Erich 1973, *The Anatomy of Human Destructiveness*, London: Pelican.

Fuglestvedt, Ingrid 2014, 'Humans, Material Culture and Landscape: Outline to an Understanding of Developments in Worldviews on the Scandinavian Peninsula, ca. 10,000–4500 BP', in *Structured Worlds: The Archaeology of Hunter-Gatherer Thought and Action*, edited by Aubrey Cannon, New York: Routledge.

Garner, Robert 2005a, *The Political Theory of Animal Rights*, Manchester: Manchester University Press.

Garner, Robert 2005b, *Animal Ethics*, Cambridge: Polity.

Giannetto, Enrico 2005, 'La rivoluzione neolitica', *Liberazioni 2*.

Godelier, Maurice 1977, *Horizon, trajets, marxistes en anthropologie*, Paris: Maspero.

Griffin, Nathan Stephens 2017, *Understanding Veganism: Biography and Identity*, Basingstoke: Palgrave Macmillan.

Grundmann, Reiner 1991a, 'The Ecological Challenge to Marxism', *New Left Review*, 187, May–June.

Grundmann, Reiner 1991b, *Marxism and Ecology*, Oxford: Clarendon Press.

Guidi, Alessandro 2000, *Preistoria della complessità sociale*, Roma-Bari: Laterza.

Habermas, Jürgen 1987, *The Philosophical Discourse of Modernity: Twelve Lectures*, translated by Frederick Lawrence, Cambridge, MA: The MIT Press.

Harding, A.F. 2000, *European Societies in the Bronze Age*, Cambridge: Cambridge University Press.

Harris, Marvin 1977, *Cannibals and Kings: The Origins of Cultures*, New York: Vintage.

Harris, Marvin 1990, *Our Kind: Who We Are, Where We Came From, Where We Are Going*, New York: HarperCollins.

Harris, Marvin 1998, *Good to Eat: Riddles of Food and Culture*, Illinois: Waveland Press.

Harvey, Graham 2014, 'Introduction', in *The Handbook of Contemporary Animism*, edited by Graham Harvey, New York: Routledge.

Hayden, Brian 2003, *Shamans, Sorcerers, and Saints: A Prehistory of Religion*, Washington: The Smithsonian Institution.

Hegel, Georg Wilhelm Friedrich 1977, *Phenomenology of Spirit*, translated by A.V. Miller, Oxford: Clarendon Press.

Hegel, Georg Wilhelm Friedrich 2008, *Outlines of the Philosophy of Right*, translated by Tom M. Knox, Oxford: Oxford University Press.

Hershkovitz, Israel, and Avi Gopher 2008, 'Demographic, Biological and Cultural Aspects of the Neolithic Revolution: A View from the Southern Levant', in *The Neolithic Demographic Transition and its Consequences*, edited by Jean-Pierre Bocquet-Appel and Omar Bar-Yosef, Berlin: Springer.

High, Casey 2012, 'Shamans, Animals and Enemies: Human and Non-Human Agency in an Amazonian Cosmos of Alterity', in *Animism in Rainforest and Tundra: Personhood, Animals, Plants and Things in Contemporary Amazonia and Siberia*, edited by Marc Brightman, Vanessa Elisa Grotti, and Olga Ulturgasheva, Oxford: Berghahn Books.

Hobsbawm, Eric 2011, *How to Change the World: Reflections on Marx and Marxism*, New Haven: Yale University Press.

Hodder, Ian (ed.) 2014, *Religion at Work in a Neolithic Society: Vital Matters*, New York: Cambridge University Press.

Hollands, Clive 1985, 'Animal Rights in the Political Arena', in *In Defense of Animals*, edited by Peter Singer, New York: Basil Blackwell.

Hornbor, Alf 2014, 'Submitting to Objects: Animism, Fetishism, and the Cultural Foundations of Capitalism', in *The Handbook of Contemporary Animism*, edited by Graham Harvey, New York: Routledge.

Horkheimer, Max 1975, 'Traditional and Critical Theory', in *Critical Theory: Selected Essays*, translated by Matthew J. O'Connell et al., New York: Continuum.

Horkheimer, Max 1978, *Dawn and Decline: Notes 1926–1931 and 1950–1969*, translated by Michael Shaw, New York: Seabury Press.

Horkheimer, Max 1985, *Dämmerung. Notizen in Deutschland*, in *Gesammelte Schriften*, Vol. 2, Frankfurt: Fischer.

Horkheimer, Max 1992, 'Traditionelle und kritische Theorie', in *Traditionelle und kritische Theorie: Fünf Aufsätze*, Frankfurt: Fischer.

Horkheimer, Max 1993, *Between Philosophy and Social Science: Selected Early Writings*, translated by G. Frederick Hunter, Matthew S. Kramer, and John Torpey, Cambridge, MA: MIT Press.

Horkheimer, Max 2013, *Eclipse of Reason*, London: Bloomsbury.

Hudis, Peter 2013, *Marx's Concept of the Alternative to Capitalism*, Chicago: Haymarket Books.

Huges, J 2000, *Ecology and Historical Materialism*, Cambridge: Cambridge University Press.

Hultkranz, Åke 1988, 'Le religioni delle grandi civiltà precolombiane', in *Le religioni dei popoli senza scrittura*, edited by Henri-Charles Puech, Roma-Bari: Laterza.

Hutchings, Monica, and Mavis Caver 1970, *Man's Dominion: Our Violation of the Animal World*, London: Rupert Hart-Davis.

Ingold, Tim 2000, *The Perception of the Environment: Essays in Livelihood, Dwelling and Skill*, London: Routledge.

Ingold, Tim 2014, 'Being Alive to a World without Objects', in *The Handbook of Contemporary Animism*, edited by Graham Harvey, New York: Routledge.

Johnson, Victoria 2011, 'Everyday Rituals of the Master Race: Fascism, Stratification, and the Fluidity of "Animal" Domination', in *Critical Theory and Animal Liberation*, edited by J. Sanbonmatsu, Plymouth: Rowman & Littlefield.

Joy, Melanie 2010, *Why We Love Dogs, Eat Pigs, and Wear Cows: An Introduction to Carnism*, San Francisco: Conari Press.

Kalechofsky, Roberta 1988, 'Metaphors of Nature: Vivisection and Pornography – The Manichean Machine', *Between the Species*, 4, no. 3.

Karatani, Kōjin 2014, *The Structure of World History: From Modes of Production to Modes of Exchange*, Durham, NC: Duke University Press.

Klein, Richard G. 1987, 'Reconstructing How Early People Exploited Animals: Problems and Prospects', in *The Evolution of Human Hunting*, edited by Matthew H. Nitecki and Doris V. Nitecki, London: Plenum Press.

Kohl, Philip L. 2007, *The Making of Bronze Age Eurasia*, Cambridge: Cambridge University Press.

Korsgaard, Christine M. 2018, *Fellow Creatures: Our Obligations to the Other Animals*, Oxford: Oxford University Press.

Kuijt, Ian 2002a, 'Life in Neolithic Farming Communities: An Introduction', in *Life in Neolithic Farming Communities: Social Organisation, Identity, and Differentiation*, edited by Ian Kuijt, Boston: Kluwer Academic Publishers.

Kuijt, Ia 2002b, 'Near Eastern Neolithic Research: Directions and Trend', in *Life in Neolithic Farming Communities: Social Organisation, Identity, and Differentiation*, edited by Ian Kuijt, Boston: Kluwer Academic Publishers.

Lee, Richard B. 1968, 'What Hunters Do for a Living', in *Man the Hunter*, edited by Richard B. Lee, Chicago: Aldine Publishing Company.

Lee, Richard B., and Irven DeVore 1968, 'Problems in the Study of Hunters and Gatherers', in *Man the Hunter*, edited by Richard B. Lee, Chicago: Aldine Publishing Company.

Lenin, V.I. 2001, *What the 'Friends of the People' Are and How They Fight the Social-Democrats*, in *Collected Works*, Vol. 1, Moscow: Progress Publishers.

Lévi-Strauss, Claude 1963, *Structural Anthropology*, translated by Claire Jacobson and Brooke Grundfest Schoepf, New York: Basic Book.

Lévi-Strauss, Claude 1966, *The Savage Mind*, Chicago: University of Chicago Press.

Lévi-Strauss, Claude 1976, *Structural Anthropology 2*, translated by Monique Layton, London: Allen Lane.

Lewontin, Richard C. 1996, *Biology as Ideology: The Doctrine of DNA*, Toronto: House of Anansi Press.

Lewontin, Richard C. 2000, *The Triple Helix: Gene, Organism, and Environment*, Cambridge, MA: Harvard University Press.

Lewontin, Richard C., and Stephen Jay Gould 2010, 'The Spandrels of San Marco and the Panglossian Paradigm: A Critique of the Adaptationist Programme', in *Philosophy of Biology: An Anthology*, edited by Alex Rosenberg and Robert Arp, Malden: Wiley-Blackwell.

Lewontin, Richard C., and Richard Levins 1985, *The Dialectical Biologist*, Cambridge, MA: Harvard University Press.

Liverani, Mario 2004, *Uruk la prima città*, Roma-Bari: Laterza.

Llorente, Renzo 2011, 'Reflections on the Perspective for a Non-Speciesist Marxism', in *Critical Theory and Animal Liberation*, edited by John Sanbonmatsu, Plymouth: Rowman & Littlefield.

Loyer, Carly, and James Ha 2017, 'Applications of Research in Nonhuman Animal Personality', in *Personality in Nonhuman Animals*, edited by Jennifer Vonk, Alexander Weiss, and Stan A. Kuczaj, Berlin: Springer.

Luke, Brian 2016, 'Animal Subjects and the Logic of Human Domination', in *Philosophy and the Politics of Animal Liberation*, edited by Paola Cavalieri, New York: Palgrave Macmillan.

Luxemburg, Rosa 1951, *The Accumulation of Capital*, London: Routledge and Kegan Paul.

Luxemburg, Ros 1993, *The Letters of Rosa Luxemburg*, edited by Stephen Eric Bronner, New Brunswick: Humanities Press.

Luxemburg, Ros 2004, *The Dissolution of Primitive Communism (Introduction to Political Economy)*, in *Rosa Luxemburg Reader*, edited by Peter Hudis and Kevin B. Anderson, New York: Monthly Review Press.

Maisels, Charles Keith 1993, *The Emergence of Civilisation: From Hunting and Gathering to Agriculture, Cities, and the State in the Near East*, London: Routledge.

Mandel, Ernest 1967, *An Introduction to Marxist Economic Theory*, New York: Young Socialist Alliance.

Marchesini, Roberto, Luisella Battaglia, et al. 1999, *Zooantropologia. Animali e umani: analisi di un rapporto*, Como: Red edizioni.

Marcuse, Herbert 1965, 'Philosophie und kritische Theorie', in *Kultur und Gesellschaft*, Frankfurt: Suhrkamp.

Marcuse, Herbert 1966, 'Ethics and Revolution', in *Ethics and Society: Original Essays on Contemporary Moral Problems*, edited by R.T. de George, Anchor: Garden City, N.Y, pp. 133–147.

Marcuse, Herbert 1972, *Counterrevolution and Revolt*, Boston: Beacon Press.

Marcuse, Herbert 1988, 'Philosophy and Critical Theory', in *Negations: Essays in Critical Theory*, translated by Jeremy J. Shapiro, London: Free Association.

Marcuse, Herbert 1998, *Eros and Civilisation*, Boston: Beacon Press.

Marcuse, Herbert 2002, *One-dimensional Man: Studies in the Ideology of Advanced Industrial Society*, London: Routledge.

Marcuse, Herbert 2005, *The New Left and the 1960s*, New York: Routledge.

Martin, Bill 2008, *Ethical Marxism: The Categorical Imperative of Liberation*. La Salle, IL: Open Court.

Marx, Karl 1962, *Das Kapital*, in MEW, Bd. 23, Berlin: Dietz.

Marx, Karl 1967, *Theorien über den Mehrwert*, in MEW, Bd. 26, Vol. II, Berlin: Dietz.

Marx, Karl 1968, *Ökonomisch-philosophische Manuskripte aus dem Jahre 1844*, in MEW, Ergänzungsband, I, Berlin: Dietz.

Marx, Karl 1971, *Einleitung zur Kritik der politischen Ökonomie*, in MEW, Bd. 13, Berlin: Dietz.

Marx, Karl 1972, *Das Elend der Philosophie*, in MEW, Bd. 4, Berlin: Dietz.

Marx, Karl 1981, *Zur Judenfrage*, in MEW, Bd 1, Berlin: Dietz.

Marx, Karl 1983, *Grundrisse der Kritik der politischen Ökonomie*, in MEW, Bd. 42, Berlin: Dietz.

Marx, Karl, and Friedrich Engels 1969, *Die deutsche Ideologie*, in MEW, Bd. 3, Berlin: Dietz.

Marx, Karl, and Friedrich Engels 1972, *Manifest der Kommunistischen Partei*, in MEW, Bd. 4, Berlin: Dietz.

Mason, Jim 1993, *An Unnatural Order: Uncovering the Roots of Our Domination of Nature and Each Other*, New York: Simon & Schuster.

Maurizi, Marco 2005a, 'Marxismo e animalismo: contributi a una discussione', *Liberazioni. Rivista di critica antispecista*, liberazioni.org.

Maurizi, Marco 2005b, 'Cos'è l'antispecismo?', *Liberazioni. Rivista di critica antispecista*, liberazioni.org.

Maurizi, Marco 2018, *Quanto lucente la tua inesistenza. L'Ottobre, il '68 e il socialismo che viene*, Milano: Jaca Book.

Mauss, Marcel, [and Henri Hubert] 1972, *A General Theory of Magic*, translated by Robert Brain, London: Routledge & Kegan Paul.

May, Allyson N. 2013, *The Fox-hunting Controversy, 1781–2004. Class and Cruelty*, Farnham: Ashgate.

Mazoyer, Marcel, and Laurence Roudart 2006, *A History of World Agriculture: From the Neolithic Age to the Current Crisis*, London: Earthscan.

McMullen, Steven 2016, *Animals and the Economy*, Basingstoke: Palgrave Macmillan.

Mendieta, Eduardo 2011, 'Animal is to Kantianism as Jew is to Fascism: Adorno's Bestiary', in *Critical Theory and Animal Liberation*, edited by John Sanbonmatsu, Plymouth: Rowman & Littlefield.

Meschiari, Matteo 2019, 'Anti-speciesist Rhetoric', in *Semiotics of Animals in Culture: Zoosemiotics 2.0*, edited by Gianfranco Marrone and Dario Mangano, Berlin: Springer.

Midgley, Mary 1995, *Beast and Man: The Roots of Human Nature*, London: Routledge.

Miller, Harlan B. 1993, 'Science, Ethics and Moral Status', *Between the Species*, 10, no. 1.

Montaigne, Michel de 1993, *The Complete Essays*, London: Penguin Classics.

Moore, Jason W. 2015, *Capitalism in the Web of Life: Ecology and the Accumulation of Capital*, London: Verso.

Nibert, David Alan 2002, *Animal Rights/Human Rights: Entanglements of Oppression and Liberation*, Lanham: Rowman & Littlefield.

Nibert, David Alan 2013, *Animal Oppression and Human Violence: Domesecration, Capitalism, and Global Conflict*, New York: Columbia University Press.

Nitecki, Matthew H. 1987, 'The Idea of Human Hunting', in *The Evolution of Human Hunting*, edited by Matthew H. Nitecki and Doris V. Nitecki, London: Plenum Press.

Noske, Barbara 1989, *Humans and Other Animals*, London: Pluto Press.

Noske, Barbara 2004, 'Two Movements and Human-Animal Continuity: Positions, Assumptions, Contradictions', in *Animal Liberation Philosophy and Policy Journal*, 2, no. 1: 1–12.

Nougier, Louis-René 1981, *L'economia preistorica*, Roma: Editori Riuniti.

O'Connor, James 1998, *Natural Causes: Essays in Ecological Marxism*, New York: The Guilford Press.

Oerlemans, Onno 2018, *Poetry and Animals: Blurring the Boundaries with the Human*, New York: Columbia University.

Pannekoek, Anton 1912, *Marxism and Darwinism*, Chicago: Charles H. Kerr & Company.

Pannekoek, Anton 1953, *Anthropogenesis: A Study of the Origin of the Human Being*, Amsterdam: North-Holland Publishing Company.

Patterson, Charles 2002, *Eternal Treblinka: Our Treatment of Animals and the Holocaust*, New York: Lantern Books.

Perlo, Katherine 2002, 'Marxism and the Underdog', *Society and Animals*, 10, no. 3: 303–18.

Perlo, Katherine 2007, 'Extrinsic and Intrinsic Arguments: Strategies for Promoting Animal Rights', *Journal for Critical Animal Studies*, 6, no. 1.

Perullo, Nicola 2018, 'When to Eat Meat? Toward a Diet of Caring', in *Semiotics of Animals in Culture: Zoosemiotics 2.0*, edited by Gianfranco Marrone and Dario Mangano, Berlin: Springer.

Petraglia, Michael D., and Ravi Korisettar 1998, 'The Archaeology of the Lower Palaeolithic: Background and Overview', in *Behaviour in Global Context: The Rise and Diversity of the Lower Palaeolithic Record*, edited by M.D. Petraglia and R. Korisettar, London: Routledge.

Plekhanov, G.V. 1940, *Essays in Historical Materialism*, New York: International Publishers.

Puech, Henri-Charles 1988, *Le religioni dei popoli senza scrittura*, Roma-Bari: Laterza.

Pyke, Susan Mary 2019, *Animal Visions: Posthumanist Dream Writing*, Cham: Palgrave Studies in Animals and Literature.

Rachels, James 1990, *Created from Animals*, Oxford: Oxford University Press.

Rees, Paul A. 2018, *The Laws Protecting Animals and Ecosystems*, Oxford: Wiley Blackwell.

Regan, Tom 2003, *Animal Rights, Human Wrongs: An Introduction to Moral Philosophy*, Lanham: Rowman & Littlefield.

Regan, Tom 2004a, *The Case for Animal Rights*, Berkeley: University of California Press.

Regan, Tom 2004b, 'How to Justify Violence', in *Terrorists or Freedom Fighters?*, edited by Steven Best and Anthony J. Nocella, New York: Lantern Books.

Regan, Tom 2004c, *Empty Cages: Facing the Challenge of Animal Rights*, Lanham: Rowman & Littlefield.

Rose, Steven P.R. 2010, *Lifelines: Life beyond the Gene*, Oxford: Oxford University Press.

Rude, Matthias 2013, *Antispeziesismus: die Befreiung von Mensch und Tier in der Tierrechtsbewegung und der Linken*, Stuttgart: Schmetterling.

Ryder, Richard Dudley 1988, *The Political Animal: The Conquest of Speciesism*, London: McFarland & Co.

Ryder, Richard Dudley 2017, *Speciesism, Painism and Happiness: A Morality for the Twenty-First Century*, Exeter: Imprint Academic.

Sahlins, Marshall 1968, 'Notes on the Original Affluent Society', paper presented at the *Man the Hunter* conference, Chicago, 1966.

Salt, Henry S. 1980 [1892], *Animals' Rights: Considered in Relation to Social Progress*, Clarks Summit, PA: Society for Animal Rights.

Sanbonmatsu, John 2011, 'Introduction', in *Critical Theory and Animal Liberation*, edited by John Sanbonmatsu, Plymouth: Rowman & Littlefield.

Sanbonmatsu, John 2013, *Animal Liberation and Critical Theory*, interview with Marco Maurizi, *Asinus Novus*, asinusnovus.net.

Sanders, Clinton R. 2006, 'The Sociology of Human-Animal Interaction and Relationships', *H-Animal*, https://networks.h-net.org/node/16560/pages/32228/sociology-human-animal-interaction-and-relationships-clinton-r-sanders

Sapontzis, Steve F. 1987, 'The Evolution of Animals in Moral Philosophy', *Between the Species*, 3.

Schmidt, Alfred 1971, *The Concept of Nature in Marx*, translated by Ben Fowkes, London: New Left Books.

Schopenhauer, Arthur 2010, *The World as Will and Representation*, Cambridge: Cambridge University Press.

Scotton, Guy 2018, 'Metaphors and Maladies: Against Psychologizing Speciesism', in *Animaladies: Gender, Animals and Madness*, edited by Lori Gruen and Fiona Probyn-Rapsey, New York: Bloomsbury.

Selz, Gebhard 2019, 'Reflections on the Pivotal Role of Animals in Early Mesopotamia' in *Animals and their Relation to Gods, Humans and Things in the Ancient World*, edited by Raija Mattila, Sanae Ito, and Sebastian Fink, Berlin: Springer.

Service, Elman R. 1971, *Primitive Social Organisation*, New York: Random House.

Shukin, Nicole 2018, 'Precarious Encounters', in *Exploring Animal Encounters: Philosophical, Cultural, and Historical Perspectives*, edited by Dominik Ohrem and Matthew Calarco, Basingstoke: Palgrave Macmillan.

Simmons, Alan H. 2002, 'Villages on the Edge: Regional Settlement Change', in *Life in Neolithic Farming Communities: Social Organisation, Identity, and Differentiation*, edited by Ian Kuijt, Boston: Kluwer Academic Publishers.

Singer, Peter 1980a, 'Utilitarianism and Vegetarianism', *Philosophy and Public Affairs*, 9, no. 4: 325–37.

Singer, Peter 1980b, *Marx*, Oxford: Oxford University Press.

Singer, Peter 1980c, 'Marx and the Giraffe', *The New York Review*, 21 February.

Singer, Peter 1981, *The Expanding Circle: Ethics and Sociobiology*, Oxford: Clarendon Press.

Singer, Peter 1982, *Hegel*, Oxford: Oxford University Press.

Singer, Peter (ed.) 1985, *In Defense of Animals*, Malden: Blackwell.

Singer, Peter 1986, 'Animal Liberation: A Personal View', *Between the Species*, 2, no. 3.

Singer, Peter 1987, TV interview with Bryan Magee.

Singer, Peter 1994, *Rethinking Life and Death: The Collapse of Our Traditional Ethics*, New York: St. Martin's Press.

Singer, Peter 1999, *A Darwinian Left: Politics, Evolution, and Cooperation*, New Haven: Yale University Press.

Singer, Peter 2015, *Animal Liberation*, London: Bodley Head.

Smulewicz-Zucker, Gregory 2016, 'Bringing the State into Animal Rights Politics', in *Philosophy and the Politics of Animal Liberation*, edited by Paola Cavalieri, New York: Palgrave Macmillan.

Sohn-Rethel, Alfred 1978, *Intellectual and Manual Labour: A Critique of Epistemology*, Basingstoke: Macmillan.

Stache, Christian 2018, 'On the Origins of Animalist Marxism: Re-reading Ted Benton and the *Economic and Philosophic Manuscripts of 1844*', *Monthly Review*, 70, no. 7.

Stanford, Craig B. 1999, *The Hunting Apes: Meat Eating and the Origins of Human Behavior*, Princeton: Princeton University Press.

Subversive Energy 2012, 'Beyond Animal Liberation', in *The Anarchist Library*, http://www.theanarchistlibrary.org.

Sztybel, David 1997, 'Marxism and Animal Rights', *Ethics and the Environment*, 2, no. 2: 169–85, http://sztybel.tripod.com/Marxism.html.

Sztybel, David 2008, Response to Katherine Perlo's 'Extrinsic and Intrinsic Arguments: Strategies for Promoting Animal Rights', *Journal for Critical Animal Studies*, 6, no. 1.

Timofeeva, Oxana 2018, *The History of Animals: A Philosophy*, London: Bloomsbury.

Timpanaro, Sebastiano 1975, *On Materialism*, translated by Lawrence Garner, London: NLB.

Trinkaus, Eric 1987, 'Hunting in Late Upper Paleolithic Western Europe', in *The Evolution of Human Hunting*, edited by Matthew H. Nitecki and Doris V. Nitecki, London: Plenum Press.

Tugnoli, Claudio, et al. 2003, *Zooantropologia. Storia, etica e pedagogia dell'interazione uomo/animale*, Milano: Franco Angeli.

Van der Leeuw, Gerardus 1986, *Religion in Essence and Manifestation: A Study in Phenomenology*, Princeton: Princeton University Press.

Vigne, Jean-Denis 2008, 'Zooarchaeological Aspects of the Neolithic Diet Transition in the Near East and Europe, and Their Putative Relationships with the Neolithic Demographic Transition', in *The Neolithic Demographic Transition and its Consequences*, edited by Jean-Pierre Bocquet-Appel and Omar Bar-Yosef, Berlin: Springer.

Wadiwel, Dinesh Joseph 2016, 'Counter-Conduct and Truce', in *Philosophy and the Politics of Animal Liberation*, edited by Paola Cavalieri, New York: Palgrave Macmillan.

Wallis, Robert J. 2014, 'Exorcizing "Spirits": Approaching "Shamans" and Rock Art Animically', in *The Handbook of Contemporary Animism*, edited by Graham Harvey, New York: Routledge.

Weber, Max 1947, *The Theory of Social and Economic Organisation*, Oxford: Oxford University Press.

Weisberg, Zipporah 2011, 'Animal Repression: Speciesism as Pathology', in *Critical Theory and Animal Liberation*, edited by John Sanbonmatsu, Plymouth: Rowman & Littlefield.

Whitebook, Joel 1994, 'The Problem of Nature in Habermas', in *The Frankfurt School: Critical Assessments, Vol. 6: Jürgen Habermas*, edited by J.M. Bernstein, New York: Routledge.

Whitehead, Amy 2014, 'The New Fetishism: Western Statue Devotion and a Matter of Power', in *The Handbook of Contemporary Animism*, edited by Graham Harvey, New York: Routledge.

Whittle, Alisdair 2003, *The Archaeology of People: Dimensions of Neolithic Life*, London: Routledge.

Wilde, Lawrence 2000, 'The Creatures, Too, Must Become Free: Marx and the Animal/Human Distinction', *Capital & Class*, 72: 37–53.

Willerslev, Rane 2007, *Soul Hunters: Hunting, Animism, and Personhood among the Siberian Yukaghirs*, Berkeley: University of California Press.

Willerslev, Rane, and Olga Ulturgasheva 2012, 'Revisiting the Animism versus Totemism Debate: Fabricating Persons among the Eveny and Chukchi of North-Eastern Siberia', in *Animism in Rainforest and Tundra: Personhood, Animals, Plants and Things in Contemporary Amazonia and Siberia*, edited by Marc Brightman, Vanessa Elisa Grotti, and Olga Ulturgasheva, Oxford: Berghahn Books.

Wilson, Edward O. 1975, *Sociobiology: The New Synthesis*, Cambridge, MA: Harvard University Press.

Wilson, Edward O. 2014, *On Human Nature*, Cambridge, MA: Harvard University Press.

Witt-Stahl, Susann 2003, 'Auschwitz liegt nicht am Strand von Malibu und auch nicht auf unseren Tellern. Kritische Anmerkungen zum "KZ-Vergleich"', *Tierbefreiung*, 43.

Wolf, Daniel 2018, 'Caesar: The Rise and Dawn of a Humanimalistic Identity', in *Animal Biography: Re-framing Animal Lives*, edited by André Krebber and Mieke Roscher, Cham: Palgrave Macmillan.

Wrenn, Corey Lee 2015, *A Rational Approach to Animal Rights: Extensions in Abolitionist Theory*, New York: Palgrave Macmillan.

Zerzan, John 1988, *Elements of Refusal*, St. Louis, MO: Left Bank Books.

Zerzan, John 1994, *Future Primitive*, New York: Autonomedia.

Žižek, Slavoj 2002, 'A Plea for Leninist Intolerance', *Critical Inquiry*, 28, no. 2: 542–66.

Žižek, Slavoj 2008, *In Defence of Lost Causes*, London: Verso.

Žižek, Slavoj 2010, *Living in the End of Times*, London: Verso.

Žižek, Slavoj 2011, *The Animal Does Not Exist*, podcast, http://www.zizekpodcast.com/2016/04/19/ziz044-the-animals-doesnt-exist/

Žižek, Slavoj 2013, 'Man as *the* Animal', *Asinus Novus*, http://www.asinusnovus.net

Index

CPSIA information can be obtained
at www.ICGtesting.com
Printed in the USA
LVHW080501110722
723092LV00005B/10